D0322560

This book is due for return on or before the last date shown below.

In the same series from Bloomsbury Methuen Drama:

BRITISH THEATRE COMPANIES: 1965–1979
Welfare State International, CAST, Portable Theatre Company,
The People Show, and The Pip Simmons Theatre Group
by John Bull
ISBN 978-1-4081-7543-9

BRITISH THEATRE COMPANIES: 1995–2014
Mind the Gap, Kneehigh Theatre, Suspect Culture,
Stan's Café, Blast Theory and Punchdrunk
by Liz Tomlin
ISBN 978-1-4081-7727-3

Related titles:

MODERN BRITISH PLAYWRITING: THE 1950s
by David Pattie
Includes detailed studies of works by T. S. Eliot, Terence
Rattigan, John Osborne and Arnold Wesker

MODERN BRITISH PLAYWRITING: THE 1960s
by Steve Nicholson
Includes detailed studies of works by John Arden,
Edward Bond, Harold Pinter and Alan Ayckbourn

MODERN BRITISH PLAYWRITING: THE 1970s
by Chris Megson
Includes detailed studies of works by Caryl Churchill,
David Edgar, Howard Brenton and David Hare

MODERN BRITISH PLAYWRITING: THE 1980s
by Jane Milling
Includes detailed studies of works by Howard Barker, Jim
Cartwright. Sarah Daniels and Timberlake Wertenbaker

MODERN BRITISH PLAYWRITING: THE 1990s
by Aleks Sierz
Includes detailed studies of works by Philip Ridley,
Sarah Kane, Anthony Neilson and Mark Ravenhill

MODERN BRITISH PLAYWRITING: 2000–2009
edited by Dan Rebellato
Includes detailed studies of works by David Greig, Simon
Stephens, Tim Crouch, Roy Williams, and debbie tucker green

BRITISH THEATRE COMPANIES 1980–1994

Joint Stock Theatre Company, Gay Sweatshop, Théâtre de Complicité, Forced Entertainment, Women's Theatre Group, and Talawa

Graham Saunders

Series Editors: John Bull and Graham Saunders

Bloomsbury Methuen Drama
An imprint of Bloomsbury Publishing Plc

B L O O M S B U R Y
LONDON • NEW DELHI • NEW YORK • SYDNEY

Bloomsbury Methuen Drama

An imprint of Bloomsbury Publishing Plc

Imprint previously known as Methuen Drama

50 Bedford Square	1385 Broadway
London	New York
WC1B 3DP	NY 10018
UK	USA

www.bloomsbury.com

BLOOMSBURY, METHUEN DRAMA and the Diana logo are trademarks of Bloomsbury Publishing Plc

First published 2015

© Graham Saunders and contributors, 2015

Graham Saunders has asserted his right under the Copyright, Designs and Patents Act, 1988, to be identified as author of this work.

British Library Cataloguing-in-Publication Data
A catalogue record for this book is available from the British Library.

ISBN: HB: 978-1-4081-7549-1
PB: 978-1-4081-7548-4
ePDF: 978-1-4081-7551-4
ePub: 978-1-4081-7550-7

Library of Congress Cataloging-in-Publication Data
A catalog record for this book is available from the Library of Congress.

Typeset by Fakenham Prepress Solutions, Fakenham, Norfolk NR21 8NN
Printed and bound in Great Britain.

CONTENTS

ACKNOWLEDGEMENTS

I would like to thank the department of Film, Theatre and Television at the University of Reading and the Arts and Humanities Research Council (AHRC) for research leave to complete this volume. Much of the material in Chapter 2 comes from time spent consulting only a fraction of the labyrinthine Arts Council of Great Britain archive. My thanks go to Dr Kate ('Sparky') Dorney and staff at the Victoria and Albert Museum's Theatre and Performance Collection for all their help (and long suffering patience) during my numerous visits to their Reading Room at Blythe House, London.

Several former members of Arts Council staff, Ian Brown, Christopher Gordon, Yvonne Brewster, John Faulkner, Jonathan Lamede, Peter and Sue Stark and Sue Timothy, were unfailingly helpful in answering any number of arcane questions relating to companies, policy and personnel over the period covered in this volume. Nassem Khan also answered questions relating to *The Arts Britain Ignores* and subsequent events following its publication.

I would also like to thank my co-editors, Professor John Bull and Dr Liz Tomlin, for their insights and practical assistance during the writing of this volume. The task was made considerably easier through their good spirits and prompt attentions.

Lastly, I would like to thank Amanda and Eva for allowing me to stay in my basket …

Graham Saunders
Bristol, 2014

SERIES EDITORS' PREFACE

In the first major study of John McGrath's theatre company 7:84 Scotland, published in 1996, Maria DiCenzo notes a curious omission in scholarship: 'While it is not unusual to find book-length studies of the work of playwrights (often an analysis of plays with a bit of socio-political context thrown in), alternative theatre *companies* in the same period have received comparatively little detailed coverage' (DiCenzo, 1996, 6). Despite the remarkable proliferation of companies that emerged from the late 1960s until the end of the 1980s, a phenomenon that undoubtedly reshaped the ecology of British theatre, the area has only ever partially been addressed in edited collections such as Catherine Itzin's *Stages in the Revolution* (1980) and Sandy Craig's *Dreams and Deconstructions: Alternative Theatre in Britain* (1980), or in monographs, principally Andrew Davies's *Other Theatres: The Development of Alternative and Experimental Theatre in Britain* (1987) and Baz Kershaw's *The Politics of Performance: Radical Theatre as Cultural Intervention* (1992). However, in all these cases, the companies themselves are rarely considered collectively, comprising instead one strand of an alternative theatre culture that included arts labs/centres, individual practitioners and dramatists.

In recent years, this situation has changed through the endeavours of Susan Croft's exhaustive online project Unfinished Histories, which concentrates on the work of companies operating between 1968 and 1988. The project seeks to archive and document materials relating to these companies including posters and photographs of productions as well as interviews with former company members. However, being a website, Unfinished Histories, despite providing both valuable focus and scope, cannot provide a clear chronological and contextual account of the overall development of these groups, how they related to each other, or how funding policies and shifts in cultural agendas changed their evolution in the course of over forty years.

This three-volume series aims to address this lacuna. Individually, each volume charts the progress – and sometimes demise – of small- to medium-scale touring companies, who from the late 1960s took to the road in a fleet of transit vans and established a network of performance venues for themselves throughout the British Isles. These included theatres, community centres, youth clubs and arts centres as well as urban and rural outdoor spaces.

These companies have been variously described as 'alternative' or 'fringe', yet over the years both their work and more significantly much of their influence, has been assimilated into mainstream British theatre culture. For some groups, including Complicité (originally Théâtre de Complicté), Cheek by Jowl and Punchdrunk, their move from the margins to international status has been easy to identify. However, more often than not, the process has been more subtle, and so consequently unrecognized and unacknowledged. A good example of this has been the gradual absorption of black and Asian work into the repertoires of many major subsidized London and regional theatres since the late 1990s. This did not happen by accident: rather it came about through a long succession of gruelling one-night stands by pioneering companies including Tara Arts, Temba and the Black Theatre Co-operative during the 1970s and 1980s.

Each volume covers a distinct historical era. The first discusses the period 1965–79; volume two 1980–94, while volume three covers 1995–2014. The format for all three includes an opening chapter written by each editor that provides a contextual political and cultural background to the period in which the companies operated. The second chapter gives a broad outline and discussion of the many types of companies operating within the given period. Here, the editors have endeavoured not only to include familiar names, but other lesser-known documented groups. The final section of each volume includes a series of case studies from chosen contributors on the work of a particular theatre company active in the period covered.

Archival sources, both from holdings dedicated to a specific company and from the Arts Council of Great Britain, largely inform the choice of companies and approach taken in volumes one and two. This has come out of a larger five-year AHRC funded project, *Giving Voice to the Nation: The Arts Council of Great Britain and the Development of Theatre and Performance in Britain 1945–95*, that the editors Bull and Saunders have been engaged on since 2009. It soon became clear that, for the period covered, between 1965 and 1994, the Arts Council archive would provide a unique and, up until recently, unexplored resource for the study of theatre companies active in those years: materials include minutes of company meetings, funding proposals for projects, records of tour dates, statistics on box-office takings and audience attendance, newspaper and magazine reviews and publicity materials, as well as Arts Council, memos, letters and records of meetings. These frequently reveal much about the Arts Council's often cryptic assessment methods and more tellingly their attitudes towards particular companies, or the types of work they produced. The archive also offers insights into wider questions relating to changing priorities in policy towards alternative/fringe theatre in Britain from the late 1960s to the mid-1990s. Contributors, where possible (and where relevant), have made use of this resource, as well as individual company archives in assessing their work.

As editors, we are mindful of what we have left out. We also fully recognize that some of our decisions will be highly contentious. For instance, with hindsight, the first two volumes could perhaps have been retitled *English Theatre Companies*, as relatively little space is accorded to Scottish, Welsh or Northern Irish companies. This has been influenced by a number of factors: for one thing, we wanted each of the volumes to look at the *kinds* of work produced, rather than the geographical location they came out of. While it also might be assumed that the Arts Council archive would have provided a detailed national survey of British companies, in reality the archive resembles more of a Domesday Book on English theatre. The reasons for this are both historical and administrative, in that the Welsh, Scottish and Northern Ireland offices of the Arts Council, while answerable to London, were in effect autonomous bodies with their own allocated budgets and set of policies. This meant (with the often-made exception for the annual Edinburgh Festival) that a company such as 7:84 Scotland would be funded on the proviso that they tour exclusively within Scotland, unless prior arrangements had been made between other regional offices, or the company had secured necessary funds to tour within England. The third volume begins as the Arts Council of Great Britain devolved into three distinct Arts Councils for England, Scotland and Wales, and so looks at how arts policy develops in each and the impact of this on the independent theatre ecology that emerges across the UK (with the exception of Northern Ireland) in this period.

The editors have also endeavoured to provide as comprehensive an insight as possible into the types of work produced in any given period; yet this will always mean that certain companies will be privileged over others. Sometimes this is reflected in the priorities operating in a given period: for instance, in volume two, the second chapter places more emphasis on black, Asian and women's companies simply because these were areas that experienced the largest growth and afforded greater priority in terms of funding allocation than companies specializing in Live Art or Theatre in Education, whereas volume three takes particular account of the participation and access agenda that supported a growth in theatre for children and young people, as well as more widespread experimentation with audience involvement.

The editors are also aware of the problems of adopting a chronological approach. While the majority of companies only enjoyed a comparatively short life span, others such as CAST, The Women's Theatre Group and Temba continued to work over several decades. While each editor's second chapter concentrates on the work of groups who were formed within the period covered by their respective volumes (with some leeway given between companies who formed on the cusp), the contributors' chapters on particular companies assess the work on the basis of what they consider to be their most significant or celebrated of the period.

Chapter 1

HISTORICAL AND CULTURAL BACKGROUND

Politics

Mrs Thatcher and Thatcherism

Any account of British political and cultural life in the period covered by this volume cannot help but be dominated by the figure of Margaret Thatcher. Her election on 3 May 1979 as the first British female Prime Minister has often been taken to mark the end of what has been called the post-war consensus. Until then, successive Conservative and Labour governments since 1945 had run the economy on broadly Keynesian lines with full employment an overriding priority and direct government control imposed over institutions such as the Bank of England, industries such as coal, iron and steel, and transport networks including railway and canal. This policy of nationalization was considered to be serving the public good; profitability was a lesser concern. The spirit of consensus politics also meant that successive Conservative governments after 1951 continued to support the radical welfare reforms instituted by Clement Atlee's 1945 Labour adminis-tration, including the National Health Service.

The election of Mrs Thatcher questioned the role of government in maintaining these systems. Influenced by economists such as Friedrich Hayek and Milton Friedman, who believed that government should play a minimal role in running the economy, Mrs Thatcher saw the existing system of consensus as, at best, a series of uneasy compromises that failed to satisfy anyone as well as being disincentives to enterprise and innovation. The cultural historian Robert Hewison has described the Thatcher government as setting out with a radical and ambitious agenda whereby 'the British soul was to be remade by creating a new myth of economic individualism to replace the old ideas of community and collectivism' (Hewison, 1995, 212).

In turn, advocates of consensus argued that direct state inter-vention in key areas of national life served as a crucial buffer against the excesses of the free market and were necessary for the creation of a socially cohesive and civilized Britain. Mrs Thatcher laid out her position on the matter in characteristically forthright language at the 1981 Conservative Party Conference:

> To me consensus seems to be the process of abandoning all beliefs, principles, values and policies in search of something in which no one believes, but to which no one objects...the process of avoiding the very issues that have to be solved, merely because you cannot get agreement on the way ahead. What great cause would have been fought and won under the banner 'I stand for consensus'? (Campbell, 2003, 122–3)

The political journalist John Cole has argued that Mrs Thatcher was elected in the expectation of provoking 'a tidal wave for change, even if her supporters were by no means clear what changes to expect' (Cole, 1987, 43), while Hewison has gone on to describe Thatcherism itself as 'a moral and ideological project that set out to release new energies and produce cultural change' (Hewison, 1995, 210). In this respect she certainly succeeded, but these new energies have been likened by Alwyn W. Turner to 'a Pandora's box [that] released forces into society over which [Mrs Thatcher] had little control' (Turner, 2010, xi). Even the most casual observer looking back to the Britain of 1979, immediately after Mrs Thatcher's resignation in 1990, would have been struck by how much the previous decade already resembled another age. Yet, mythologizing Mrs Thatcher as the sole architect of these monetarist forces also risks exaggerating both the speed of change and the Prime Minister's ideological clear sightedness, especially in the early years of her administration. It is also worth remembering that the 'Thatcherite' policies that take her name came about relatively slowly and in a more piecemeal manner than is generally assumed.

The Thatcher government is also defined by many contradictions: despite winning three successive general elections with large majorities in 1983 and 1987, her party only won 42.9 per cent of the popular vote in the first of these – far less than the Conservatives had achieved between 1945 and 1979 – and throughout its time in office Mrs Thatcher's government only ever succeeded in attracting a third of the population at election time (Morgan, 2001, 466). Despite a call for a return to living within one's means, high street banks and building societies encouraged an unprecedented increase in personal borrowing after the deregulation of the City of London. Despite welcoming economic libertarianism, there were frequent calls for a return to moral responsibility and a blanket condemnation of the social reforms of the 1964–70 Wilson administration such as abortion, divorce reform and legalization of homosexuality that had produced the moral laxity of the 'permissive society'. And, while frequently asserting that her government would play a less intrusive part in people's everyday lives, legislation related to curbing local government, such as rate capping and the abolition of the six metropolitan authorities in 1986, made the Thatcher administration one of the most centralized in post-war politics.

The First Term 1979–83
Cuts to government spending defined the first years of the Thatcher government, and with it an economic downturn as monetarist policies began to take effect: their aim was to limit the supply of money in the economy, which had caused crippling inflation since the mid-1970s. Monetarist policy had in fact been introduced during the final years of the previous Callaghan government, and the touring theatre company Foco Novo's 1977 *Tighten Your Belts* by Jon Chadwick and John Hoyland was an agitprop-style protest play directed against proposed Labour cuts to public services. However, what defined the Thatcher government's economic policies was both their speed and severity.

Mrs Thatcher's fortunes were revived in April 1982 when a small group of islands in the South Atlantic known as the Falklands, with a population at the time of 1,800 people and 600,000 sheep, were invaded by Argentina, who held a long-standing historical claim to the territories. Despite setbacks to the British forces such as the sinking of HMS *Sheffield* and four other ships by the Argentine air force, UK land forces, assisted by heavy bombing from its own ships and aircraft, landed troops on the islands. Resistance from the Argentinian forces was poor and by 14 June the Falklands were once more back in British hands.

Despite a prevailing wave of jingoistic patriotism, encouraged by tabloid newspapers such as the *Sun*, some of the most critical voices at the time came from theatre. These included Peter Cox's play *V Signs* (1983), written for the company 7:84 England, and Louise Page's *Falkland Sound / Voces de Malvinas* (1983), produced at the Royal Court and an early example of verbatim drama that used interview sources to dramatize issues around the conflict. Tash Fairbank's play for the women's theatre company Siren, *From the Divine* (1983), criticized the exultant mood of nationalism that followed the end of the hostilities[1] and Steven Berkoff's play *Sink the Belgrano* (1986) was an excoriating treatment of a controversial incident when the Argentinian ship that gave the play its name was torpedoed by a British submarine after it had left a military exclusion zone and was returning to Argentina. The *Sun*'s infamous headline for the sinking, 'Gotcha!', obscured the reality of the 360 lives lost. The Falklands precipitated the fall of the military junta in Argentina and marked a significant boost to Mrs Thatcher's fortunes. Until then, the government's economic policies had made it increasingly unpopular, but victory in the Falklands seemed to restore a sense of national pride that had been in steady decline since the gradual dismantlement of the Empire and Britain's erratic economic fortunes since 1945. The Falklands also gave Mrs Thatcher a reputation for firm resolve and decision-making, which she capitalized upon.

The Second Term 1983–7
Although the Thatcher government, during its early years, was largely seen as both ineffectual and unpopular, the Conservatives won a 140-seat majority in the election of 1983, boosted by Mrs Thatcher's handling of the Falklands conflict and signs that the economic recession had ended (although levels of Gross Domestic Product, the main marker of a nation's economic health, had not yet returned to the level of 1979). Also, this period witnessed conditions that led to a consumer boom, due to the abolition of credit and hire purchase restrictions that had previously made it difficult to obtain loans. The privatization of formerly nationalized companies and industries also gathered momentum. This process had, in fact, already begun during the government's first term, starting with British Aerospace in 1981, and was followed by British Telecommunications in 1984, British Gas in 1987, British Airways and the electricity industry in 1989. By the end of the decade more people in the UK owned shares than belonged to a union (Turner, 2010, 229).

This period also saw the deregulation of financial markets (known collectively as the Big Bang) and the switchover in October 1986 to on-screen trading in the stock market; banks were also deregulated, and with this move came a reduction in the amount of capital they were required to hold in order to cover against bad debt. This meant that capital could leave the country without the approval of the Bank of England, which encouraged speculative dealing. Although its manufacturing base continued to decline, the UK rose to prominence as a world financial centre, providing services such as banking and investment. Simultaneously, an erosion of identity and function between retail and investment banking took place: the mortgage market, an area that had formerly been the preserve of building societies, was now included as part of the services provided by high street banks. All these factors created the perfect conditions for a financial bubble that would eventually burst, with disastrous consequences, by the end of the decade.

The Third Term and Resignation 1987–90
Caryl Churchill's 1987 play *Serious Money* ends with the song 'Five More Glorious Years'. Produced in election year, it was a satirical attack on the culture of greed and amorality that some interpreted as taking place with the government's blessing; yet, it was also an ironic paean to what had seemed like the invincible progress of Thatcherism. However, even as the Conservatives won a convincing third term in office, subsequent events revealed that Mrs Thatcher had feet of clay.

The first portent came in October 1987, soon after the election, in what came to be known as Black Monday, when world stock markets crashed because of debt in South America and Eastern Europe. In the following year withdrawal of mortgage interest tax relief raised householders' monthly repayments considerably. This was exacerbated further by a rise in the Bank of England base interest rate in order to prepare Britain for entry into the European Monetary Fund (EMF). Rates increased to 13 per cent in 1988, and then up to 15 per cent from October 1989. By October of the following year, 43,000 homes had been repossessed, compared with just 5,000 in 1980. Not surprisingly, by 1989 financial conditions had created a major slump, leaving many householders in negative equity and struggling to pay their monthly mortgage.

Another financial burden for many was the threat of the Community Charge, or poll tax, as it was more commonly known. This was an ambitious initiative to reform the system of rates by which a local council could raise money to pay for amenities. Many small businesses and property owners had long argued that they bore the brunt of these costs, and the original aim of the Community Charge was to spread the burden more fairly. However, the system devised went the other way and penalized those on low incomes while reducing the costs for wealthy homeowners in large properties.

In 1989, the poll tax was piloted in Scotland, where its implementation produced mass civil disobedience and refusal to pay. In March 1990, a major demonstration in London led to a riot in which over 400 police officers were injured, and its introduction in England and Wales in April 1990 also led to widespread demonstrations and unrest.

While many attribute Mrs Thatcher's fall from power to her refusal to abandon the poll tax, her increasing unpopularity, both within her own party and across the country, came mainly from the economic downturn. Her stance against Europe, where she seemed to renege on the idea of Britain joining the EMF after being a signatory, saw her Chancellor, Nigel Lawson, resign. Six weeks later Sir Anthony Meyer, a relatively unknown Conservative MP, challenged her leadership. Although Mrs Thatcher easily won, it was significant that more than 60 of her own MPs had voted against the Prime Minister.

After another resignation, this time from Foreign Secretary Geoffrey Howe on 13 November 1990 during a speech in parliament in which he effectively called upon others to challenge Mrs Thatcher's leadership, the former Defence Secretary Michael Heseltine immediately put himself forward as a candidate for leadership. Although Mrs Thatcher only lost by four votes in the first ballot, she failed to obtain the required majority. Despite wishing to fight on, losing the first ballot meant that 178 members of her own party had failed to vote for her, so Mrs Thatcher was forced to resign. She left office on 22 November 1990.

Industrial Relations

In 1979 trade union membership in Britain reached 12 million, its highest-ever level. Yet, Mrs Thatcher's election that year had come about, in no small measure, because many (including those with broadly socialist leanings, such as the theatre director Peter Hall and the playwright Harold Pinter) were frustrated by the behaviour of the trade unions. A long series of disputes had bedevilled the National Theatre since its opening in 1976, and at the beginning of 1979, when the country was still in the grip of the so-called Winter of Discontent, Hall wrote in his diary:

> The country is gradually coming to a standstill … We are a society of greed and anarchy: no honour, no responsibility, no pride. I sound like an old reactionary, which I'm not, but what we have now isn't socialism, it's fascism with those in power injuring those who do not. (Hall, 1983, 407)

The dispute had begun in late 1978, when members of the National Union of Public Employees (NUPE) went on strike after a one-per-cent cut had been imposed on government public expenditure. This had become necessary after the Callaghan government had been forced to take out a £2.3 billion loan from the International Monetary Fund. One of its conditions had been reductions in public spending.

Reform of the unions was to be a priority for the new Thatcher government, although changes were brought in cautiously via two employment acts, in 1980 and 1982, that placed significant curbs on union power.

The Miners' Strike 1984–5

This 12-month dispute was among the most bitter and prolonged in British industrial history. It also marked a watershed: by defeating the National Union of Mineworkers, who had all but ended the 1974 Conservative administration under Edward Heath, it achieved one of the Thatcher government's key aims breaking union power nationally, and at the same time removing them from their central place in promoting socialist values.

Three years before the strike, 7:84 England had toured a play that in hindsight was prescient. John Burrows' *One Big Blow* (1981) was partly about the miners' resistance to pit closures and was inspired by events earlier that year when the National Coal Board (NCB) had announced proposals to close 23 mines and make 13,000 miners redundant. However, under the threat of a national strike, the government had backed down.

In September 1983 Ian MacGregor, a fierce supporter of Mrs Thatcher's free-market economic policies, was appointed Chairman of the NCB and by March 1984 it had announced once again its intention to close 20 mines with the potential loss of 20,000 jobs. Supporters of the miners argued that the plan had been put into action before viability reports had been received, yet, from the very start, the call for a strike by the NUM's leader, Arthur Scargill, was controversial; it took place without a national ballot and even in areas where it was supported, only 18,000 members voted in favour while 405,000 voted against. More importantly, it allowed opponents to accuse the NUM of being undemocratic and using the strike for political ends – to overthrow an elected government.

Nevertheless, the strike received widespread moral and practical support from the public and, if anything positive could be said to have come out of this bitter and protracted dispute, the *Financial Times* observed that it was 'the biggest and most continuous civilian mobilization to confront the government since the Second World War' (Turner, 2010, 184). For miners, the strike was always far more than simply an industrial dispute: it was part of a wider struggle to preserve their communities and a way of life that had existed for several generations.

However, the strike had no real support from the Trades Union Congress (TUC) and Arthur Scargill's hope that it might trigger a general strike never materialized. Coal continued to be produced from Nottinghamshire, South Derbyshire and Leicestershire, where the miners refused to strike. The government, with long memories going back to their defeat in 1974, had made plans in readiness for the confrontation: stockpiles of imported coal meant that power stations could supply the country throughout the winter of 1984. The timing of the strike at the beginning of spring also meant that demand for coal was lower than if it had taken place in winter.

Both Mrs Thatcher and Scargill saw the strike in ideological terms. For Scargill, it represented not just a battle over miners' jobs but revolutionary socialism in action and a way of defeating the government's monetarist policies and belief in the free market. For both, compromise was unthinkable. Mrs Thatcher also made her position regarding the strike clear in a speech she delivered to the 1922 Committee on 19 July 1984, in which she likened the miners to insurgent fifth columnists: 'We had to fight an enemy without in the Falklands. We have to be aware of the enemy within, which is more difficult to fight and more dangerous to liberty' (Young, 1989, 371).

The NUM used the tactics it had employed in the 1974 strike, sending mass pickets from other areas into the Nottinghamshire coalfields to prevent coal production. The government responded in like, drafting in thousands of police officers from other areas and setting up roadblocks to prevent anyone suspected of being a picket. Not surprisingly, the tactic met accusations that the government was using the police as a neo-military force to break the strike.

Mass use of the police, together with recent employment and social security legislation, played a significant role in diminishing the impact of the strike: because the miners' union had not taken a national ballot, the government's employment laws meant it could ask the courts to sequester the union's financial assets. The NUM responded by moving the majority of its assets abroad, but this meant it had no means of providing strike pay to its members.

The dispute ended in March 1985 with 63 per cent of the striking miners marching back to work. The outcome was not only a humiliating defeat, but also marked a definitive turning point in the history of the Labour movement. Although, Nigel Lawson believed it 'essential that the government spent whatever was necessary to defeat Arthur

Scargill' (Brown, 1997, 137), the following year 36 mines had been closed, with significant job losses. Between 1979 and 1986 the NUM lost 72 per cent of its members and trade union membership in the UK declined from 13.5 million members in 1979 to 10.5 million in 1986 (Evans, 2004, 39). By the time Mrs Thatcher left office the figure had reduced further to ten million.

Many theatre companies supported the strike. Joint Stock produced Jane Thornton's play *Amid the Standing Corn* (1985), a celebration of the 1984 Women Against Pit Closures movement in Barnsley; Gay Sweatshop set up a reading of Noël Greig's play *The Dear Love of Comrades* (1979) – a gesture of solidarity reciprocated by the miners, who marched with the company at the 1985 Gay Pride festival, replete with brass band – while 7:84 England produced Peter Cox's play *The Garden of England* (1985) about the Kent miners during the dispute, seen from the perspective of the strikers' families. Yet, as D. Keith Peacock has commented, even at the time, 7:84's production seemed to be a demonstration of 'a form of political theatre which … was no longer effective or relevant' (Peacock, 1999, 138). Other companies opted to provide alternative responses, to both the issue of the strike and what had traditionally been understood as political theatre. For example in a documentary play *Six Men of Dorset* (1984), 7:84 England tackled the history of the Tolpuddle Martyrs, a group of nineteenth-century Dorset farm labourers convicted of swearing a secret oath as members of the Friendly Society of Agricultural Labourers who were subsequently transported to Australia. This play was directed by Pam Brighton and the project was sponsored by several trade unions, including the Transport and General Workers Union, who donated £45,000. By contrast, the company Welfare State International, which had been in existence since 1968 (longer in fact than 7:84, which formed in 1972) also set out to commemorate this important event in the history of the British trade union movement, but in a different way. Their Tolpuddle project had been commissioned by the Darlington Trades Council with help from the Darlington Centre for the Unemployed. The project involved seven company members together with 100 local residents in a half-mile procession that culminated in a garden party in a local park. As well as staging historical events, topical issues of the time were also represented by means of six-foot-high effigies of Mrs Thatcher and Ian MacGregor, as well as a miners' brass band and a parade of the unemployed. The miners' dispute also helped directly to set up a number of new theatre companies. One of these, the ReSisters Theatre, was active during the period of the strike in Nottinghamshire and Derbyshire. Set up by two women, Cordelia Ditton and Maggie Ford, their 1985 play *About Face* looked at the under-representation of women in Britain. Using stand-up and documentary sources, with Ditton playing all of the characters herself, the play toured to non-theatre venues (Goodman, 1993, 104).

In some ways, the fates of 7:84 and the miners' strike were closely intertwined. For John McGrath, 7:84's founder, the strike demonstrated that revolutionary socialism would not be brought about directly by the workers, or political companies like 7:84, who since the early 1970s, like latter-day evangelizers, had seen themselves preparing the way for full-scale socialism in Britain. They were now forced to reassess their position. McGrath also saw the potential of the approach taken by Welfare State and European practitioners such as Ariane Mnouchkine and Jerome Savaray's Magic Circus, who adopted a more anarchic, carnivalesque approach to political theatre, but, by the time McGrath attempted to incorporate these ideas into the project *All the Fun of the Fair* (1985), 7:84 England had been forced to break up after withdrawal of funding by the Arts Council.

Poisoning the Waters
The opening chapter in John McGrath's 1990 book *The Bone Won't Break* (originally a series of lectures given at the University of Cambridge) is entitled 'Poisoning the Waters'. Here he argues that throughout her three terms in office Mrs Thatcher maintained a concerted effort to contaminate 'the sea of Britain, with the purpose of asphyxiating socialism' (McGrath, 1990, 2). Since 1945, albeit hesitantly and often in highly compromised forms, Britain had come some way in adopting certain socialist principles, yet Mrs Thatcher had made it abundantly clear at the start of her administration that she intended to 'roll back the frontiers of socialism'(McSmith, 2011, 10). McGrath believed that a sustained campaign was being carried out by the government on the network of closely interrelated systems crucial to the implementation of socialism: these included weakening the power of trades unions through legislation, culminating in the defeat of the miners' strike in 1985; gaining financial control over socialist councils and the abolition of the GLC the following year, and using the threat of unemployment during its first term to divide communities. In addition, sophistry was called upon, with the promotion of 'popular capitalism', such as the sale of council houses and share options in the formerly nationalized industries, that appealed to working-class families who saw it as a way towards social betterment. Nationalist sentiments were aroused during the Falklands conflict and, throughout the Thatcher years, the

use of propaganda, smear tactics and sympathetic opinion formers in the media produced a slow erosion of collective spirit throughout socialist networks. These included the trade union movement, as well as liberal-leaning organizations such as the BBC and the Arts Council of Great Britain. As we shall see, these effects directly impinged on touring theatre companies, especially those with a political agenda like McGrath's own 7:84.

While D. Keith Peacock believes that theatre was never 'considered subversive enough to be singled out by the Thatcherites for especially harsh treatment' (Peacock, 1999, 60), if one considers political theatre as being connected to a larger oppositional network, then more than a grain of truth exists in McGrath's argument. The playwright David Edgar, commenting specifically on the effects of Thatcherism on the arts, seems to share McGrath's belief that an ideological shift was being engineered but believes the means employed were far less naked, in that, while there were no direct political assaults on the arts, 'dramatic economic shrinkage, in combination with gentle but consistent political pressure ... prised open the cracks sufficiently to let the sap of Thatcherism through' (Edgar, 1988, 17). Whatever the methodologies employed, the political journalist Peter Jenkins argues that Mrs Thatcher genuinely believed socialism to be the chief reason for Britain's economic and moral decline and saw her government as the first since 1945 'not to postpone or mitigate the advance of collectivism but to reverse it'(Jenkins, 1987,168).

Mrs Thatcher largely succeeded in her objective of dismantling the complex, symbiotic network that gave rise to the collectivist spirit of socialism. If one were to look, for example, at the path that the Labour government took after 1979, starting with the removal of the word 'socialist' in its 1991 election manifesto followed by Clause 4 in 1995 (which had formerly pledged common ownership of the nation's wealth), socialism as an understood practice had withered by the mid-1990s.

The Thatcher government was abetted by a weak and divided Labour Party which, after its defeat in 1979, went through a tumultuous period of internal strife. In the analysis that took place immediately after the election, many on the left blamed the defeat not on factors such as industrial relations and the Winter of Discontent, but on the party abandoning its socialist principals after 1974. Just as the Conservative party witnessed an unprecedented shift to the right after 1979, with the resignation of James Callaghan as its party leader in 1980, Labour, under its new leader Michael Foot, saw an equally unprecedented shift to the left. At its 1980 conference, the party voted for a policy of unilateral disarmament on nuclear weapons, the closure of American airbases on British soil and only narrowly avoided a motion to withdraw from NATO. While embracing socialism, some of these policies, especially the issue of unilateral disarmament and withdrawal from the European Common Market, alienated many moderate members of the party.

The extreme faction in the Labour party was known collectively as the Militant Tendency, who, after 1979, gained control of the Young Socialists. The group was strongest in London and other large cities such as Liverpool and Sheffield. For those on the left of the party the Millitant Tendency represented its conscience and the roots of the Labour movement. For moderate party members the group was an alienating presence and it was not until the first of a series of expulsions in May 1986 that the Labour Party finally began to appear at ease with itself.

Labour also lost voters with the formation of the Social Democratic Party (SDP), created in March 1981 when four former Labour Party cabinet ministers – Shirley Williams, Bill Rodgers, David Owen and Roy Jenkins – left to form a new party. While the SDP enjoyed early successes in the opinion polls and at by-elections – in Crosby for Williams and Glasgow Hillhead for Jenkins – its fortunes went into decline after the Falklands victory in 1982, leading to a merger with the Liberal Party in 1988. Despite this, the creation of the SDP reflected badly on the Labour Party as it harshly exposed ideological differences within its own leadership and crucially drew away some of Labour's traditional electorate.

The second election victory for the Conservatives in 1983 marked a low point for Labour. Looking back now, given the swell of national spirit after the successful resolution of the Falklands conflict, it was perhaps inevitable that Labour would lose. Even taking into account high unemployment, John Cole believed Labour would still have lost the election, as 'it seemed improbable … [that] the electorate would jump straight from the frying pan of monetarism-plus into a fire of massive public ownership and protectionism' (Cole, 1987, 4).

Dennis Kavanagh has identified traditional core support among working-class communities already beginning to fall after the 1974 election (Kavanagh, 1987, 168–9). In part, this had followed the decline of unionized industries in northern England, Scotland and Wales, and although this process had been taking place ever since the end of the Second World War, the 1980s and 1990s saw a rapid transition to service industries that were represented either by non-politicized unions or by no union at all. However, an awareness of these changes had not seemed to have reached the Labour Party by 1983. Kenneth O. Morgan estimates that less than half of those unemployed voted for Labour in the 1983 election (Morgan, 2001, 466), while Eric Evans estimates that between 1979 and 1983 thirty eight per cent of manual workers and thirty nine per cent of trade union members voted for the Thatcher government, groups who saw policies such as tenants' right to buy council houses as aspirational (Evans, 2004, 27).

An early piece of Thatcher legislation, the 1980 Housing Act, had given council house tenants the right to buy their property at a substantial discount. At that time, just under one third of British families lived in council properties; when Mrs Thatcher left office nearly one-and-a-half million of those properties were subject to a mortgage (Turner, 2010, 13). The policy's outcome may have encouraged aspiration, but its true aim can be seen as ideological. A 1987 survey revealed that 40 per cent of new council house owners voted Conservative against 25 per cent of their neighbours who were still tenants (Evans, 2013, 44). David Eldridge's play, *Market Boy* (2006), set in the Essex town of Romford, captures something of this working-class admiration for Mrs Thatcher very well. In one scene, a prospective Labour candidate is jeered and pelted by market traders, who declaim 'We're with Maggie' (Eldridge, 2012, 144). Mrs Thatcher's later onstage appearance also juxtaposes Romford market as a working miniature for her experiment with 'popular capitalism': at one point she asserts, 'This is my market, do you understand me? Mine! No one preaches in this free market except me!' (Eldridge, 2006, 53).

After the 1983 defeat, and under its new leader, Neil Kinnock, Labour underwent a period of internal reform. This included its first serious engagement with media and image consultants – figures who had played such an important part in the Conservatives' presentation strategy since 1979. Under the party's new Campaigns and Communication Directorate, run by Peter Mandelson, the first tangible sign of movement came with the introduction of the red rose emblem at Labour's 1986 conference. This replaced the traditional socialist symbol, the red flag, to represent the party. Despite these moves, Labour suffered a further major election defeat in 1987, failing once again to make any inroads into the south east or south west of the country. Even after the resignation of Mrs Thatcher, Labour still lost the 1992 election (an event that forms the basis of David Hare's 1993 play *The Absence of War*). The reasons for this may be attributed to John Major, who as Mrs Thatcher's successor appeared to be a more emollient figure, and the electorate's lingering reservations over Neil Kinnock's suitability as a potential prime minister.

Kenneth Morgan also observes that in the 1992 election less than 12 per cent of working-class voters supported Labour and that the Conservatives increased their vote by over 14 million, the highest poll any party had obtained since 1945 (Morgan, 2001, 512). Thatcherite reforms also continued, such as the privatization of what remained of the coal industry in 1994.

Society

Unemployment

Richard Viner, in his analysis of the Thatcher government, has commented: 'unemployment haunted British culture in the early 1980s' (Viner, 2009, 125). Despite being aware that one of the symptoms of their experiment with monetarism would be a rise in unemployment, most Conservative politicians after May 1979 believed that the rise would stop at around 100,000. However, by the end of 1980 unemployment was just short of two million, peaking at over three million in January 1982 and falling to just under that figure by the election of June 1983. Unemployment on such a scale had not been experienced in Britain since the 1930s and the situation remained static until 1987. In fact, the lowest unemployment levels recorded during Mrs Thatcher's time in office only appeared near the end, with a figure of 1,596,000 recorded in April 1990 (McSmith, 2011, 30). Unemployment also followed specific geographical patterns with high figures recorded in cities such as Liverpool and Sheffield, while areas such as Essex, Berkshire and Kent – all within commuting distance of London – experienced financial prosperity during the Thatcher years.

In theatre, Major Road, a company based in the north of England, produced Barry Lyon's play on this subject, *Divided Kingdom*, which went on national tour in 1989. Elsewhere, unemployment's corrosive effect on masculinity was explored in plays such as Jim Cartwright's *Road* (1986) and Peter Cox's *Jimmy Riddle* (1983), a monologue play for 7:84 England about the effects of long-term redundancy after the closure of the British Leyland car works in Liverpool. Jane Milling points out that women also addressed unemployment and the changing nature of the workplace in plays such as Kay Adshed's *Thatcher's Women* (1987), Debbie Horsfield's *Red Devils* (1983) and most famously Caryl Churchill's *Top Girls* (1982) (Milling, 2012, 73).

However, it was through television drama that these issues were most widely and forcibly brought to public attention. Undoubtedly the most well-known and powerful example was Alan Bleasdale's BBC series *Boys From the Blackstuff* (1982), set in Liverpool, but also influential was the new Channel 4 soap opera *Brookside*, launched that same year, set in the same city. Youth unemployment even found its way on to children's television drama, such as the BBC's *Tucker's Luck* (1983–5), while in pop music beat group The Specials reached number one in the hit parade with their single 'Ghost Town' (1981), written about the effects of unemployment in the band members' home city of Coventry.

Even though unemployment was a public preoccupation and a cause for serious concern among many, Mrs Thatcher's government won a convincing second term in 1983. Although the Falklands victory was significant, unemployment at the time only affected 13 per cent of the population, while the standard of living for the majority in employment had risen continually since 1979 (Turner, 2010, 118).

Inner-City Riots

The first wave of disturbances broke out in April 1981. They were alleged to have started when a young black man was arrested in Brixton, south London, outside a minicab office. Rioting lasted two days and led to damage amounting to £6.5 million. There were also hundreds injured, with police casualties outnumbering civilians by three to one (Turner, 2010, 91). Further outbreaks of civil unrest followed that July in Toxteth, Liverpool (where rioting was fiercest and CS gas was used for the first time on the British mainland), Southall in West London, the Moss Side district of Manchester, Chapeltown in Leeds, Handsworth in Birmingham, St Pauls in Bristol, Preston, Wolverhampton, Hull and once again Brixton. Rioting was to reoccur four years later, in September 1985, in Tottenham, Birmingham, Bristol, Liverpool and London.

David Edgar saw the rioting's principle cause as being high unemployment (Edgar, 1988, 132), and it is telling that the *Sun*, a newspaper that took a highly critical stance on multiculturalism and which was a firm supporter of the Thatcher government, reported on a 47.5 per cent increase in unemployment among black people against 37 per cent amongst the rest of the population in late 1980 (*Sun*, 1980). One study in Handsworth revealed that over half of its unemployment benefit claimants came from the ethnic minorities (Spencer et al., 1986, 42). Meanwhile, cities such as Leeds, Newcastle and Glasgow, where unemployment figures were also high, but which did not have high numbers of ethnic minority residents, did not experience riots. While this is not to say that economic policy did not play its part in the social unrest, it seems likely that ethnic tensions also had a role. Lord Scarman's conclusion in his 1981 report on the riots identified another cause: long-standing tensions between ethnic communities and the police. The government's response, however, was that race and unemployment were no more than potential factors and identified the riots' causes as principally cultural. David Edgar lists these as 'inadequate schooling, single parenthood ... and crucially the residual influence of 1960s permissiveness' (Edgar, 1988, 14). When the issue of unemployment was raised, newly appointed Employment Secretary Norman Tebbit brushed it aside: 'I grew up in the 1930s with an unemployed father. He didn't riot. He got on his bike and looked for work' (*The Times*, 1981).

Responses by theatre companies to the riots took various forms. 7:84 England toured a revival of Barrie Keefe's *Sus* (1979), a prescient play set on the eve of Mrs Thatcher's election. Its title refers to the power of the police to stop and search individuals; in areas such as Toxteth and St Pauls, a disproportionate number of young black men were targeted. Foco Novo, originally formed in 1972 and often associated with large-scale productions of work by European dramatists such as Brecht, added a new strand to its work in 1982: following the riots, the company applied for an Arts Council Special Initiatives Grant to produce a show on the effects of youth unemployment in south London. Known originally as The Peckham Project, the grant, together with funding from Greater London Arts (GLA) and Southwark Council, saw the development of work by the British born black dramatist Tunde Ikoli in plays such as *Sink or Swim* (1982) and (in collaboration with Howard Brenton) *Sleeping Policeman* (1983), which originated from a series of workshops devised with the local community.

Kwesi Owusu, in his book *The Struggle for Black Arts in Britain*, was sceptical of such responses, seeing them as doing little more 'than reiterating anti-racist slogans and polishing up their "multicultural" profiles'. While not specifically naming initiatives such as Foco Novo's Peckham Project, Owusu reserves particular scorn for what he calls 'half-baked sociological diagnoses of the 1981 uprisings and a stigmatisation of the Black community through favoured terms such as "Problems of black youth" ... "Youth and culture in Babylon" [and] "police harassment"' (Owusu, 1986, 96).

These approaches arose in part out of the Arts Council's increasing commitment during the 1980s to black and Asian arts. However, Clare Cochrane believes that this policy lent more to a growing awareness, following the 1981 and 1985 inner-city disturbances, that the government expected the Arts Council to contribute towards social amelioration rather than adhere to its former practice of supporting artistic merit simply for its own sake (Cochrane, 2006, 163).

For example, in a paper prepared for the Arts Council in 1985 entitled 'Ethnic Arts – Proposals for Development', the Deputy Secretary General writes about how 'the Arts Council, as a public agency, has been widely criticized for failing to make its contribution (if an indirect one) to the resolution of this crisis by the active encouragement of the best Afro-Caribbean and Asian arts' (ACGB, 1985e, 99/46/2). The paper also cites an article published in November's 1985 edition of the *Economist* that talks about 'blackspots in England's inner cities' as 'festering and dangerous' and calls upon the Arts Council to subsidize the sort of 'black arts groups the Arts Council fights shy of' (*Economist*, 1985). In what seemed like a response to such pressures, in that same year the Arts Council announced a 4 per-cent increase in overall funding to black and Asian arts over the next two years, followed by a further half a million pounds being made available to specific projects in 1988–9. In 1988, the Arts Council also published a report, *An Urban Renaissance: The Case for Increased Public and Private Sector Co-Operation*, which set out the direction that funding criteria for the arts would increasingly take in the 1990s.

Feminism: 1980–94

In her book *Hyenas in Petticoats* Angela Neustatter makes a pertinent observation about the differences between feminism in the 1970s and 1980s: 'Where the Seventies had been the heady days of optimism, of group activity, and a sense of compatibility at the shared feelings about a woman's lot, the Eighties were the days when women were looking far more critically at what feminism was about' (Neustatter, 1989, 51). The 1980s, while a period of unprecedented social and political activism for women, was also one of constant re-evaluation.

The election of Mrs Thatcher in 1979 was a case in point. While this was a clear demonstration of change, Mrs Thatcher's own attitude to women's issues was completely opposed to radical feminism. As in many other areas, the Prime Minister proved to be a divisive figure. In one speech she proclaimed: 'The battle for women's rights has largely been won. The days when they were demanded and discussed in strident tones should be gone forever. I hate those strident tones we hear from some Women's Libbers' (Campbell, 1987, 25). Mrs Thatcher seemed to assume that the battle for women's rights had been won shortly after the First World War, and that agitations made by second-wave feminists of the 1960s and 1970s were just one more unwelcome symptom of the permissive society.

Yet many women also admired Mrs Thatcher. As the 1980s gave way to the 1990s a schism opened up: known widely as post-feminism, it favoured women's individual achievement over the collectivist ideals of the 1970s. Caryl Churchill's *Top Girls* is not only a remarkable play for the clear-sighted analysis it anticipated regarding the effects and costs of Thatcherism, but also for its early anticipation of post-feminism. Its central figure, Marlene, dismisses collectivism in favour of a bourgeois feminism that privileges individual achievement; in the play she adopts and exploits male thinking strategies in order to succeed within patriarchal culture and refuses to acknowledge women as a group meriting special pleading. Marlene makes pronouncements including 'I don't believe in class' (Churchill, 1990, 140); the working class 'doesn't exist anymore' (Churchill, 1990, 139); and 'anyone can do anything if they've got what it takes' (Churchill, 1990, 140). Little wonder that Elaine Aston believes '*Top Girls* shows the dangers of feminism without socialism' (Aston, 2003, 20). However, post-feminism did not begin its ascendency until the beginning of the 1990s and, while not all women's theatre in the 1980s was directly opposed to Thatcherism, a spirit of collectivism prevailed. Ideas generated by Anglo-American feminism during the 1970s and 1980s included not only consciousness-raising groups, but also elements of political activism that in Britain included a number of 'Take Back the Night' marches during the Yorkshire Ripper murders of the late 1970s and early 1980s. An understandable sense of threat produced a sense of solidarity among women living in a number of northern towns and cities. The theatre company Siren dramatized this activism in its play *Curfew* (1981–2), as did Julia Kearsley's *Waiting* (1982), produced at the Lyric Studio Theatre, Hammersmith. Andy McSmith, in his history of the 1980s, argues that the Ripper case and the issues it raised about police incompetence, together with the issue of male violence against women, 'reached a wider and more receptive audience than all the debates about gender-specific language and patriarchal structures ever had' (McSmith, 2011, 37). As Siren member Jane Boston recalls, 'I always felt in my bones, if there was any time we were speaking for a movement that was tangible this was the time' (Hart and Phelan, 1993, 188). Peter Sutcliffe was tried in 1981 and convicted of murdering 13 women and of attempting to murder another two.

While the fears and anxieties caused by these murders did at least produce a sense of solidarity and strength within companies such as

Siren, elsewhere, in plays such as Sarah Daniel's *Masterpieces* (1983) and Claire McIntyre's *Low Level Panic* (1988), anxieties based on the threat of physical or sexual assault by men were clearly dominant concerns. Feminist activists in America, such as Andrea Dworkin and Catharine MacKinnon, and Catherine Itzin in the UK, also made associations between pornography and a wider repressive patriarchal system that feared, desired and oppressed women.

New ways of thinking about pornography, rape and body image were further promoted and disseminated through the burgeoning number of women's presses that had appeared during the 1970s and 1980s, together with the increasing presence of Women's Studies being taught as a degree subject in British and American universities. Yet in theatre, despite a willingness to question everything that had come before, when it came to issues of representation, clashes arose. Clean Break was a theatre company formed in 1979 by a group of women prisoners. In a 1980 show report for the Arts Council's Drama Panel, the theatre academic Jill Davis, who did much to champion the work of feminist and lesbian playwrights, objected to one particular performance.[2] This was less over questions of artistic quality and more about wider issues of representation within a framework of feminist politics:

> What really turned me off, though, was not the poverty of material or its performance but the very high level of verbal and physical violence in the piece. The rest of the audience at Action Space (mostly women, mostly feminists, a lot of gays) were visibly disturbed too. Several women left. There was a sense in the audience that the first rule of feminist ethics has been broken – sisters don't hit sisters, not even in plays, unless they have good reason, unless something is being demonstrated by it. And the violence in this show seemed completely gratuitous. Very nasty. (ACGB, 1980, 41/49/1)

One debate awakened by the more radical domains of second-wave feminism (a movement often seen as developing out of Kate Millet's book *Sexual Politics* in 1970) that directly affected artistic policy for a number of women's theatre companies in the 1980s was the question of separatism. Barbara Caine quotes one activist who stated the position clearly:

> We wanted to leave men no matter what, we started squatting so we could live with other women, we acquired by necessity new 'male skills' of plumbing, electricity, carpentry and car maintenance,

setting up our own discos and then forming bands to dance to. We cut our hair very short and stopped wearing women's clothes, we stopped smiling and being 'nice'. (Caine, 1997, 266)

This position was taken up by separatist lesbian feminists during the mid-1980s. Although their number has been estimated at no more than 10,000, the academic Emily Hamer believes that 'their influence on what it meant to be a lesbian was profound' (Hamer, 1995, 200). Influenced by the first major work on the subject, *Love Your Enemy?*, published by the Leeds Revolutionary Feminists in 1981, a position was taken that was similar to that of the Black Panthers in America over race in the late 1960s. Its central belief was that men and women were always going to be fundamentally in conflict with one another. Importantly, lesbianism itself was not necessarily seen as same-sex desire but more a political statement or, as Hamer puts it, 'a bond which excluded men' (Hamer, 1995, 201). Paradoxically, this meant that you did not need to be sexually attracted to women in order to become a lesbian feminist and, in some quarters, genuine lesbian relationships were treated with suspicion as they were said to confirm patriarchal hegemony, whereas political 'lesbianism was resistance to power' (Hamer, 1995, 201).

Anti-nuclear protests brought different groupings within the British Women's Movement together. Also known as Women's Liberation, this sought to obtain political, social, cultural and financial equality for women. These have been called 'the decade's most enduringly visible manifestation of feminist activism' (Brooker, 2010, 176), and one that succeeded for the first time in bringing '[to] public awareness feminist separatism and lesbianism hitherto unseen in the mass media' (Turner, 2010, 159).

In June 1980, Defence Secretary Francis Pym announced that American cruise and Pershing missiles would be sited in Britain as a consequence of NATO's defence policy in Europe. In return, the Americans would offer Britain the opportunity to purchase Trident missiles, albeit at the high price of £10 billion, as a replacement for its ageing nuclear Polaris submarine-launched warheads. Jane Milling points out that, while this did not start out as an explicitly feminist campaign, the first 40 demonstrators who marched from Cardiff to establish a women-only peace camp at Greenham military base in Berkshire provided the momentum for a protest that would last 20 years (Milling, 2012, 180). The camp attracted most attention in 1982 for a demonstration involving 30,000 women who encircled the air base, hanging photographs and personal mementos on the perimeter wire.

Theatre also played a part in this long-running dispute. Gay Sweatshop's touring production of *Poppies* (1983), itself a play concerning anti-nuclear issues, supported the Greenham women with a benefit reading at the Albany Empire in London on 10 and 11 March 1984, while six women at the Greenham camp set up a theatre group called Common Ground. Despite having no previous experience and disbanding, in 1985 their play *The Fence* (1984) was performed outside the perimeter of Greenham air force base and at St Paul's Church in Hammersmith. The establishment of the Women's Peace Camp also informed two significant plays from the same period – David Edgar's *Maydays* (1983) and Sarah Daniels' *The Devil's Gateway* (1983).

However, by the early 1990s, once-clear feminist positions began to falter. In literature, Dominic Head notes that, as the 1980s gave way to the 1990s' 'serious British fiction ... [moved] away from women's rights ... towards human rights' (Head, 2002, 111). Susan Faludi's book *Backlash: The Undeclared War Against Women* (1992) was amongst the first to discern that gains made in the last two decades were already under attack by the same patriarchal forces they had attempted to overthrow. Books such as David Thomas's *Not Guilty: The Case in Defense of Men* (1993), which variously blamed feminism for the breakdown of society since the 1960s and a corresponding marginalization of men's roles, made their position very clear. At the same time, feminist writing, such as Naomi Wolf's *Fire with Fire: The New Female Power and How it Will Change the 21st Century* (1993), also openly criticized elements of feminist theory and activism.

Allied to this, and perhaps as a direct result of the attention feminism had already paid to analysing patriarchal structures in society, attention now turned to questions and definitions of masculinity. Put crudely – if the 1980s was the decade when women's issues occupied a prominent place in mainstream culture, then the 1990s saw the spirited re-emergence of masculinity, particularly within popular culture and the arts.

David Edgar has argued that in British theatre, a number of male centred plays appeared in the early 1990s, including Nick Grosso's *Peaches* (1994) and Joe Penhall's *Pale Horse* (1994), and marked an important development that

address[ed] masculinity and its discontents as demonstrably as the plays of the early 1960s addressed class and those of the 1970s the failures of democracy ... The decline of the dominant role of men – in the workplace and in the family – is probably the biggest single story of the last thirty years in the western countries. (Edgar, 1999, 27–8)

However, if theatre did at least attempt to provide thoughtful, if violent, explorations of male identity, elsewhere films such as Quentin Tarantino's *Reservoir Dogs* (1992) and Danny Boyle's *Shallow Grave* (1994) appeared to celebrate violent and reckless forms of masculinity, where women seemed notably absent, or held up for abuse.

British theatre itself was not entirely immune from the same trend and, while this period saw plays such as Jonathan Harvey's *Beautiful Thing* (1993) and Kevin Elyot's *My Night with Reg* (1994), which explored homosexual identity often in touching and humorous ways, as in film other dramatists focused on wild sprees of violent male behaviour. Rather than being about men 'in crisis', plays such as Anthony Neilson's *Penetrator* (1994), Tracey Letts' *Killer Joe* (1995) and Louis Mellis and David Scinto's *Gangster No. 1* (1995) often seemed to advocate, and indeed celebrate, violence.

The celebration of irresponsible male behaviour also manifested itself, albeit less violently, in British popular culture during the early 1990s. This ranged from the launch of the men's magazine *Loaded* in 1994 to television series such as *Fantasy Football League* (1994–6) and *The Word* (1990–95). These programmes embraced 'traditional' male pursuits such as drinking, football and ogling (via the non-threatening distance of the printed page and television screen) scantily clad women.

The media quickly found a term for this form of masculinity – 'The New Lad': taken from a phrase coined in 1993 by the journalist Sean O'Hagan in an article for *Arena* magazine, Aleks Sierz defines this group as 'middle class men posing as sexist, anti-intellectual beer swilling brutes' (Sierz, 2012, 12). While often university educated and from the professional classes, familiar with feminist discourse and broadly in agreement with its aims, the 'New Lad' still celebrated unashamed forms of regressive 'male' behaviour. James Brown, the editor of *Loaded*, provided a rationale of sorts:

We like football, but that doesn't mean we're hooligans. We like drinking but it doesn't mean that as a soon as the pub shuts we turn into wife beating misogynists. We like looking at pictures of fancy ladies sometimes, but that doesn't mean we want to rape them. (Southwell, 1998, 101)

Imelda Whelehan provides an alternate view to this composite of the 'New Lad' in the following terms: 'Self-centred, male identified, leering and obsessed by sport, the new lad was naughty but nice; he proved himself a domestic catastrophe, but a certain boylike vulnerability supposedly made up for his deficiencies' (Whelehan 2000, 5).

Whelehan goes on to argue that this figure was also symptomatic of a gender conflict that had been identified since the end of the 1980s in books such as Joan Smith's *Misogynies: Reflections on Myths and Menace* (1989) and the aforementioned *Backlash* by Susan Faludi. In short, a counter-insurgency had been launched against the gains made by feminism, and the rise to prominence of the 'New Lad' was but one manifestation of a wider attempt to undermine and wrest power from women. Some sort of 'equality' came in the form of a counterpart – or perhaps accessory – to the 'New Lad': the so-called 'Ladette'. This startling figure was not entirely new, and in some ways was reminiscent of the 'Roaring Girls' of Jacobean drama. In the 1990s, its most high profile representation came through the brief, but immensely successful career of The Spice Girls, who formed in 1994, and their association with a loose ideology (if it could be termed so) named 'Girl Power'. Elaine Aston succinctly assesses this as 'a contradictory mix of feminist and anti-feminist discourses that promoted an image of aggressive "sisterhood" and feminine glamour through a creed of selfish individualism designed to "get what you want out of life"'. (Aston, 2003, 6)

AIDS

June 1983 stood out, not only as the month of Mrs Thatcher's re-election, but also because it was, as Alan Hollinghurst described in his novel *The Swimming Pool Library* (1988), 'the last summer of its kind there was ever to be' (Hollinghurst, 1988, 3). Hollinghurst is referring to the moment when AIDS reached the UK. That year, the BBC had screened a documentary, *Killer in the Village*, about the effects of AIDS among the homosexual community in Los Angeles. In July of the previous year, a 37-year-old man, Terry Higgins, became the first recorded victim of the disease in the UK. By 1989, there were 2,296 cases of diagnosed AIDS in the country (Turner, 2010, 221).

When male homosexuals were identified as the highest risk group, the backlash was almost immediate. For instance, when the Criminal Law Revision Committee decided in 1981 not to lower the age of homosexual consent to 16, (the same age as heterosexuals), offering instead a compromise of 18, the Police Federation condemned the committee's recommendations. Long-held prejudices could even be seen at the time in an episode of the popular television police series *The Gentle Touch* (1980–4). Here, the programme's central protagonist, Detective Inspector Maggie Forbes, despite herself being part of a minority group within the police, as a woman, warns her son Steve, who is training to be an officer, to best avoid a pub frequented by homosexuals lest it prejudice his future.[3] When diagnosed cases of AIDS started to emerge in the UK, James Anderton, the Chief Constable for Greater Manchester, spoke publicly of the crisis being self-inflicted and of victims 'swirling around in a cesspool of their own making' (David, 1997, 261–2).

Ironically, homophobia and the hysteria surrounding AIDS provided a rallying call and justification for activist theatre groups such as Gay Sweatshop, whose staging of Andy Kirby's play *Compromised Immunity* (1985), while largely addressing the homosexual community, was an important early attempt to remove some of the myths and prejudices that surrounded the disease. Despite these attempts, the company experienced reactionist homophobia when, during an engagement at the Taliesin Theatre in Wales, cleaning staff expressed concerns over their safety. The theatre manager, in an effort to generate publicity, leaked the story to the press and was photographed in the local paper wearing a white overall, rubber gloves and holding a bottle of bleach to allay fears. Unfortunately, the story was picked up by several national newspapers: one headline in the *Sun* read 'Gays Put Mrs Mopps in a Sweat', which reinforced and propagated existing myths about AIDS (Osment, 1989, ivii). These events subsequently informed Noël Greig's 1988 play for Gay Sweatshop, *Plague of Innocence* (1989), with its theme of press hysteria over the issue. Other companies, not exclusively associated with a homosexual constituency, also produced work on the subject, such as Red Ladder's *Who's Breaking* (1989), a play by Philip Osment about a young man coming to terms with a diagnosis of being HIV positive, which toured to youth clubs throughout Derbyshire.

The self-help approach by Gay Sweatshop and other organizations such as The Terrence Higgins Trust, London Lighthouse and Body Positive provided a bulwark in the absence of direct government intervention. It was not until 1987 when it looked as though the heterosexual community might also be at risk, that the Department of Health and Social Security were given a budget of £2.5 million to publicize the threat (Cook et al., 2007, 206); and not until 1989 that government funded AIDS campaigns directly addressed the homosexual community (David, 1997, 259), with grants to organizations such as London Lighthouse, The Mildmay Mission Hospital as well as local authorities (Cook, 2007, 206).

Section 28

Introduced by the Thatcher government as part of the Local Government Act in 1988, this piece of legislation seemed driven as much by ideological imperatives as by law reform. Although prompted in part by the moral panic over AIDS, Section 28 in fact owed more to the government's long-standing antipathy against teachers' organizations such as the Inner London Education Authority (ILEA) in the late 1970s and the activities of Labour-run councils, particularly the GLC in the early 1980s. Both had actively sought to combat discrimination against homosexuality through raising awareness of the subject; for example, in 1986 the London borough of Haringey sent out letters to all head teachers asking them to provide positive images of homosexuals and lesbians to students. The funding of theatre companies such as Gay Sweatshop, Sexual Outlaws and Consenting Adults had always been a contentious issue, even before the advent of AIDS. For example, in June 1979 the Conservative MP Brian Mawhinney, one month after the election victory, wrote to the Chairman of the Arts Council and the Arts Minister on behalf of one of his constituents who complained about Gay Sweatshop (and Monstrous Regiment) being in receipt of Arts Council funding. While the exact nature of the complaint was never articulated, the inference was clear – public money was irresponsibly being given away to support gay and feminist drama. This was the conclusion reached by the Arts Council's Chairman, Kenneth Robinson, who, in a memo to the Drama Director, summarizes, 'one company deals very largely with homosexual problems in a dramatic context and the other has a strong feminist line' (ACGB, 1979, 38/26/4).

However, it was a book by Susanne Bosche, *Jenny Lives with Eric and Martin*, published in 1983, that acted as one of the major triggers for Section 28. Bosche's book, an account of homosexual parenting aimed at children, had been made available in a number of schools within ILEA and other Labour-controlled councils. However, the book provoked an uproar: Joseph Brooker comments in his survey of the period, *Literature of the 1980s*, that 'aside from [Salman Rushdie's] *Satanic Verses*, Susan Bosche's book was perhaps more embroiled in public controversy than any other work of fiction this decade' (Brooker,

2010, 204). Section 28 was a deliberate measure to curb what it termed the promotion and 'teaching in any maintained school of the acceptability of homosexuality as a pretended family relationship' (Unfinished Histories).

The reason why the legislation caused such disquiet for people working with young people such as teachers and youth workers came from perceptions that merely by discussing the subject of homosexuality – even in the context of a class on Oscar Wilde's *The Importance of Being Earnest* or Christopher Marlowe's *Edward II* – they risked the danger of prosecution.

The year in which Section 28 was introduced also saw the greatest number of convictions against homosexual men on charges of soliciting since the mid-1950s. However, the legislation both united and galvanized the gay and lesbian community who during the 1970s had grown estranged from one another over lifestyle attitudes ranging from pornography to advertisements in the gay-male press for the services of sex workers. These differences were put aside while setting up a number of different initiatives to resist Section 28, such as the formation of the activist organization Stonewall. Several high-profile figures, including the actor Ian McKellan, spoke out against the government and there were many colourful acts of protest, including one group of lesbians abseiling into the House of Lords and another breaking into the BBC to disrupt a live news broadcast.

The legislation also prompted swift responses from a number of theatre companies. Philip Osment's play for Gay Sweatshop, *This Island's Mine* (1988), looked at discriminatory tactics used against homosexuals, Channel 4 commissioned the physical theatre company DV8 to respond to Section 28 in a piece entitled *Never Again* (1989) while the Gritty Theatre Company, set up by Maro Green, produced a play about the subject entitled *Memorial Gardens* (1988).

Section 28 was finally repealed, first in Scotland in 2000 and then in England three years later. Philip Osment, in his history of Gay Sweatshop (written in 1989 while the legislation was still in existence), conceded that despite widespread fears, in practice Section 28 failed to interfere with work such as Jackie Kay's 'coming out' play *Twice Over* (1990) that had toured schools (Osment, 1989, lxiv). Also, by the time of its repeal, no individual had ever faced prosecution, yet it is easy to see why this piece of legislation might have led to self-censorship and not difficult to understand the hostile message it sent out to homosexuals.

The Major Years 1990–4

Politics

Despite early popularity, and with the appearance of being a more consensual figure than Mrs Thatcher, those expecting a significant change of direction in policy under John Major would be disappointed. Further privatization of assets continued: most significantly of British Rail in 1993.

However, John Major's premiership was turbulent from the outset. Almost immediately after Mrs Thatcher left office in 1992, a two-year period of economic recession began, initiated by a run on sterling on 16 September. Despite interest rates rising that day from 12 to 15 per cent in order to support the pound, it continued to fall in value. In 24 hours, the Bank of England had sold over £30 billion of its reserves and Britain had left the European Exchange Rate Mechanism (ERM). Now that the pound was no longer pegged to the Deutschmark, its value was determined by world markets, and this effectively led to its devaluation. 'Black Wednesday', as this became known, was seen as a political humiliation, losing the Conservatives any reputation they may have secured for financial competence, and ending any aspirations on John Major's part to influence events within the European Union.

Europe also became the subject of a long and fractious dispute within the Conservative Party over the Maastricht Treaty, which was viewed by its British critics as a move towards greater political integration with Europe and associated loss of national self-determination. Although the treaty was ratified in 1993, the decision caused a split in the Conservative Party that undermined John Major's authority irrevocably. It was from this point that public opinion began to swing in favour of Labour, which had a new leader, John Smith, following Neil Kinnock's resignation after the 1992 election defeat. This improvement was continued after Smith's sudden death in May 1994 with his replacement by Tony Blair.

Culture: 1980–94

Theatre

While this volume is principally concerned with independent theatre companies, their place needs to be assessed in relation to a wider theatre ecology: this includes major subsidized venues such as the National

Theatre, The Royal Shakespeare Company and the Royal Court as well as the network of regional theatres, the West End and the commercial sector. As the next chapter and the individual company case studies hope to show, it is a mistake to think of all of these elements as separate entities; for example, a touring company such as Foco Novo frequently performed at the Royal Court's Theatre Upstairs and also mounted co-productions with other major regional theatres such as Howard Brenton's *Bloody Poetry* (1984) at the Leicester Haymarket, or Tunde Ikoli's adaptation of Maxim Gorky's *The Lower Depths* (1986) at the Birmingham Repertory Theatre.

The 1980s are generally seen as a time of crisis and retreat for the theatre. The critic Martin Esslin, in an essay written in 1980 in which he looked back over the achievements of British theatre in the last decade, concluded that it had been a golden period, characterized by innovation and experimentation. By contrast, 1980, for Esslin, was notable only for the increased array of what he called 'shoddy entertainments for tired businessmen – and footsore tourists' (Esslin, in Trussler, 1981, vii). In the same vein, John McGrath saw British theatre in the 1970s as 'a blossoming bough' that had been 'clumsily hacked off' in the 1980s (McGrath, 1990, viii), and it is certainly true that a number of practitioners struggled to survive in the new economic climate. For instance, Gillian Hanna, one of the founding members of the feminist company Monstrous Regiment, spoke of going into the new decade fully expecting it be one of continuity, and soon discovering instead that it would be one of retrenchment and compromise (Hanna, 1990, 56).

Yet the period between 1980 and 1994 is a contradictory one – especially in the area of women's theatre. Here, the 1980s were marked by a sustained period of growth that built upon gains established during the 1970s. As the playwright David Edgar puts it, 'the third wave of new playwrights – those who emerged in the early to mid-1980s – didn't answer to names like David [Hare/ Edgar], John [Osborne] and Howard [Brenton] but to names like Sarah [Daniels], Bryony [Lavery], Louise [Page] and Clare [McIntyre]'. Taking the output of new plays at the Royal Court as an example, Edgar notes that whereas between 1956 and 1980, 8 per cent were presented by women, by 1989, it had risen to 38 per cent (Edgar, 1999, 8). Women's drama also made inroads within the mainstream, when in 1981, 1984 and 1988, Nell Dunn, Sharman MacDonald and Timberlake Wertenbaker, respectively, won the Evening Standard Most Promising Playwright award for *Steaming* (1981), *When I was a Girl I used to Scream and Shout* (1984) and *Our Country's Good* (1988). All three plays subsequently transferred to the West End, although as Tom Maguire observes, the boom in women playwrights during the 1980s was a phenomenon largely confined to England, whereas their Scottish counterparts (with the exception of Sharman Macdonald) such as Liz Lochead, Marcello Evaristo and Rona Munro encountered difficulties in getting their work produced. Maguire also notes a scarcity of Scottish women's theatre groups (with the exception of the short-lived Mother Hen formed by Jules Caulfield, Tot Brill and Sue Armstrong), in comparison to the situation in England (Maguire, 2011, 157).

The sense of purpose and increasing prominence of women in the 1980s also served to emphasize what seemed like a collective loss of nerve by several of the major political dramatists of the late 1960s and 1970s: figures such as Edward Bond, Howard Brenton and Trevor Griffiths, who had embraced a broadly Marxist /socialist position. Critics have been unforgiving over their collective silence and failure to adapt to the rapid changes in British political life after the election of Mrs Thatcher. Vera Gottleib, for instance, maintains that 'in some respects it became easier to write about the collapse of Eastern Europe than about domestic politics' (Gottleib, 2004, 422), while Richard Boon comments that when 'faced with a "real" enemy … the most dangerously reactionary right wing government of recent times, their work seem[ed] to have lost momentum and their voice some of its authority' (Boon, 1993, 325–6).

This sense of impotence was not solely confined to drama, but seemed to infect the entire British artistic landscape during the 1980s. The critic D. J. Taylor, writing at the end of the decade on developments in the novel, concludes that 'most of our "great writers", those masters of modern English literature, are simply not capable of defining the 1980s' (Taylor, 1989, 16), while Leonard Quant in his assessment of British cinema states that while many films 'expressed a revulsion with Thatcherism … their anger rarely turned to … schematic politics' (Quant, 1993, 33). Kenneth O. Morgan, in his book *The People's Peace*, also observed that 'the new generation of novelists and playwrights … were increasingly prone to introspective analysis without a social cutting edge' (Morgan, 2001, 439). For Vera Gottleib, only British television drama provided any real outlet for political resistance during the 1980s. She praises 'series after series [that] set itself in opposition to the policies of the radical New Right' (Gottleib, 2004, 414). These included Troy Kennedy Martin's *Edge of Darkness* (1985) and M. S. Power's *Children of the North* (1991).

As all these critics note, the chief problem was that, with a few exceptions, there was a basic failure to understand the nature of Thatcherism and the changes it was making to British life: in particular, many of these artists fell into the trap of crude representation, ignoring or failing to comprehend Thatcherism's complexities and contradictions. Crucially, they seemed blind to the attractions it held to large sectors of traditionally Labour voting communities. Instead, Howard Brenton and Tony Howard's *A Short Sharp Shock* (1980), resorted to early 1970s agitprop techniques and broad satire as an early response to the new government. Edward Bond's trilogy *The War Plays* (1985) was more concerned with apocalyptic nuclear dystopias than the state of 1980s Britain, while David Edgar spent much of the decade either writing plays about the post-war failure of the British left to achieve socialism, or visiting the mid-nineteenth century in *The Life and Adventures of Nicholas Nickleby* (1980) and *Entertaining Strangers* (1985). This same retreat to the past has also been observed in the work of novelists such as Peter Ackroyd and Graham Swift (Taylor, 1989, 16), and while Edgar did address the 1984–5 miners' strike in *Maydays* (1983) and later made it central to *That Summer* (1987), the future utopias of Brenton's *Greenland* (1988) and dystopias of Bond's *The Tin Can People* (1984) seemed more preferable than confronting the present.

Edward Bond could justifiably retaliate by saying that his concerns arose out of the preoccupation of other dramatists with what they saw as the more pressing crisis of the Cold War and nuclear conflagration in plays such as Howard Brenton's *The Genius* (1983), Edgar's aforementioned *Maydays*, Nick Darke's *The Body* (1983), Robert Holman's *The Overgrown Path* (1985) and Barry Hines' BBC drama *Threads* (1984).

Michael Billington observes that it was not until the 1984 miners' strike and the full effects of unemployment that political dramatists began to fully regain their voices (Billington, 2007, 309). Yet their relative silence for the first part of the decade did have the beneficial effect of allowing female dramatists and theatre companies the chance to become established.

The 1980s also managed to produce some notable work that dissected some of the changes Thatcherism sought to bring about. Churchill's *Top Girls* has already been mentioned, but David Hare and Howard Brenton's collaboration entitled *Pravda: A Fleet Street Comedy* (1985) managed, through the figure of the newspaper proprietor Lambert La Roux, to capture both the energy and ruthlessness of such individuals who flourished under Thatcherism. Also, Caryl Churchill's *Serious Money* (1987), set on the trading floors of London's Stock Exchange, demonstrated with remarkable wit and clarity how the new American system of trading had swept away the established gentlemanly order of the British stock market to be replaced by a new breed, forged out of the brutal logic of the free market. Perhaps less successful in finding its target, but nevertheless accurate in identifying the bourgeois family unit as one of Mrs Thatcher's key voting groups, was Alan Ayckbourn's *A Small Family Business* (1987).

In Jane Milling's account of British theatre culture in the 1980s she maintains, 'if the 1970s had been the decade of the small-scale alternative theatre company, the 1980s were primarily concerned with the large scale' (Milling, 2012, 41). However, it is perhaps more accurate to describe the situation as one resembling a state of polarization. Michael Billington also sees grand-spectacle as the governing characteristic of the period, for example, the so-called 'mega-musicals' such as Andrew Lloyd Webber's *Cats* (1981) and *The Phantom of the Opera* (1986), shows that Billington dubs 'Thatcherism in action' (Billington, 2007, 284). Other epic projects included ambitious adaptations of classic novels, such as David Edgar's *Nicholas Nickleby* (1980), or sweeping director-led history cycles, such as Peter Hall's *The Oresteia* (1981) or John Barton's *The Greeks* (1980). These were far removed from the gaudy pleasures of the mega-musical. However, as Billington points out, many of these grand theatre projects were in fact the progeny of the 1970s, having originally been conceived in that decade (Billington, 2007, 298). Yet, despite their impressive scale, Billington argues that these productions represented little more than palliatives, offering their audiences only a fleeting 'spiritual affirmation in a time of disillusion' (Billington, 2007, 296).

While no doubt taking issue at his adaptation of *Nicholas Nickleby* being considered little more than a temporary analgesic, David Edgar, writing at the time, identified the same trend. He terms these events 'celebratory theatre', which he describes as 'large-scale spectaculars, performed at the great institutional theatre[s] which have sought to comfort rather than agitate, to conform rather than disturb' (Edgar, 1988, 141). Edgar also sees the process as evolutionary, in that the seriousness of Barton and Hall's staging of Greek myths unwittingly spawned what he terms 'The New British Musical', that was 'even more dazzling in form, even more empty of content' (Edgar, 1988, 230).

By the end of the 1980s the mega-musical had also developed (if one can call it that) a further offshoot that began with *Buddy: The Buddy Holly Story* (1989). Later dubbed a 'jukebox musical', this loosely biographical account of the 1950s rock and roll musician was merely a device, or excuse, to perform Holly's most popular songs from the hit parade. This format became increasing popular during the 1990s and reached its apogee (or nadir, depending on your view) with Ben Elton and Queen's *We Will Rock You* (2003).

Spectacle, albeit on a lesser scale, was also the hallmark of a number of ornate RSC productions of Shakespeare and Chekhov during the 1980s. This produced a dichotomy, whereby bombastic musicals and lavish productions of classical drama thrived, while elsewhere a slow inexorable struggle for survival took place within what could be loosely called alternative, or fringe theatre.

After Mrs Thatcher's resignation, the 1990s marked a slow but progressive process of re-evaluating the previous decade in plays such as David Hare's *Racing Demon* (1991), *Murmuring Judges* (1991) and *The Absence of War* (1993) 'trilogy', as well as *Skylight* (1994). This reappraisal even extended to Stephen Daldry's celebrated 1992 revival of J. B. Priestley's *An Inspector Calls* (1944) that ran for almost six years in the West End. Priestley's morality tale about society's personal responsibility for the less fortunate came to be seen as making a pointed critique of the Thatcher decade.

Daldry, who had taken over as Artistic Director of the Royal Court in 1992, also encouraged a new group of dramatists to stage what came to be seen in retrospect as a remarkable season of plays at the Theatre Upstairs in 1994: names included Joe Penhall, Judy Upton and Nick Grosso. Their plays, *Some Voices*, *Ashes and Sand* and *Peaches*, also looked at the aftermath of Thatcherism on a number of communities and organizations; these included the closure of long-stay hospitals for the mentally ill and the rarely reported social effects of economic decline on seaside resorts in south-east England. The last play in the Royal Court season entitled *Coming on Strong* more than lived up to its promise: *Blasted*, written by a twenty-three-year-old playwright called Sarah Kane, not only become the subject of a hysterical media controversy owing to its depiction of sex and violence, but would come to define much of the content of new theatre writing throughout the latter part of the 1990s. While at the Royal Court, Daldry took advantage of funding opportunities made available through the newly inaugurated National Lottery in order to renovate the building.

Changes in new-writing culture could also be seen in the success of two small London theatres in the early 1990s – The Almeida and The Donmar Warehouse. Two actors, Ian McDiarmid and Jonathan Kent, formed the Almeida in 1990, while the Donmar opened in 1992 under its artistic director Sam Mendes. Both venues were dubbed 'boutique theatres', owing both to their size and their ability to attract 'star names'. Both offered programmes that included classical revivals, such as the

Almeida's productions of *Medea* with Diana Rigg in 1992 and Terence Rattigan's *The Deep Blue Sea* with Penelope Wilton the following year, and new work, such as its premieres of Harold Pinter's *Party Time* (1991) and *Moonlight* (1993).

Elsewhere, another small theatre in London's Kilburn district, the Tricycle – with a long-standing reputation for producing politically orientated drama – staged, in 1994, *Half the Picture*, a collaboration by John McGrath and the journalist Richard Norton-Taylor that dramatized parts of the Scott Report. Commissioned in 1992, this government inquiry investigated accusations that British companies had been exporting arms to Iraq, despite the existence of an embargo. This genre of dramatization became a hallmark of the Tricycle's output during the 1990s and 2000s, with plays such as *The Colour of Justice* (1999) and *Guantanamo – Honour Bound to Defend Freedom* (2004) becoming known as tribunal or 'verbatim' plays.

Funding and Subsidy in Theatre 1980–94

As Michael Billington observes in his history of post-war British theatre, the 1980s began with a 2.9-per-cent cut in arts funding and ended with a further reduction of 4.8 per cent (Billington, 2007, 322). In fact, funding for the arts was one of the first items of public spending to be cut when the Thatcher government entered office. As early as October 1979, the magazine *Private Eye* had leaked news that the Arts Council's Drama Panel were being asked to consider the withdrawal of funding to a number of repertory theatres including Watford, Coventry and Crewe and, perhaps most controversially, the English Stage Company at the Royal Court. Smaller companies on the list included Belt and Braces, Pirate Jenny, Stirabout and Clown Cavalcade (*Private Eye*, 1979). This was the first time in its 35-year history that the Arts Council had been forced to consider making substantial cuts to its budget. Up until then, its policies had been based on an assumption (much like the core belief of capitalism itself) of exponential growth. This sudden reversal came as a shock to both the Arts Council and the clients it supported. While the government was able to justifiably claim that spending on the arts increased on an annual basis during its time in power – and large-scale capital projects such as the new British Library were amply supported – overall, funding did not keep up with the rate of inflation. For many theatre companies this meant that, at best, funding was at a standstill and more often than not suffered a cut in real terms.

On Christmas Eve 1980, faced with what amounted to a 1-per-cent cut to its annual budget, the Arts Council's Drama Panel announced it was to discontinue funding for 41 of its clients (18 of whom were theatre companies), to take effect in April 1981. The timing of the decision was a public relations disaster of the highest order. Although this action was intended to give artists and companies enough time to consider their budgets before the end of the financial year, dispatching the letters on Christmas Eve had unfortunate Dickensian associations, casting the Arts Council as a misanthropic Scrooge against the good-hearted band of impoverished Bob Cratchits who relied on their mean-spirited employer. What made the cuts appear even worse in the eyes of many working in fringe theatre was that companies such as the Royal Opera House remained unaffected by the cuts, and it became easy to agree with D. Keith Peacock's observation that it was far easier to withdraw funding from small-scale touring companies than established building-based ones due to the latter's greater visibility (Peacock, 1999, 37). In the end, only three companies lost their funding, but the Christmas cuts were an early portent of what the arts could expect under Mrs Thatcher's government. For example, whereas in the financial year 1977/8 the Arts Council supported 109 revenue clients and 58 project clients in Drama, by 1981/2 these had decreased significantly to 83 revenue clients and 50 project clients (ACGB, 1981a, 38/32/13).

Despite pledging to continue the existing model of distributing funds through the Arts Council, Mrs Thatcher's new Arts Minister, Norman St John-Stevas, introduced a caveat in December 1979 – one that would increasingly assume importance during the 1980s – that expected artists to 'look to the private sphere to meet any shortfall' (Sinclair, 1995, 248). Elizabeth McLennan recalls how this new culture soon affected 7:84 Scotland, when in 1980, at the behest of their Drama Officer, Mary Picken, its board was encouraged to attend a conference on sponsorship of the arts. Yet efforts to supplement its Arts Council grant only ever saw the company secure £100 from the *Daily Record* newspaper (Maclennan, 1990, 90). By 1986, companies were routinely asked to seek sponsorship in addition to receiving subsidy – for example, the physical theatre company Trestle was 'recommended' by its drama officer to seek sponsorship from British Petroleum and the independent television company TV South (ACGB, 1986a, 41/45/7) and Complicite, one of Trestle's contemporaries, attracted £3,000 from Beck's beer for a national tour (ACGB, 1986, 41/45/2). In reality, sponsorship and private donation were only ever viable options for major national companies such as the RSC and National Theatre. While the British Museum (an institution that the Association of Business Sponsorship in the Arts estimated received more than 10 per cent of all sponsorship in the UK) received over £3 million in sponsorship for 1987/8, this was never going to be a serious proposition for small, touring companies, especially 7:84 Scotland, which was against many of the values of capitalism.

Yet the picture of British theatre in the 1980s being in a state of permanent retrenchment is grossly misleading. Baz Kershaw, while clearly hostile to Thatcherism, points out (using statistics from the Policy Studies Institute's *Cultural Trends* series) that in broad terms overall subsidy across the theatre sector increased, while both commercial and regional theatre saw overall box-office takings rise. Kershaw concludes:

> whatever it *felt* like to be making theatre under Thatcher – and there were rising cries of 'crisis' throughout the 1980s and into the 1990s – the theatrical system generally, and especially in London, responded well to the tough new fiscal challenges of monetarism and value for money. (Kershaw, 2004, 311)

In a similar vein, histories of theatre in the 1980s depict the Arts Council simply as a willing accomplice in the demise of companies through funding cuts and the development of an increasingly bureaucratic and managerial culture. Nadine Holdsworth, in an article on the history of 7:84 England, gives a typically damning assessment: 'increasingly the Arts Council fulfilled its obligations as an agent of the state, enforcing free-market ethics and enacting a political and cultural policing mechanism' (Holdsworth, 1997, 39). However, investigation of the archival records of the Arts Council's Drama Department during this period tells a far different story: rather than being complicit agents of the Thatcher government, Arts Council drama officers as well as senior figures in the organization did their best to resist pressure from the government and actively sought to help and defend companies perceived as being under attack.

Nevertheless, misgivings over the creeping influence of Thatcherite values in the running of the Arts Council were confirmed for many by the appointment in 1982 of William Rees-Mogg as its new Chairman. However, charges of bias against the former editor of *The Times* are unsubstantiated when one considers that he was certainly not as closely bound to the government of his day as previous chairmen had been.

For example, Lord Goodman, one of the longest-serving and well-known chairmen, had from 1965 to 1970 also acted as Harold Wilson's solicitor. However, the writer and academic Richard Hoggart, who was appointed Vice-Chairman of the Arts Council in 1980 was under no illusions as to the reasons for his forced resignation the following year. While ostensibly down to the fact he had fulfilled his allocated time for serving as a Council member, Hoggart, in his autobiography, recalls being told by the Arts Minister that he was disliked by 'Number 10' – an incident that in his eyes 'confirmed that government intervention in the work of such bodies started very early in the Eighties' (Hoggart, 1994, 232).

The appointment in 1983 of Luke Rittner (who had formerly been a founder/director of the Association for Business Sponsorship of the Arts [ABSA]) as the Arts Council's Secretary General also seemed to confirm such fears. Rittner (together with the Minister of the Arts, Richard Luce) in the opinion of some 'turned native' during his time at the Arts Council (Lamede, 2013) by coming round to see the virtues of subsidy – his appointment took place at a time when public subsidy as the only stream of income available for the arts was beginning to be seriously questioned.

Rittner's arrival also coincided with the implementation of management culture into the Arts Council, especially when it came to the procedure for companies applying for funds. Previously, this had been done on an informal basis, as in the story told by Howard Brenton about how, in the early days of Brighton Combination during the late 1960s, Dennis Andrews, one of the Arts Council drama officers, paid a visit 'giving us several hundred pounds in cash, hand-to-hand, to keep the Combination going' (Rees, 1992, 219). By the mid-1980s funding became increasingly dependent on a company providing detailed accounts of its staffing and finances. This often necessitated appointing an administrator to keep abreast of applications and providing the necessary level of administration required for the Arts Council's increasing insistence on companies attempting to find matching funding from business and local authorities.

These changes could be seen most directly through the makeup of company personnel. For example, Siren was joined by Rose Sharp in 1985, who became their full-time administrator, whereas previously members of the company had shared this task. Arguably, the Arts Council's insistence on professional administration allowed artists to concentrate on creative work, but it also produced a culture that seemed increasingly to look towards financial accountability and organizational skills as key factors in assessing the health and viability of a company. In the past, artistic standards alone had been the most important criterion. By 1994, it had also become common for companies to be required to demonstrate a social or educational function for their work in order to secure funding.

Further confirmation of this shift in policy came in 1985 when the Arts Council, the Gulbenkian Foundation, the Office of Arts and Libraries, the Museums and Galleries Commission and the Crafts Council commissioned John Myerscough's report entitled *The Economic Importance of the Arts*. Essentially, this was a detailed audit of arts funding in the UK that sought to produce a new way of justifying artistic practice: instead of arguing for its merit in terms of its cultural value, or even its civilizing effects, Myerscough and many who came after him made a case for the importance of the arts entirely from an economic basis in terms of the income it generated, or ways a deprived inner-city area could be transformed through knock-on effects achieved by the establishment of an arts centre or theatre. The Arts Council's commissioning of the report to justify the need for increased funding was based on a strategy of using a set of arguments that Mrs Thatcher's government could readily understand, but as Jane Milling points out, 'without irony, the initially critical term "cultural industry", coined by the philosophers of the 1950s Frankfurt School to ascribe a totalising force that reduced art to mass consumption controlled by market forces, became part of a lexicon of defence for government subsidy for the arts during the 1980s' (Milling, 2012, 38). Writing a year before the Myerscough Report, the cultural critic John Pick had already described key elements of the new managerial culture taking place within the arts:

The notion that the arts must now be regarded solely and with no other purpose as an *Industry* is everywhere about us. Books, pictures, symphonies and plays are *products*; their readers, watchers and listeners merge into one hapless consumer … Grants are no longer seen as a form of welfare, a disinterested concern for truth and brevity, but as *investments* that are ultimately profitable to the sponsors. No longer do critics search for the quality of their art, instead experts assess the managerial *efficiency* of any organisation… In other words, armament factories, sweetshops and arts centres are all judged by the same criteria. (Pick, 1987, 2)

As already mentioned, despite the shift in culture within the Arts Council, it is important to note that many working within the organization resisted these outside pressures as best they could and fought to retain its guiding principles. Writing in 1988, David Edgar could still report that the 'arm's length principle' that guaranteed the Arts Council autonomy from government interference in the distribution of funds had 'been more or less preserved' (Edgar, 1988, 18).

However, one early use to which Mrs Thatcher's government put the 'cultural industries' to work was as an ameliorative measure in the aftermath of the 1981 riots. For example, the Manpower Services Commission, with the use of government money, funded a Youth Training Scheme that offered financial support for artists. Also, the Enterprise Allowance scheme, set up in 1982, provided the necessary start-up capital that allowed a number of theatre companies to become established, including Red Stockings and Rejects Revenge in Liverpool and Hogwash, an all-women's company in Sheffield (Milling, 2012, 54).

Another key event in the Arts Council's history during the 1980s was the publication of a report, *The Glory of the Garden*, which set out an ambitious ten-year national strategy from 1984 to 1994. An earlier report in 1982 by the Policy Institute, *A Hard Act to Swallow*, had shown the disparity between the Arts Council's distribution of funds to London compared to the regions. The aim of *Glory* was to address and remedy this long-standing gap. The report proposed that £6 million be transferred from London to the regions and 44 of its clients be devolved to the Regional Arts Associations (RAAs), the semi-autonomous satellite bodies of the Arts Council.

The report also sought to address the problem of the Arts Council's growing list of regularly funded drama clients. A popular car sticker at the time reminded the public that 'A dog is not just for Christmas – it's for life', a responsibility that seemed to also sum up the policies of the Arts Council whenever it decided to take on a new client in drama for revenue funding. Anthony Field, the Arts Council's former Financial Director brought this problem to wider attention when in 1984 he replied to a public letter from John McGrath in the *Guardian* newspaper, who accused the Arts Council of political bias in its withdrawal of funding from 7:84 England. Field rejected McGrath's argument, saying that cuts had long been in the offing due to the growing number of fringe companies, who had been in receipt of funding since the 1970s. While it had been possible to accommodate such a large number of companies when annual government grants to the Arts Council had been higher, the reductions after 1980 and high inflation had made this unsustainable and a situation had occurred that resulted in 'many new excellent groups having to be turned down for subsidy while annual subventions were continuing to many groups who had run out of artistic impetus' (Field, 1984, n.p).

Field had said the unsayable. Interviewed in 1992 for Roland Rees's book *Fringe First*, David Aukin, a founding member of Foco Novo and later Director of the Hampstead Theatre Club, Leicester Haymarket and former Executive Director of the National Theatre, echoed Field's sentiments when he commented, 'I have always felt about Fringe companies generally that they do not know when to stop. That there is a certain energy which lasts for a certain time, and without any loss of face they should stop': speaking in particular about Foco Novo, Aukin believed it 'got cautious and worried about the impact of what closing down might mean' (Rees, 1992, 56). Although Foco Novo had been in receipt of regular Arts Council subvention since 1976, the decision was made in 1988 to withdraw its revenue funding. It is interesting to note that Roland Rees, Foco Novo's Artistic Director, simply cannot comprehend Aukin's argument.

This refusal to abandon subsidy once in receipt of it was the very problem that Field believed led to creative stagnation. His proposed solution was to fund a company for five to six years before assessing its artistic viability, and if this had declined, funding should be withdrawn to make way for new companies. While this policy was never adopted in practice, this did occasionally happen voluntarily. Cliffhanger, a Brighton-based company who had produced a number of popular shows including *They Came From Somewhere Else* (1982) and *Gymslip Vicar* (1984), despite being granted £35,000 for their next show, wrote to the Arts Council in 1985 following a tour of Australia, saying they had decided to return the money, explaining 'the company has spent the bulk of the last five years touring, and we feel that the time has come when a break in the pattern of work would be beneficial to us all' (ACGB, 1985d, 99/46/2). Members of the company were true to their word and went on to pursue individual and collaborative projects for BBC Radio 4 and Channel 4 television. However, Cliffhanger was an exception: the majority of companies, if not in receipt of revenue subvention, applied regularly each year for project funding. In some ways this trapped the companies into a state of dependency on the Arts Council, where the need to produce work, whatever the quality, was its only means of support. Field felt companies assuming lifelong support from the Arts Council was detrimental to the long-term quality of work produced, but it is worth noting that his proposed policy only applied to small- and middle-scale touring companies such as 7:84 England and not building-based companies such as the RSC and National Theatre, who seemed able to assume continued funding for perpetuity.

The *Glory of the Garden* report also noted that the list of drama companies in receipt of regular funding had risen from 30 in 1950 to over 80 by 1984. With finite resources at its disposal and the need to make a 10 per cent saving to its £1.2 million drama budget, *Glory* questioned whether a company deserved continued support, especially if the quality of work was no longer at the level of past artistic achievement, or when a leading member left. Established policy was seen by some as blocking the development of newer companies, and *Glory* asked 'whether it has been spreading its resources too widely and hence too thinly' (ACGB, 1984).

A policy deriving from *Glory* was thrashed out at a hotel in Ilkley, Yorkshire in 1984, and a strategy was rapidly (and to its critics hurriedly) instituted five months afterwards (Rittner, 1984). However, in the end, *Glory of the Garden* failed to satisfy anyone, and its proposals were quietly dropped by the end of the same year. Despite honourable intentions, attempts at redistributing funding from London to the regions meant gains for some and very real losses for others. *Glory* had assumed that supplementary funds would be made available by government to facilitate its proposed policy changes, but with no extra money forthcoming, *Glory*'s more controversial proposals seemed to make matters worse. These included withdrawal of subsidy from building-based companies including the Tricycle in London, Chester Gateway, the Yvonne Arnaud Theatre in Guilford and five touring theatre companies (CAST, M6, Mikron, 7:84 England and Temba). Even the Royal Court was put on notice that it might lose its annual subsidy. No new clients were to be taken on in London, due perhaps to the realization that the GLC was still providing much of their funding. Using the garden metaphors that regularly occur in the report, Dickon Reed, the Arts Council's Drama Director, stressed that out of the ten building-based and five touring companies facing withdrawal of subsidy 'in almost all cases these companies are of value; they are not dead wood' (ACGB, 1984, 28/32/5). Nevertheless, the Arts Council planned to get its garden under control by lopping off some of its long-established clients to allow fresh companies to start up in their place. However, in reality this meant a smaller number of companies would be allocated more money. The proposals led to the widely reported resignation of seven members of the Drama Panel. Many of the companies, especially those in regular receipt of revenue subsidy were also unhappy about the plan to devolve them to the RAAs, as they were suspicious that continuity of funding provided under the central body of the Arts Council would be lost. This was especially felt by black and Asian companies, who harboured suspicions that regional arts bodies might be more conservative in their tastes and questioned whether they would be represented on the governing boards. By the end of the decade, Andrew Feist and Robert Hutchinson in their book *Cultural Trends of the Eighties* could report that arts spending still remained stubbornly concentrated in London (Feist and Hutchinson, 1990, 14–15).

By the time of *Glory*, it was clear that funding for theatre had reached crisis point. As a response, the Arts Council commissioned The Cork Report in 1986. This was the first comprehensive assessment on the state of English theatre since 1970 and provides a snapshot of dominant trends in the period as well as the perilous state in which theatre found itself. Ian Brown and Rob Brannen, who worked on the original report, helpfully updated its statistics in a subsequent article to provide a picture of the whole decade. Commissioning of new plays fell slightly (from 35 per cent in 1976–80 to 32 per cent in 1986–90), while there was a significant rise in the number of adaptations of novels (5 per cent in 1976–80, rising to 20 per cent in 1986–90) and a smaller increase in musicals staged at national and regional theatres (9 per cent in 1976–80 compared with 12 per cent in 1980–6). Productions of Shakespeare remained constant, but there was a decline in presenting lesser-known classical work (18 per cent in 1976–80 and 11 per cent in 1986–90) (Brown and Brannen, 1996, 381). The report recommended that an extra £13.4 million be spent annually and that increased provision be made for black theatre, touring work, theatre for young people and community projects as well as the setting up of a series of national companies in the regions. A recommendation was also made that local authorities take on more responsibility for arts provision by matching Arts Council funding from rates revenue.

The Cork Report also revealed that a clear pecking order had established itself in terms of funding priorities. The undoubted 'jewels in the crown' (as they were often referred to) were the Royal Opera House, the Royal Shakespeare Company and the National Theatre: statistics in The Cork Report revealed that in 1985–6 the RSC and the National Theatre had devoured 47 per cent of the total drama budget. Yet, even the National Theatre struggled during this period, with Peter Hall being forced in February 1985 to close the Cottesloe stage as well as cut jobs. At the bottom were the fringe and small-scale touring companies who, from the mid-1980s onwards, found their existence increasingly precarious.

The Greater London Council and Theatre

Although the Greater London Council (GLC) had been in existence since 1965, it was the election in 1981 of the socialist Labour group under its leader Ken Livingstone that brought the authority to national prominence. While Labour only took 42 per cent of the vote with the Conservatives close behind (and even by Livingstone's own reckoning, out of the 50 Labour councillors elected, only 22 were broadly left wing), the new administration at the GLC succeeded in controlling not only the leadership, but all the major offices (Turner, 2010, 79). Unlike previous administrations, under Livingstone the GLC's ambitions went considerably beyond its formally recognized function of administering public services for Londoners to what Alwyn W. Turner called 'a new style of local government, overtly political in its desire to change society' (Turner, 2010, 79).

While earlier socialist councils, such as the West Midlands district of Walsall in the early 1980s, were an irritant to the government, the GLC's prominence in London, combined with Ken Livingstone's ability to attract media attention, became a problem for the government. Kenneth Baker, the Conservative Minister for Local Government at the time, has written:

> A new generation of hard-left activists replaced the old style Labour moderates and deliberately decided to use town halls as a weapon against the Conservative government. Local government was to become a 'state within a state', the vehicle for delivering Socialism locally in the face of electoral rejection nationally. (Baker, 1993, 112)

There was a strong element of popular socialism in the GLC's policies, such as its Fares Fair scheme, which introduced a 32 per cent reduction in public transport ticket prices, together with a system that simplified travel across the various London zones. Its spending on the arts and culture was another popular policy. Despite the Arts Council being an early target for spending cuts after Mrs Thatcher's election in 1979, many of the Labour-controlled authorities made a commitment to support the arts: this meant that, until the abolition of the GLC in March 1986, the arts experienced a boom time. By making use of the powers granted to all local authorities by the Local Government Act of 1948, authorities were able to raise provision for the arts out of rates revenue from a penny in the pound to sixpence in the pound. Few authorities had ever made use of these powers, but the GLC and other

Labour-controlled councils, for example Sheffield, found that this gave them the ability to completely transform arts provision. Between 1980 and 1985 the GLC and six other Labour-controlled authorities spent over £100 million on the arts (Peacock, 1999, 37), far outstripping the money that the government provided to the Arts Council.

Robert Hewison believes that the most radical initiative in the GLC's policy towards arts funding was the establishment of a new Arts and Recreation Committee under the leadership of Tony Banks, who before becoming a Labour MP worked as a trade union official. Here, radical practitioners were given representation on the Committee's sub-panels. The most influential of these was the Community Arts Sub-committee, which crucially proposed 'communities of *interest* rather than geographical communities as the focus of support' (Mulgan and Worpole, 1986, 75). In practice, this involved funding arts projects by the needs of 'minority groups' such as the unemployed, youth sub-cultures (particularly girls), women's groups, gay men's groups, ethnic minorities (who were served by the Ethnic Arts Sub-committee) and the elderly. This sometimes meant that theatre companies such as Bedside Manners, a group who put on shows in hospitals, were formed exclusively to address a particular need in the community rather than evolving naturally, and the artistic content of the work was often considered secondary to the work it did for the particular needs of its constituency.

The flamboyant Banks ensured London's arts organizations were made aware of the funding opportunities available to them as well as the priority given to community projects when he invited them all to a major conference in November 1981, shortly after Labour's victory in the GLC elections (Hewison, 1995, 238). This not only marked a radical move in terms of reassessing the function of art and culture, but also a new form of politics, one that Stuart Hall described as a 'test-bed ... to build a broad popular base for radical change' (Hall, 1988, 236), drawn from the aforementioned constituency groups. Hall's use of the term 'test-bed' for this policy very much applies to the GLC rather than other Labour-controlled authorities such as Sheffield or Liverpool, who saw the concerns of identity politics (and especially the recognition of women's issues) as peripheral to the real aims of socialism (Turner, 2010, 156–7).

Whereas the Arts Council's 'arm's-length policy' based its decisions (ostensibly at least) on artistic merit alone, the GLC's attitude to the arts was unashamedly ideological: by funding a large number of minority groups, it believed that a powerful constituency would be created that could be called upon to support the Labour administration at council elections. As we shall see in the next chapter, questions of artistic quality became an issue for the Arts Council when it came to funding some of these new theatre companies, especially so, when it took over many of the GLC's former clients after the latter's abolition in 1986.

This is not to say that the GLC only supported community arts initiatives; sometimes artistic and community interests overlapped. For instance, in 1985 the newly formed theatre company Talawa proposed an ambitious idea to mount C. L. R. James's play *The Black Jacobins*, about the first Haitian revolution. Despite being a new company, Yvonne Brewster, one of its founding members, put in a proposal budgeted at over £80,000: this included a cast of 25, a long period of paid rehearsal and a three-week booking at the Riverside Studios (Goodman, 1996, 123). Amazingly, all of these requests were met by the GLC, who launched a company still in existence today. Although Talawa was in discussions with the GLC for six months before the bid was approved (ACGB, 1986, 92/1/1), to have commanded such resources from the Arts Council, especially for a new company's first production, would have been unthinkable. Under the Arts Council it would have taken Talawa's members several years to have proved their worth; in 1985, not even the Council's long-established clients who specialized in new writing, such as Foco Novo and Monstrous Regiment, were funded at such levels. Whereas Talawa received over £80,000 for *one* production, Foco Novo's *entire* annual Arts Council budget for 1985 was £78,000, and Monstrous Regiment's £63,000 (ACGB, 1987, 34/43/9). Talawa were in many ways in the right place at the right time, able to benefit from the GLC's largesse, who, earmarked for abolition seemed to have gone on a final spending spree knowing it had nothing to lose.

More established arts such as classical music also continued to receive funding from the GLC, although an emphasis was given to widening public access. Like the Arts Council, the GLC made sure that the work it supported carried its name on all publicity materials. In return for this acknowledgement, many of the companies in receipt of funding often gave fiercely partisan support in ways they would never have done for the Arts Council. Siren, for example, who often used music in performances, even wrote a panegyric called *GLC*, which praised the organization for its promotion of 'democracy/opportunity for you and me'. In the song the establishment of a community centre leads to 'girls nights', where one young woman learns to play bass guitar on 'reggae or Afro Night', while her mother's DIY classes allow her to 'fix the central heating/do a loft conversion/and fix the immersion'.[4]

However, the GLC's arts policy also had drawbacks for some of the theatre companies it supported. Mulgan and Worpole point out that local government funding meant that very few of these groups, unless in receipt of additional sources, were able to tour outside London. Additionally, the GLC's widespread policy of funding single projects meant that despite the availability of money many companies did not benefit from the security and sustainability that Arts Council revenue funding secured for a number of its clients. Consequently, when the GLC was abolished, it was easy for the Arts Council to justify not taking on its former companies.

Resentment against the GLC could be glimpsed as early as 1984. For example, The *Glory of the Garden* report strongly implied that the GLC's generosity removed any obligation on the Arts Council's part to take on new revenue clients in London (*Glory of the Garden*, 1984, 6). Evidence of this attitude, albeit in less-formal terms, can also be found in the Arts Council's archives: for example, in a letter to Pippa Smith, one of the Senior Combined Arts Officers, Jatinder Verma from Tara Arts points out that despite receiving a positive assessment, the company had been placed on standstill funding for that year. In the letter, Verma asks the leading question: 'what new Asian or Black arts clients in London, for example, are now offered support?' (ACGB, 1984b, 41/30/4), with the clear inference that the Arts Council had washed its hands of clients who it felt the GLC could now fund.

Mrs Thatcher's government may have considered the GLC's spending on the arts and schemes such as Fares Fair to be profligate, but the popularity of this funding helped to reduce the Conservatives chances of getting re-elected in London. In October 1983, shortly after their second victory in the polls, a White Paper entitled *Streamlining the Cities* set out a plan to abolish the GLC and the six other metropolitan authorities. At first, the government tried to bring high-spending authorities to heel by introducing ratecapping as a way of controlling how much money local authorities could collect from their constituents through the rates. This measure was brought into legislation through the Rates Act of 1984, which came into force in spring 1985, making it illegal to set rates beyond a level imposed by government. In total, 18 local authorities were rate capped, all but two of them under Labour control. The House of Lords also abolished the Fares Fair scheme in December 1981, and on 31 March 1986 the GLC and six other metropolitan authorities were abolished.

While the government gave the Arts Council a post-abolition grant of £25 million in 1986/7 and £24 million in 1987/8 to cover the many projects that had been funded by local authorities, it was estimated that in reality more like £37 million was required in order to support the GLC's former clients (Feist and Hutchinson, 1990, 13). As a consequence, D. Keith Peacock points out that 60 GLC-funded organizations failed to receive any of these extra funds (Peacock, 1999, 40) and from 1987 onwards many theatre companies began to run into real financial difficulties (ACGB, 1987b, 38/32/2).

A case in point was the Women's Theatre Group (WTG). The WTG had received assistance from the GLC, but found that post-abolition funding from the Arts Council only increased its funding by 2 per cent for 1987–8. Although the group was successful in its application to the Arts Council's three-year revenue funding scheme in 1989, it needed to attract money from additional sources, including the London Borough Grants Scheme, and gain project funding for touring from various Regional Arts Associations.

However, with its adoption of some of the GLC's former clients, something of the community arts ethos of the former regime seemed to have passed into the Arts Council's bloodstream. New priorities established in project funding after 1985 included black and Asian theatre which now received 27 per cent of all theatre project funding (ACGB, c. 1990c, 38/32/2), women's theatre, and young people, the disabled, the latter being marked out as a priority for 1988/89 (ACGB, 1987b, 38/32/2).

Another legacy of the GLC's arts policies was, paradoxically – given its socialist politics – the emphasis it placed on seeing art and culture as an *investment* that could yield economic, social and political dividends, rather than the model that the Arts Council subscribed to in which the quality of work produced was of paramount consideration. Looking at GLC policy retrospectively, it is curious to see how far, in this respect at least, it shared Thatcherism's preference for a business model in arts policy rather than the argument for subsidy enabling artistic excellence. The GLC saw investment in the arts as beneficial to all concerned (not least themselves in securing office), and its activities provided a working pilot that echoed many of the findings of the 1988 Myerscough Report.

Funding and the Arts under John Major 1990–4

Robert Hewison points out that funding for the arts in terms of Arts Council grant in aid after Mrs Thatcher left office increased by 20 per cent from 1990 to 1993 (Hewison, 1994, 420). However, Michael

Billington also points out, 'There was an attritional spirit about theatre in the Eighties which carried through into the Nineties' (Billington, 2007, 338), and in 1991 Tim Renton, the Minister for the Arts, publicly mooted the case for the abolition of the Arts Council. Nevertheless, in the run-up to the 1992 general election, the Arts Council received a boost of £192 million, an increase in funding of 14 per cent. However, little of this money reached individual theatre companies, with much being diverted into writing off the RSC's accumulated deficits that had caused the closure of its operational base at the Barbican in London. It should also be noted that regardless of budget rises between 1990 and 1993, funding was only restored to 1979 levels (Hewison, 1994, 429).

The catastrophic events of Black Wednesday in 1992 also necessitated cuts in public expenditure and the Arts Council saw a below-the-rate-of-inflation increase of 1.8 per cent in 1993–4: cuts that translated to £5 million. This ended the well-regarded three-year theatre franchise scheme recommended by the Cork Report. Additionally, in April 1994, ten Regional Arts Boards were created, with clients redistributed between them and a central office. However, as Robert Hewison points out, the reorganization meant that 'many of the specialist units that the Arts Council had developed in the 1980s to promote general policies such as cultural diversity, the role of women in the arts and attention to disability, were wound up' (Hewison, 1995, 303). This loss of financial security coupled with administrative structures that took account of the needs of touring theatre led to a further decline in older companies and the formation of new companies.

Under the Major administration a new Department of National Heritage was established in 1992, with responsibility for the performing arts, museums and galleries. Other areas such as English Heritage (formerly looked after by the Department of the Environment), sport (formerly under the Department of Education), film (under the Board of Trade) and tourism (formerly under the Department of Employment) now all came under the umbrella of this new leviathan department, and, with its budget of nearly £1 billion, the considerable influence it brought.

The Department of National Heritage also devised the UK's first National Lottery, from which a proportion of the money collected would go to charities (in what was called the Millennium Fund) and heritage projects. Hewison describes the National Lottery as a means by which the government could 'pay for various British versions of the grand projects that had been created in socialist France during the 1980s' (Hewison, 1994, 422). The Lottery Act was passed in October

1993 and the lottery itself launched the following year. The Arts Council was given responsibility for distributing the funds allocated to the arts, and, while undoubtedly beneficial for many organizations, the money was only made available for capital projects, such as buildings. This automatically disqualified many theatre companies, especially those such as Monstrous Regiment, which toured, from applying. In the year that the Lottery Act was passed, the company finally lost its Arts Council funding and was forced to disband. In April 1994, the Arts Council itself was devolved, with Wales and Scotland receiving their funding directly from the Scottish and Welsh Offices.

Chapter 2

BRITISH THEATRE COMPANIES: 1980–1994

Graham Saunders

A New Golden Age?

In July 1980, the theatre critic Michael Billington, reporting on what some still called the Fringe, gave a pessimistic assessment of its future: the influence of what had once been regarded as the vanguard of political and cultural change had been steadily eroded during the economic recession of the mid-1970s, to the point where even its most ardent supporters now realized it would take more 'than performing a clown-show in Willesden High Street' (Billington, 1993, 157–8) to transform society. While possibly right about the revolutionary potential of clown shows, Billington makes almost no mention of theatre companies in his survey, confining his recognition of fringe theatre to include playwrights such as Howard Brenton and David Hare, or particular London venues such as the Bush, in Shepherd's Bush and the Half Moon in Putney.

Yet, such an omission should not be seen as surprising: when theatre companies are discussed in the context of the 1980s and early 1990s, they are always compared with what has come to be seen as the golden age of the late 1960s and 1970s, a period characterized by bold experimentation and supported by a climate of unprecedented levels of funding. To some extent, this assessment is true: modest Arts Council seed-corn funding in 1968/9 allowed groups such as Portable and The Brighton Combination to become established and by 1972/3 had led to more than 29 other companies gaining subsidy. While the critic Martin Esslin has questioned the whole project of 1970s alternative theatre with its 'ambulatory, truck based pioneers of a truly working class theatre [who] did *not* reach the bulk of the working class audience' (Trussler, 1981, vii), it is often forgotten that exponential growth continued into the 1980s, and by 1981 there were more than 60 companies receiving annual funding of £2.5 million (Field, 1984). This progression continued steadily until 1985 with the creation of a further 50 new companies (Kershaw, 2004, 365). Despite noting their brief lifespan, especially that of the many political groups who failed to last the course of the decade, Baz Kershaw notes that by 1987 the total number of companies had reached over 300 and concludes, 'as the 1980s drew to a close, it is clear that this sector of British theatre was in some ways well suited to the newly harsh economic environment' (Kershaw, 2004, 365).

Regardless of Kershaw's important re-evaluation, British theatre after 1979 was dominated by companies struggling to survive through a miasma of steadily increasing financial hardship, going precariously from project to project, many being dissolved by the end of the decade. While pioneers of the fringe such as Howard Brenton had been proclaiming its death since the mid-1970s (Brenton, 1975, 10–11), this all-too-ready acceptance comes with hindsight, knowing the unhappy fates that many of these companies ultimately met. Consequently, there is an understandable resistance to acknowledge that the first half of the 1980s continued the forward momentum of the previous decade.

Moreover, in spite of increasingly harsh economic conditions after 1979 that saw yearly decreases in arts funding after inflation had been taken into account, as the last chapter discussed, many companies in fact flourished in the sustaining microclimates provided by Labour-controlled metropolitan authorities, most notably the GLC. In terms of their combined spending during the first half of the 1980s, these authorities outstripped the Arts Council's entire annual budget until their abolition in 1986; this meant that the first half of the 1980s saw a proliferation of new companies that was every bit as remarkable as the expansionist period of the 1970s.

Constituency Companies

In her survey of British theatre in the 1980s, Jane Milling principally defines the period by its *diversity*, as 'a host of resistant voices ... in community and school halls, in fringe and alternative venues, in regional theatres, as well as on the major subsidised national stages: voices whose resistance was not always based on a readily interpretable left-wing agenda' (Milling, 2012, 262). Here, she is referring to *constituency theatre* that included gay, feminist, black, Asian and other companies, specializing in cabaret, performance art, mime and community work. Crucial to their identity was a deliberate targeting of specific types of audience, as opposed to the practice of political companies such as North West Spanner and Broadside Mobile Workers' Theatre, who performed (in theory at least) to a broadly defined working-class audience.

While the rise of constituency theatre has been associated with the decline of political theatre (Kershaw, 2004, 367; Peacock, 1999, 59), Jane Milling argues that the 1970s were only partially a golden age for political theatre, given the significance of what she calls 'leftish male-authored drama as the marker of true political art' (Milling, 2012, 89), while at the same time largely ignoring 'those voices that were heard more insistently during the 1980s' (Milling, 2012, 89). By this, Milling means the constituency companies who increasingly challenged former models of political theatre in favour of a 'new politics ... based on utilising the grossly underrated strength and power of specific constituencies of people and movements, including the elderly, youth, black people, women, people with disabilities and the peace and gay movements' (Owusu, 1986, 85). Robert Hewison sees these constituencies as representing 'an alternative form of mobilisation' (Hewison, 1995, 238) and Baz Kershaw, despite certain misgivings, also recognized that it had been the constituency companies who offered the most effective opposition to Thatcherism (Kershaw, 2004, 368).

At the same time, Kershaw makes it clear that things had changed, and not necessarily in a desirable way, as growth of constituency companies also meant 'a general weakening of alternative politics as companies competed for diminishing audiences' (Kershaw, 2004, 367). John McGrath of 7:84 (an exemplar of 1970s politically committed theatre) held, like Kershaw, conflicting views about constituency theatre: while on the one hand recognizing its value in putting forward the voices and interests of minority groups, McGrath could say 'alternative theatre of all kinds was making the running in England' (McGrath, 1990, 30), yet at the same time dismiss these as 'essentially a defensive assemblage of the powerless' (McGrath, 1990, 94).

Writing in 1983, Michael Billington also expressed concern over 'the growing tendency to sectionalize and compartmentalize' and, while agreeing that particular interest groups had their place in theatre, still admitted, 'if I confront a company calling itself, say, Single Parent Masons in Milton Keynes I tend to feel that I am being excluded or the territory covered will be, shall we say, a little narrow' (Billington, 1993, 199). While this is no doubt a journalistic exaggeration, such exclusivity was troubling to some.

While constituency theatre undoubtedly became the distinguishing feature that set the companies of the 1980s apart from their predecessors,

David Edgar identifies its origins in 1971, when gay men and women from the theatre company General Will left due to growing dissatisfaction over its attitude to work based on sexuality. Many who broke away went on to become founding members of Gay Sweatshop in 1977. Edgar also believes that elsewhere a number of other groups formed out of established political companies to produce more specialized work (Edgar, 1988, 27–8). A further development of the 1970s that acted as an impetus for constituency theatre in the 1980s was Nasseem Khan's 1976 report for the Arts Council, *The Arts Britain Ignores*. This highlighted a flourishing arts culture within numerous immigrant communities, yet these had largely been excluded from receiving funding. While Khan's report was in many ways a highly welcome development, Kwesi Osuwu has argued that it also provided a convenient way for the Arts Council to make the 'formulation of a blanket category of "deprived peoples" … to [which was] add[ed] women, gays, disabled people and the unemployed' (Owusu, 1986, 57). Writing later, Khan also showed awareness of the problems her report had created, and while believing that 'naming categories is a powerful act … [that] brings an individual into the social body', institutions such as the Arts Council and the GLC had used her report to form 'a kind of subsection of loonies, women, Disableds and ethnic arts … [and] by making a special case of ethnic arts [it] … paradoxically succeeded in painting them into a corner where they only have each other to contend with for grants, that by the basic laws of life are never large enough' (Khan, undated).[1]

A good example of the institutional prejudices towards one of these groups – 'the Disableds' – as Khan calls them, can be found in the Arts Council's attitude to the early work of Graeae. While now a highly regarded company and one of the few survivors from this period, in a 1983 Arts Council show report for Graeae's production of *M3 Junction*, the assessor's openness about his initial prejudices is highly revealing:

> Right and proper as it is for disabled people to be able to practise their chosen art / craft as actors, this is the province of the Social Services not the Arts Council: and if their aim was to offer their audience some understanding of the problems of the disabled then – right and proper as this also is – this is best achieved by good professional actors who have researched their subject but who are not necessarily disabled themselves. (ACGB, 1983b, 41/42/2)

Due to the strength of Graeae's performance, Guy Slater, the assessor in question, undergoes nothing less than a Pauline conversion, but his initial reservations were certainly not unrepresentative of thinking at the time.

Spare Tyre and Mrs Worthington's Daughters: Case-studies in Constituency Theatre

This question of artistic standards became a recurring issue for the Arts Council when assessing constituency companies and D. Keith Peacock concludes that ultimately many of the groups failed to generate what he calls 'a body of work that conform[ed] to critical standards of excellence claimed by mainstream theatre' (Peacock, 1999, 145). These criticisms were often based on a theatre's lack of literary qualities – values that constituency companies often deliberately rejected; yet these yardsticks were often the ones by which a company were assessed when it came to funding decisions.

Spare Tyre was an all-female company who formed in 1979 when founder member Clair Chapman advertised in *Time Out* for women interested in dramatizing Susie Orbach's bestselling book *Fat is a Feminist Issue* (1978) and related issues concerning women's relationships with food, including bulimia and anorexia. The company saw themselves as performers, but also as facilitators, helping to establish self-help groups during their tours that could continue providing support for women. As well as performing in theatres and arts centres, the group also visited non-theatrical venues that included health centres, the London Radical Nurses Conference and even the American Embassy Wives Coffee Morning (ACGB, 1982b, 41/30/1).

Yet the work of Spare Tyre is illustrative of criticism frequently levelled at constituency theatre – namely that the work rarely went beyond the mutual vindication of a shared set of beliefs between performer and audience. For example, in *How do I Look?* (1980) the theatre academic Jill Davis, in an otherwise complimentary show report, notes that the performers relied on the audience having prior knowledge of Susie Orbach's work (ACGB, 1980b, 41/30/1). Drama officer Jonathan Lamede (who noted that Orbach's publishers had donated £100 to the company) also saw this as a failing, observing that 'the show was virtually ancillary to something which couldn't be experienced in the stage event itself' (ACGB, 1979, 41/30/1). Even by 1983, reporting on their show *Just Deserts*, which Lamede describes as 'a mixture of revue and cartoon agitprop', he concludes that once again the group were 'playing entirely to the converted' (ACGB, 1984, 41/30/1).

Converted or not, Spare Tyre often attracted large and enthusiastic audiences. Despite being described as a small-scale touring company, whose audience size could be expected to number below 50, Lamede's report of *Just Deserts* at the Hampstead Community Centre, whatever his other misgivings, talks of it being 'packed to the rafters with about 150 people, mainly women, mainly middle class' (ACGB, 1984, 41/30/1). Jill Davis, reporting in 1980 for *How Do I look?* at the Oval House, also reports a capacity audience with people being turned away at the box office and she concludes that Spare Tyre have already 'acquired a large following' (ACGB, 1980b, 41/30/1).

Yet, even from their earliest shows the company were aware of the need to be more ambitious. In an application for an Arts Council Project Grant, Clair Chapman spoke about the need to appeal 'across the classes to women with problems of self-image and compulsive eating while remaining entertaining and accessible to mixed audiences' (ACGB, 1980a, 41/30/1). Graeae, who formed a year after Spare Tyre in 1980, were by 1983 also talking to the Arts Council about 'drawing away from disability as the explicit theme of shows' (ACGB, 1983a, 41/42/2).

Another group who encountered similar difficulties in this area was Mrs Worthington's Daughters, which had formed in 1978 by director Julie (Jules) Holledge and the actors Anne Engel and Maggie Wilkinson. In an interview given in 1993, all three revealed that their original intention was to exploit the Arts Council's willingness to fund work by neglected female playwrights of the late-nineteenth and early-twentieth centuries; in fact, their main intention was to produce 'experimental feminist work, a sort of women's hit and run theatre', with the drama projects on earlier women's theatre functioning 'as a reliable income'(Goodman, 1993, 55). However, a vogue for the reclamation of women's drama at the time, together with the group being amongst the first to specialize in this area, ultimately determined their direction. Notwithstanding, the group tried to persuade the Arts Council to allow them to pursue these two very different strands of artistic policy. In 1983, they put forward two projects to the Arts Council: one was Peta Masters and Geraldine Griffiths *Wyre's Cross* (1983), a pastiche soap opera in four nightly parts, described in their project application as 'what happened when popular television styles collide with feminism?' (ACGB, 1982, 41/25/1). Although the project was turned down by the Arts Council, the production was able to secure funding from other sources and was also reviewed by Arts Council assessors: Jonathan Lamede, for example, found it to be little more than 'a performer's romp', concluding, 'We [The Arts Council] had turned down the project for subsidy and I think we were right to do so. It was fun but considering all the other more important claims on Council funds this was not really subsidisable material' (ACGB, 1983, 41/25/1). The other submission, a play by Jenny Sprince called *Greece,* also failed to get produced. The script was sent to director Jenny Topper for her opinion, who dismissed it in the opening sentence of her reader's report: 'I cannot pretend to have read this play thoroughly or completely but, anyone doubting the fairness of this report has only to read four or five pages of this miserable attempt at playwriting to see how arch, impenetrable, leaden and intellectually lazy the whole exercise is' (ACGB, 1983, 41/25/1). Although never stated in any correspondence, it is not difficult to understand the Arts Council's reasons for not supporting this kind of work: with groups such as Monstrous Regiment and the WTG already commissioning similar work, the value of Mrs Worthington's Daughters (and as a consequence their funding) came from their reclamation of historical drama by women dramatists – not from new writing.

In truth, neither Spare Tyre nor Mrs Worthington's Daughters could ever realistically expect to escape from their constituency status, as it was this identity that justified their continued funding. Even companies not normally associated with addressing niche work started to see the benefits of taking this approach. WTG, who in the 1970s had been associated with a broader feminist theatre, were by 1985 producing work that, like Spare Tyre, focused around issues associated with bulimia, anorexia and agoraphobia.

Although the Arts Council seemed willing to fund constituency theatre, they sometimes expressed concern about its exclusivity. In July 1980, for example, they were forced to respond to Spare Tyre after they had been turned down for project funding after Clair Chapman had spoken out publicly to the press. In a memo to the Secretary General Sir Roy Shaw over the matter, Drama Director John Faulkner reported, 'most advisors allow that the group has performing talent; the major criticism has been of the reliance on a comparatively limited subject matter – over eating' (ACGB, 1980, 41/30/1c). In response to this, Lamede comments that he and his fellow officers Jean Bullwinkle and Ruth Marks had all been in agreement over the poor quality of Spare's Tyre's last show. He continues with some frankness, 'although we did not say so in blunt terms, what it amounted to was that their [Spare Tyre's] application and past work were simply not good enough' (ACGB, 1980d, 41/30/1).

Spare Tyre's work also marked the start of a wider cultural shift during the 1980s, by which the personal started to become increasingly detached from the political and, assisted by more than a decade of Thatcherite values, seemed to become increasingly solipsistic.

Issues in Touring Theatre

The theatre director Yvonne Brewster provides a vividly disconsolate personal recollection about touring in the early 1980s:

> Small-scale touring was something I loathed. Driving a large white van back from Bristol at 3 o'clock in the morning after the final curtain on a three night run of Barry Reckford's *Streetwise* produced by Carib Theatre at a tiny venue, The Inkworks I think it was called. Delivering the six members of cast to their respective homes far flung across Greater London I finally landed up alone in Kilburn. Finding no space to park the van full of props and collapsed set, I left it in the middle of the road thinking, hoping more like, that next morning it would have been towed away. No such luck. [The theatre director] Ken Chubb parked it for me on his way to the Tricycle. But that marked the end of my small-scale touring days. (Brewster, 2011)

Despite starting out as an innovative practice, small-scale touring had run into trouble by the end of the 1970s and the Arts Council had become increasingly aware that many others shared Brewster's sentiments that, while in reality they had no real interest in touring, they felt forced to do so as a condition of funding.

Arts Council show reports routinely requested that assessors supply approximate audience numbers, and that companies submit box-office returns for each show. Both provide useful indicators by which to assess the popularity of a given company and sometimes it is surprising to discover just how small audiences were. For example, in 1984 Ian Kellgren, who at the time was Artistic Director of Liverpool's Everyman Theatre, reports that Monstrous Regiment's production of Bryony Lavery's play *Calamity!* at Darlington Arts Centre had been cancelled owing to only four people attending, while during the two remaining nights audience figures did not exceed 40 (ACGB, 1984, 41/53/18).

Sometimes, there was a reluctance shown by local authorities to fund groups who were based outside their area, or of venues to take the risk of paying booking fees to companies who played to audiences of below 50. Even before the reduction in arts spending after 1979, many companies were already facing yearly deficits that were not met by guarantees against losses incurred during a show, and even costs associated with van depreciation became a significant issue. When taken together all of these factors risked the long-term future of small-scale touring (ACGB, 1979, 38/9/23). An example that illustrates this is Foco Novo's 1983 tour of Brecht's *Puntilla and his Servant Matti* and its visit to Theatre Clwyd. The theatre's administrator Patric Gilchrist, despite admiring the production, questioned whether touring a little-known play by Brecht with a cast of 12 unknown actors to audiences averaging only 28 each night was a sustainable model, and expressed his concern as to whether 'the Arts Council can afford to tour medium/large-scale productions to small-scale audiences for an indefinite period' (ACGB, 1983, 41/53/4).

Audience numbers could be erratic, sometimes going to both extremes. When, for example, WTG produced another play by Lavery, *Her Aching Heart* (1990), at the Town Hall Studios Swindon, a touring report by Southern Arts records that only 38 tickets were issued – 5 of which were complimentary – in a venue with a capacity of 92. The average audience size during this tour was 42. The company's booking fee was £500 and their only means of support apart from the Arts Council grant was a regional supplement by South East Arts amounting to a further £250 (ACGB, 1990, 41/15/8). These statistics give credence to arguments about the financial unsustainability of small-scale touring. Yet, Lavery's *Her Aching Heart* has subsequently become an important work in lesbian drama, and indications of its later reputation can also be found in statistics: when the tour reached the Pavilion Theatre Brighton, a town with a considerable lesbian community, Philip Bernays (who at the time was working as an administrator for the Independent Theatre Council) notes in his show report that the 200-seat venue was sold out 'with queues round the corner for returns' (ACGB, 1990b, 41/15/8). These examples demonstrate the fine line between unsustainability and viability of small-scale scale touring – they show that viability could be sustained providing a company was able to build an audience from among a particular grouping or constituency.

As mentioned, as early as 1975, some individuals once associated with the start of alternative theatre had already grown disillusioned with it as a political enterprise as well as with the practical difficulties of life on the road (Rees, 1992, 219). While Howard Brenton may have been among the first to publicly voice doubts about the rationale of small-scale touring, he was not alone. The Arts Council archive reveals that other individuals were also expressing similar doubts. In 1982

Jude Kelly, who at the time was Artistic Director of the Battersea Arts Centre in London, wrote to John Faulkner about the problems arts centres faced in booking suitable touring companies: 'I have felt for a considerable time that small-scale touring groups who are generally available for booking are, by and large, unsuitable both in terms of scale of production and, unfortunately, often in the standard of production'. Kelly adds, 'I know that this is a problem which Jenny Harris from the Albany Empire also experiences' (ACGB, 1982b, 38/9/23). Faulkner's reply is interesting as he asks for names to be named and even includes a list of companies for Kelly to identify and suggests that if Battersea Arts Centre simply stops booking poor work the problem will be eradicated. Faulkner is also keen to meet and discuss the matter further as 'a number of people say what you are saying. They shy off naming names and mistake an analysis of the problem for its solution. If you suggest remedies on paper you would be the first to do so and we would have something to talk about!' (ACGB, 1982c, 38/9/23).

Sadly (at least based on extant Arts Council records) nothing was committed to paper,[2] yet evidence that the Arts Council was thinking along the same lines can be found in a discussion paper written the year before by Ruth Marks, who was then head of the Touring Department. Here, she addressed both this particular issue and other long-standing problems in uncompromising terms, by raising the question of whether in 1981 small-scale touring was still relevant after more than a decade in existence. In blunt language, she points out that if the Arts Council believes it to be 'a notional activity' then the logical outcome would be that some companies 'be allowed to fade away'. The founding Keynesian ideas of artistic excellence being the guiding principle is also challenged in Marks's recommendation for a long hard look to be taken at the ratio between audience numbers and existing levels of funding to determine not only 'whether or not a company should continue to receive revenue subsidy', but also whether there are 'more touring companies doing work of a certain type than the market can genuinely stand' (ACGB, 1981, 99/46/2).

In 1985, touring officer Jodi Myers, in a memo to the Regional Director David Pratley, reveals that serious thought was being given to abandoning small-scale touring altogether and devolving 'all responsibility for the funding of small-scale touring companies and venues to the RAAs (Regional Arts Associations), leaving only a small fund for exceptional projects within the drama department. That would leave us to concentrate on what we can, alone, do: the large- and middle-scale' (ACGB, 1985, 99/46/2). Following this course of action would have meant the complete abandonment of a national touring strategy for the smaller companies. Fortunately, this did not come to pass, and it was not until 1988 and the withdrawal of revenue funding from Foco Novo and Joint Stock that the Arts Council actually started to implement some of its original proposals made earlier in the decade.

The Curse of Project Funding

Fifty per cent of all the Arts Council's drama clients were designated as project status. The scheme had started out in the 1970s with noble intentions. In those early days of alternative theatre, when many of the companies themselves did not imagine sustaining any kind of longevity, the system was well suited to the culture: groups could form, produce a piece of work, disband and move on to something else. The system of project funding fell into disrepute once alternative theatre started to become professionalized, with individuals seeing the company as their long-term career.

This led to a situation where often long-established and respected companies still had to approach the Arts Council on a show-by-show basis. This in turn meant that artistic policy could never be developed long-term, together with the additional insecurity of never knowing whether a current application would be funded, or by how much. While project companies were not forced to produce new work each year, as revenue companies were required to do, they lacked financial security and were often expected to undertake significantly more touring than revenue clients or those designated as middle-scale. This exploitative system forced many members of project companies to take up other part-time jobs or to claim unemployment benefit between periods of production work. Even when funded, wage rates were frequently below the Equity minimum and working conditions were often inadequate. Companies on project funding also lost the 'right to fail'. Whereas revenue-funded companies could afford to produce more experimental work, or weather an unsuccessful show, for those on project status, work deemed unsatisfactory often resulted in the rejection of their next application, wasting time and effort as well as endangering the future of the company.

In an informal report to the Arts Council on the problems companies were facing with project funding, Andy Jordan, founder of the new-writing company Bristol Express, noted in 1986 that instead of being rewarded, he, together with groups such as The Theatre of Thelema and Trestle, who had been on the scheme for three consecutive years, seemed indefinitely consigned to project status. Jordan calls this 'the sin of survival', which often culminated in older companies being overlooked in favour of new groups who were either creating a name for themselves, or others who met designated Arts Council priorities for revenue funding, such as black or Asian work (Jordan, n.d., ACGB 99/36/1).

The criteria for project funding, taken from the minutes of the advisory panel for the New Applications and Projects Committee (NAPS), make interesting reading:

1. demonstrate a satisfactory level of artistic achievement and maturity
2. have sound administrative capabilities; it was important they should be incorporated and have submitted audited accounts for previous years
3. demonstrate that there was a demand for the company's work through bookings and earned income (ACGB, 1983, 38/32/4).

Despite the much-vaunted emphasis on artistic standards, if administrative competence is taken to include a demonstration of audience demand through touring returns and audience figures, then the last two criteria override artistic quality. Demand for work often favoured companies such as Shared Experience and Cheek by Jowl, who worked in adaptation and classical revivals, or groups like Hull Truck and The National Theatre of Brent, who had no interest in playing to niche constituency audiences and who set their sights firmly on the mainstream. John McGrath has also argued that when auditing procedures and funding policy started to favour mass audiences over social and political activism, then this was always going to disadvantage companies such as 7:84 and CAST, who McGrath believed the Arts Council had always viewed as 'bureaucratically inconvenient, apt to have messy books and to give away tickets to the unemployed' (Holdsworth, 2002, 146).

As discussed in the previous chapter, the 1986 Cork Report set out to address some of these problems. One of its recommendations was a shortlist of companies who should make the transition from project to revenue status: these were Century (who became the English Touring Theatre), Cheek by Jowl, The Oxford Stage Company and Cambridge Theatre Company (who changed name to Method and Madness). Yet even these choices revealed other priorities being addressed. Putting to one side the clear Oxbridge dominance, these companies mainly concerned themselves with revivals of the classics, and in some respects, it is not difficult to see this confirming some of John McGrath's concerns.

However, one of the Cork Report's other recommendations that was subsequently adopted had more lasting value for those companies wishing to make the transition between project and revenue funding. It had been noted that between 1975 and 1980, eleven companies had made the transition, whereas between 1981 and 1986, only two had done so and 13 had lost their funding entirely. The proposed solution was the establishment of a small-scale touring franchise system. This meant that instead of receiving an annual grant, seemingly for perpetuity, revenue clients were funded for three years, after which they had to reapply. Likewise, if project clients had made three successful bids in a row, they would automatically become revenue clients on the three-year scheme.

The system had the advantage of deterring complacency and took account of major changes, such as the detrimental effect the change of artistic director might have on a group's work. Whereas previously a 'bottleneck' had existed, the new scheme gave greater flexibility and enabled companies to progress to revenue status more easily, despite finite resources (Brown and Brannen, 1996, 374). Although it had many advantages over past practice, the new scheme also introduced a Thatcherite spirit into the system, which meant companies were effectively placed in competition with one another. It also meant that there were now clear winners and losers, with some long-established revenue clients including Foco Novo and Joint Stock losing revenue funding after review: both companies disbanded almost immediately after the scheme was introduced. Brown and Brannen also noted a further erosion of budget allocated to projects, despite the Cork Report's recommendations, and the scheme itself ended after only three years when a further series of public-spending cuts were announced early into the John Major administration.

Dwarfs in Giant's Boots: Foco Novo and the Transition from Small-Scale to Middle-Scale Touring

A problem in small-scale touring that gave rise to a great deal of discontent was the absence of a clear progression between the categories of middle- and large-scale. A typical situation was where a company originally designated as small-scale, after having succeeded over time in building up audiences and a critical reputation for itself, now wished to progress on to the next tier. The Arts Council faced problems concerning the long-term financial commitment of supporting an increasing number of middle-scale companies on less money.

Not unsurprisingly, this led to a great deal of frustration from companies who felt they had now earned the right to play to larger audiences and be funded at levels that would enable them to develop work in more ambitious new directions. Foco Novo provides a useful case study here. The international success of Bernard Pomerance's 1977 play *The Elephant Man* had understandably widened the company's ambitions and now gave them a timely opportunity to pressurize the Arts Council into funding their move into middle-scale touring. Foco Novo were able to mount Bernard Pomerance's next play *Quantrill in Lawrence* (1980) as a middle-scale production, funded largely out of the proceeds from the Broadway royalties accrued from *The Elephant Man*. While the production was poorly received, it demonstrated to the Arts Council that Foco Novo were capable of mounting ambitious productions, and so Brecht's *Edward II* (1982) was funded on a trial basis as a middle-scale production.

The tour of *Edward II* played at four venues – Theatre Clwyd in Wales, Basildon in Essex, Croydon and London – to mixed reviews. While there was praise for aspects of the production, with Michael Billington declaring 'it is heartening to see Foco Novo entering the big league', Billington and others also felt that an early play by Brecht was a poor choice (Billington et al., 1982). Audience numbers were also disappointing, and despite letters to the company from Theatre Clwyd and the Towngate Theatre, in Basildon, Essex, praising the production and wanting to see Foco Novo return, as one manager pointed out, 'Brecht is not easy to market even to Theatre Clwyd audiences' (ACGB, 1982, 34/43/5). The Arts Council also saw *Edward II* as conclusive evidence that Foco Novo was unsustainable as a middle-scale touring company. In a letter to the company, John Faulkner pointed out that based on returns for the entire tour, audience figures only averaged 185 a performance, far short of the 300 minimum that would justify promotion to middle-scale (ACGB, 1982, 34/43/6).

British Small-Scale Companies in Europe

The more favourable environment that existed abroad also exacerbated theatre companies' resentment at home. Material poverty can be demonstrated in the response that the physical theatre company (or 'mime', as it was designated by the Arts Council at this time) Trickster gave to the 1986 Cork Theatre Inquiry, providing an account of its financial state. Despite being in receipt of project funding, company members were still forced to claim state unemployment benefit, or to take on weekend and part-time freelance work in addition to working for the company (ACGB, 1986, 41/45/6).

Elsewhere, a number of British companies found that tours in Europe, either through the auspices of the British Council or by invitation to festivals or venues such as The Mickery Theatre in Amsterdam, provided far more generous remuneration in terms of booking fees. Kaboodle, at one time a clown company (who changed their name to The Theatre Exchange in 1980), were an eclectic group of performers who produced a wide range of work including devised Theatre in Education (TIE) and community projects with physically and mentally handicapped adults. During a NAPS interview, the company revealed that in Germany it had received £250 per performance and £700 for a community show in Rome, compared to UK work, pay for which ranged from £25 to £100 per night (ACGB, 1979, 41/22/2).

Knowing this, it is of little surprise that companies such as Forkbeard Fantasy chose to spend much of the 1980s touring Europe rather than the UK. However, there is also evidence to suggest that companies who looked towards Europe for financial support risked burning their boats with the Arts Council. One company who took this route was Hesitate and Demonstrate, a pioneering live art company formed by Geraldine Pilgrim in 1975. In 1983 the company was shortlisted to become permanent Arts Council revenue clients, yet, while the NAPS Committee felt that the 'work was unique and had consistently been of high quality [and] were very ripe for revenue funding … some committee members remained uneasy about the wholeheartedness of their commitment to work in this country, rather than abroad' (ACGB, 1983, 38/32/4). Artistic and financial recognition abroad paradoxically seemed to involve paying a cost at home.

Women's Theatre Companies

If a golden age could ever said to have existed for women's theatre companies, it would be the ten-year span between 1975 and 1985, and many of these groups entered the 1980s with a burst of confidence. In a show report for a 1980 production of Dacia Maraini's play *A Dialogue Between a Prostitute and one of her Clients*, Jonathan Lamede commented, 'I'm in no doubt whatsoever that, in twenty five years of theatre going, this was the most successful show of its kind that I've ever seen' (ACGB, 1980, 41/51/3). Writing in 1978, David Edgar had predicted that women's companies would come into their own in the next decade – not only acting 'as a bridge between the Royal Court and a wider audience' (Edgar, 1988, 45) but also 'between the literary, cerebral, intellectually vigorous but visually dry work of the 1960s and 1970s, and the visually stunning but intellectually thin experiments of the performance artists in and from the arts schools' (Edgar, 1988, 175). This approach was also crucial in distinguishing how women's companies formed and organized themselves.

In 1980, many companies could still be found adhering to a collectivist way of working; however, this ethos steadily eroded during the decade. Janelle Reinelt believes that whereas collectivism had once addressed 'the social scope of a community', this distinguishing practice of many of the women's groups had now given way to types of work that addressed the concerns of 'internal psychological experiences' (Reinelt, 1993, 161). While collectivism allowed, in theory at least, a democratic means by which everyone could contribute artistically, in a web broadcast that brought together former members of several feminist companies, Clair Chapman from Spare Tyre commented, 'We would do a scene and us four – *us four* [my emphasis] will write this scene! ... We'd come back with two lines at the end of an hour ... The whole collective scene was so crazy and stifling' (Argument Room, 2013). Anna Furse, who from 1980 to 1986 was part of the all-woman Bloodgroup, even felt collectivism may have been partly responsible for preventing feminist groups developing further: 'It was considered in our politics evil and wrong to put yourself out front as a director as it implied a male dominating position. I actually think that the collective movement – brilliant though it was ... also inhibited a sense of entitlement' (Argument Room, 2013).

Gender exclusivity was often integral to identity. While Monstrous Regiment had seen men involved in the company during the 1970s, between 1980 and 1981, the group's working praxis became all female. Although Gillian Hanna recalls that this was not a deliberate policy and had evolved out of men leaving to pursue other projects, she believes that, with the change, life became easier (Goodman, 1993, 35). Other companies were less doctrinaire, as in the Sadista Sisters' proposal to the Arts Council in 1983 for a show called *Rachel and the Roarettes*, where the group planned to work with a male director, David Sibley (ACGB, 1983, 42/28/11).[3]

Oh Bondage. Up Yours!

Michael Billington saw 1983 as the year when women playwrights came to the fore in British theatre, or more specifically the Royal Court, in work such as Caryl Churchill's *Top Girls* and *Fen*; Sarah Daniels' *The Devil's Gateway* and, the following year, *Masterpieces*. Yet, it should be remembered that the most profound impact came from the touring companies and that the Royal Court itself was only just beginning to reflect something of the nature of work that had already been taking place nationally since at least 1975.

Groups who formed in the late 1970s and early 1980s often came from an entirely different background from the generation who formed WTG and Monstrous Regiment. Writing in 1993, Lizbeth Goodman saw these new groups as part of a process where 'year by year, slightly younger women begin to develop their own feminist theatres' (Goodman, 1993, 82). The rise of punk rock in the mid-1970s was also a significant factor, producing a different sensibility. Noelle Janaczewska identified 'a mass of energy, humour, outrageousness' (Janaczewska, 1989, 109) and performance styles that favoured cabaret, where live music played a significant part. Siren's founder members Tash Fairbanks and Jane Boston were both originally members of a Brighton-based, female punk band called Devil's Dykes, while The Sadista Sisters, a group who had originally started in 1974 but who reformed in 1978, also incorporated music into their shows. Michelene Wandor noted how one of their performances involved 'throwing food around and disembowelling a doll' in a style she described as 'a chaotic kind of sexual aggression' (Wandor, 1981, 46).

The humour and physical nature of this work, often combined with radical feminist politics, could polarize opinion. For example, in his report for The Sadista Sisters' 1981 show *Red Door Without a Bolt*, a performance described in its publicity leaflet as 'a collection of bleak modern fables innocent music, violent lyrics, crude actors, filthy humour and sex' (ACGB, 1981c, 42/28/11). Guy Slater, who at the time worked as Artistic Director of the Horseshoe Theatre in Basingstoke, was bewildered by the show's sexual politics:

> The fact remains that if the Sisters are as sincere and passionate as they are strident they inhabit a world I simply don't recognize. A battle cry of 'poison the fuckers' (men, need I explain?) I find sufficiently mindless to leave the withers unwrung. (ACGB, 1981b, 42/28/11)

By contrast, two years earlier, the theatre academic Jill Davis in her show report for the Sadista Sisters' rock musical *Duchess*, had described it as '*Sensational* ... They could seduce even the heaviest chauvinist, I'm quite certain. Excellent. Fantastic. Amazing. *Give them the money*' (ACGB, 1979b, 42/28/11). However, Jonathan Lamede, who alongside Jill Davis had been approving of *Duchess* (ACGB, 1979a, 42/28/11), found the show *Red Door Without a Bolt* (1981) 'so atrocious it hardly deserved a show report [and that] apart from a few card carrying feminists who applauded as a matter of routine obligation ... It would surely have been an insult to the Women's Movement to call this show feminist' (ACGB, 1981a, 42/28/11).

While the Arts Council was generally supportive of women's companies, sometimes concern was expressed when feminist politics seemed to be coming before considerations of artistic practice. For example, at one point, Jonathan Lamede questioned Jill Davis's work as an assessor for the Arts Council after Clair Chapman from Spare Tyre had publicly criticized its decision not to support one of her projects. In a memo to the Drama Director John Faulkner, Lamede comments that he and fellow officers Jean Bullwinkle and Ruth Marks had all been in agreement over the poor quality of Spare's Tyre's last show, whereas Davis had been unflinching in her support. Lamede concludes, 'Considering the discussion you and I have had about Jill Davis's bias in relation to gay or women's work, I do think it is a pity we are giving so much weight to her opinion' (ACGB, 1980, 41/30/1). Lamede continues with some frankness, 'although we did not say so in blunt terms, what it amounted to was that their [Spare Tyre's] application and past work were simply not good enough' (ACGB, 1980, 41/30/1).

The newer women's groups also saw themselves as different from the more politically committed feminist groups. Cunning Stunts, who combined cabaret-style sketches with circus skills, commented in a 1980 interview: 'There's enough agitprop theatre around. We want to show how women can entertain without necessarily acting "female"' (*Sunday Times*, 1980). Jude Kelly, in her show report for Spare Tyre's *Just Deserts*, also commented that despite weaknesses in technical ability and acting, the company was 'undoubtedly fulfilling a need for unashamedly light hearted mild feminist comedy ... in comparison with other worthier and more technically skilled women's theatre' (ACGB, 1983, 41/30/1).

Sometimes differences between the two approaches could be seen when new members joined an existing company. For example, in December 1980 Cunning Stunts saw the arrival of four new members, including Helen Crocker, who had previously worked for 7:84, Interplay and Mutable. Whereas earlier shows such as *Hamfat-on-the Turn* (1978), *Homer Sweet Home* (1979) and *Runts on the Stoad* (1980) had titles that were indicative of their comic sensibility, the company's new show, *The Opera*, was a departure. Described as 'using our versions of archetypal symbols and mythological characters drawn from astrology, matriarchal societies, magic and our revitalizing female imaginations we will use the image of the opera to express the experiences of living as wimin in a male strangulated world,' (ACGB, 1980a, 41/17/5). *The Opera* was clearly intended to be a more serious piece of feminist theatre. In his review, the critic Charles Spencer noted 'just when everything seems to be verging on the plain silly the company gleefully emphasise that indeed it is' (Spencer, 1983), which suggests that the group had not entirely abandoned its trademark of comedy. Still, the production is illustrative of the ways new personnel could pull a company towards a new identity.

Decline and Fall

The abolition of the GLC and other socialist metropolitan authorities in 1986 marked an end to the financial buffer they had provided against cuts in public spending. Thus began the long struggle for survival for many theatre companies, including women's theatre. Lizbeth Goodman's survey of 223 feminist companies conducted between November 1987 and September 1990 reported 161 groups still in operation, with 62 disbanding (Goodman, 1993, 39). Yet it was not until after 1990 that decline really gathered pace.

The Arts Council, following its *Glory of the Garden* initiative in 1984, seemed increasingly concerned with questions of profession-alization. By this, it meant encouraging and, more frequently, coercing small-scale companies to adopt the same working practices employed in mainstream theatre. In practice, this meant taking on a hierarchical approach, appointing figures such as a full-time administrator and artistic director. This broke with the earlier model of collectivism, since the artistic director now held overall responsibility for policy decisions.

This was to be fate for both WTG and Monstrous Regiment. In 1989, the former changed its collective status to an operation based around a small, all-female management team. In 1991 Monstrous Regiment was forced to appoint Clare Venables as Artistic Director, which likewise changed the group's status from a theatre-collective to a collective-management. These shifts led to a loss of solidarity that in turn resulted in loss of direction, prompting Gillian Hanna from Monstrous Regiment to write in an introduction to a book on British poetry, 'It is 1988 and I no longer feel I know what "feminist" means' (Hanna, 1988, 77).

A Case-Study in Decline: Cunning Stunts

In retrospect, all these growing pressures can be identified as far back as 1981 in the relationship between Cunning Stunts and the Arts Council. Formed in April 1977, Cunning Stunts operated as a women's collective who specialized in using circus skills to produce a form of popular cabaret. The group's approach was eclectic, and in the course of their career they produced community projects, children's shows, street theatre and toured a variety of different venues. Although John Maynard Keynes, in his founding vision for the Arts Council in 1945, spoke blithely of a world where 'The artist walks where the breath of spirit blows him. He cannot be told his direction; he does not know it himself' (Keynes, 1982, 368), by the early 1980s romantic notions of the artist going wherever the muse took him – or her – was now being positively discouraged.

An example of this in practice can be found in Cunning Stunts' 1981 show *Winter Warmer*. While drama officer Clive Tempest's show report comments positively on 'the loose and easy way they worked', at the same time he was 'disappointed by their general lack of direction and purpose', while his suggestions for future improvement could be seen as prophetic for later decisions taken towards theatre collectives: 'If they [Cunning Stunts] wish to entertain simply as an all-woman clown company, I suspect they will have to work very hard on their skills ... If they are interested in narrative, they will have to find ways of creating stronger material. And some directorial authority, no matter how it is arrived at, seems necessary' (ACGB, 1981, 41/17/5c).

The problem with Cunning Stunts as far as the Arts Council was concerned was that members simply wanted to do too many different things. When, for instance, the group put in an application for a Theatre Training Scheme in May 1981 in order to set up a series of workshops for the public, alarm bells sounded. In a memo to Jonathan Lamede, Senior Education Officer Peter Mair, who acted as the group's drama officer, concludes, 'I don't feel they [Cunning Stunt's] have worked out clearly enough exactly what their aims are nor how they are to be achieved ... I also wonder whether they're really drama ... and whether some other department would be more appropriate.' Lamede's reply is equally revealing: 'Very worrying. I wonder whether these portents aren't simply the symptoms of an enervating diffusion of purpose. CS [Cunning Stunts] do seem to be floundering' (ACGB, 1981b, 41/17/5). Lamede, an early champion of the company, expressed his concerns more formally the following month after seeing two performances of *The Opera*:

> Cunning Stunts started as a bunch of talented, zany women doing crazily funny things because they liked doing them to amuse an audience ... What Cunning Stunts seem to want to do at the moment ... encompasses several not necessarily compatible things. First, they want to entertain ... second they want to use some fairly progressive musical means; third, they want to perfect a form of theatre using physical skills akin to those of the circus; fourth, and by no means least, they want to delve deep into the lore of femininity and re-animate some mysteries; finally, they want to create shows that are visually stunning. No doubt, you can aim at all these things and you can do some of them some of the time, but it would take a lifetime's genius to fulfill them in one body of work. (ACGB, 1981b, 41/17/5)

The message seems clear: to stay in favour a company needed to decide on its artistic direction and stick to it, as was the practice employed in mainstream theatre of bringing in an outside director, or someone with equivalent authority from within the company. For Cunning Stunts, after completing *The Opera*, the company cancelled all further plans to perform that year citing exhaustion (ACGB, 1981, 41/15/5). After doing one more show, *Winter Warmer*, Cunning Stunts formally disbanded in 1982.

Stand-Up or Die

Changing fashions also played a considerable part in the demise of women's groups. Theatre critic Carole Woodis believed that the generation of young women who had reached maturity by the end of the 1980s now preferred to see stand-up female comedians than attend a play or a devised performance on lesbian sexual politics (Goodman, 1993, 292). Woodis's comment is significant, as the deleterious impact of stand-up comedy on many of the cabaret-style feminist companies has generally been overlooked in existing accounts of the period. In the early years both cultures grew together, influenced collectively by the energy, chaos and confrontation of punk rock. The Comedy Store in London opened in 1979, shortly followed by another club, The Comic

Strip, the following year. The subsequent proliferation of stand-up can be likened in some ways to the Arts Lab movement in the late 1960s and Baz Kershaw observes that while at first confined to a small number of London venues, they 'quickly mushroomed into a national orthodoxy' (Kershaw, 2004, 370). Alwyn W. Turner also observes that 'by the mid-1980s there were an estimated 50 clubs in London alone [and] a network of live venues that never seemed to stop growing' (Turner, 2012, 57). Stand-up comedy also increasingly dominated the Edinburgh Festival, at one time considered the stronghold of fringe theatre groups.

Early on, a number of performers such as Peter Richardson and Nigel Planer (as The Wild Boys) and French and Saunders were associated with the work of some of the theatre companies, and a number of these acts even started making applications to the Arts Council's Drama Panel for project funding. This began around 1978 with Mel Smith and Bob Goody (as Smith and Goody), but reached full momentum around 1985 with applications from among others Dross Bros (featuring future playwright and screenwriter Patrick Marber) and Mularkey and Myers (Neil Mularkey and the future comic film actor Mike Myers). However, applications started to diminish after this point as the comedy performers abandoned the circuit of venues associated with theatre groups in favour of the new comedy clubs and university gigs. Audience allegiances also transferred to the stand-up comedians rather than the theatre groups, and television channels and producers also saw the potential for stand-up comedy as a cheap way of filling their schedules. First amongst these was the newly inaugurated Channel 4, in 1982, which at first sought out fringe theatre for transposing existing work (such as Black Theatre Co-operative (BTC)'s *No Problem* and Cliffhanger's *They Came From Somewhere Else*) as a way of fulfilling its remit to represent minority tastes. However, the ascendency of performers associated with the new comedy clubs can also be discerned on Channel 4's first night of broadcast, when Peter Richardson, Ade Edmondson, Dawn French and Jennifer Saunders, as The Comic Strip, performed in *Five Go Mad in Dorset*. It was a sign of things to come.

The theatre groups most affected were the new wave of feminist companies such as Cunning Stunts, Clapperclaw, and Beryl and the Perils. Comedy was also central to their style and identity, but they saw themselves as more performance-led and collective in structure compared to the individualized world of stand-up comedy. In an internet discussion with former members of feminist groups working at that time, Clair Chapman from Spare Tyre remembers when feminist groups began to be supplanted by stand-up comedians:

> There was a very clear time when suddenly people stopped coming to our shows and it seemed to be around about the time of stand-up. Suddenly there were guys on mikes – talking about not very much. And then we would come on with our songs about stuff and audiences just fell away ... It was very violent and very sudden and very male and people didn't seem to want to think anymore. (Argument Room, 2013)

In the discussion that followed, Didi Hopkins from Beryl and the Perils expressed her belief that here was a case of a different sensibility prevailing in stand-up comedy, where 'the microphone came into play, whereas we made theatre where you could hear a pin drop. We didn't have any amplification ... I remember playing in Brixton in a pub and the following week it was French and Saunders who were miked up' (Argument Room, 2013). Anna Furse of Bloodgroup added:

> The mike was mostly the drama graduate's route to very cheap communication. We were cheap but we still had some production values and we still had some budgets. We needed to put some stuff on our stages. The mike was just you and your voice down the mike – perfect in a Thatcherised economy. The Comedy Store opened up and suddenly the whole culture changed. (Argument Room, 2013)

In one show report for Beryl and the Perils' 1980 show, *Wot's Cooking*, Jill Davis commented, 'I have a few doubts about the material, which in this show is really just a reiteration of a few of the major feminist concerns – male progression, the politics of women's health etc. If the show didn't proceed at a grand prix pace and wasn't packed with so much comedy, I might have had time to quarrel with some of the simplifications' (ACGB, 1980, 41/13/6). Davis was a long-term admirer of the company, but her comments about the show's feminist content go somewhat deeper than attempts to blame the amplification of microphones for the reason that audiences abandoned feminist groups like Beryl and the Perils: while political comedy had been in vogue during the 1980s, later audiences appeared to have grown weary of the doctrinaire.

Feminism and Funding: The 'F' Words

By 1993 Gillian Hanna of Monstrous Regiment had also come to recognize these changes in culture: namely, that the feminist politics that had once been the motivating force behind the formation of so many women's companies now seemed to be considered 'so unfashionable, so *uncool'* by younger audiences (Goodman, 1993, 37). Claire Venables, who in 1991 became the new Artistic Director of WTG, evidently felt the same way: one of her first decisions was to change the company's name and with it associations of a feminist past that now seemed burdensome. In a telling letter from its marketing officer (a new but increasingly powerful figure as the arts began to incorporate the language and practices of business), the company was informed that the name WTG carried associations of amateurism to some audiences (Goodman, 1993, 68). That a name change was deemed necessary also suggests that, by the early 1990s, companies that drew attention to their feminist identities were considered old-fashioned. Funding policy, always prone to the fickleness of changing tastes, also saw a change of priorities. Whereas 'minority' groups, into which the women's companies fell, were once fêted by the GLC, after its abolition Arts Council priorities shifted in favour of groups specializing in physical theatre and the ethnic minorities.

It could also be argued that by the early 1990s the need for women's touring companies had come to its natural end with the incorporation of many of their ideas and practices into mainstream theatre. By drawing attention to feminism, regional theatres, together with new-writing venues such as the Royal Court, Soho and the Bush in London, that had frequently hosted tours from these companies, now started commissioning women dramatists to produce similar work for themselves. Dimple Godiwala has argued that interest in the 1990s for what she terms as formerly 'ghettoized women's theatre' (Godiwala, 2003, 52) should be seen as a vindication and natural completion of the project undertaken by women's touring companies during the 1970s and 1980s.

Another contributory factor in the demise of women's theatre companies may also have come through the Arts Council's criteria governing artistic standards in drama and performance. Lauren Kruger saw this as detrimental to many women's companies, with the imposition of deliberately vague but nonetheless pervasive criteria that resulted in what she calls 'the legitimation of marginalization' (Kruger, 1990, 30). These were dominated mainly by Leavisite values, theatrical only in the sense of recognizing assessable standards based on the mainstream in terms of acting or technical abilities. Show reports from the Arts Council archive indicate that these were the benchmarks drama officers and assessors most frequently employed. For example, in a report on Spare Tyre's *Woman's Complaint* in 1982, Jonathan Lamede aimed his criticisms directly at the performance skills of the company members. Harriet Powell, the company's musician, was 'no kind of stage performer', while

> Katina Noble showed signs of acute strain, to the extent I winced with discomfort at some of her work. As for Clair Chapman, I must confess to finding her the kind of performer who seems to be forever demonstrating how she thinks things ought to be done ... without ever being capable of actually doing it herself. *In other words an amateur performer* [my italics] perhaps strayed in from an American college drama group. (ACGB, 1982a, 41/30/1)

Amateurism is the cardinal failing, and Lamede makes professional criteria chief among his objections to funding the early work of Clean Break. The company, who are still in existence today, were formed by Jennifer Hicks and Jacqueline Holborough in 1979, and specialized in working with female prisoners. In his show report on *In and Out* and *Killers* (1981) Lamede describes one of the actors giving 'the sort of self-indulgent performance that would pass for bravura acting at secondary school but had little place in professional theatre' (ACGB 1981, 41/49/1), while for their show *Avenues* the following year Lamede commented, 'spending time inside is not necessarily a qualification for the professional stage' (ACGB, 1982, 41/49/1). Not unsurprisingly, it was not until Clean Break began using professional actors and directors rather than drawing exclusively on the personal experiences of inmates attached to the company that it began to attract regular Arts Council funding.

However, this view on professionalism did not entirely prevail within the Arts Council. Some understood that 'amateurism' was a deliberate part of these groups' identities and the distinguishing quality that made their work so fresh and exciting. For example, when the Drama Panel was reluctant to commit large sums of money to Cunning Stunts after poor reviews for their 1982 show *Winter Warmer*, Jill Davis argued that by following advice from successive show reports to become more professional, Cunning Stunts had 'lost their original "spark" and were in danger of becoming mediocre' (ACGB, 1982, 41/17/5).

However, the degree of conflict between the two strands of thinking can be seen when the novelist, critic and journalist Marghanita Laski attended Cunning Stunts' 1980 *Christmas Show* at the Tricycle Theatre: 'it is incredible that this company should purport to be professionals ... not only can they not speak audibly, this anti-capitalist, anti-nuclear show they chose to present is gibberish. They cannot tap dance. They cannot synchronize anything. Their attempted audience participation is dreadful or impertinent' (ACGB, 1980b, 41/17/5).

By the end of the 1980s and faced with growing financial pressures, the Arts Council seemed to increasingly adopt a 'portfolio' approach to theatre clients, choosing one or two companies who could be said to represent a particular interest group, such as Tara Arts or Talawa. Yet with this in mind, speaking after Monstrous Regiment finally lost funding in 1993 Gillian Hanna noted ruefully that they were not replaced by another women's company (Aston, 1995, 36).

Political Theatre Companies

In some ways, this is an erroneous category, as the majority of companies working in the 1980s identified themselves as somehow oppositional to the values of Mrs Thatcher's government, although at times dissent became almost a studied reflex. When, for instance, WTG toured a production of Julie Wilkinson's *Pinchdice and Co* (1989), despite the play being set during the Crusades, the programme notes talk of the dispossessed of 1148AD struggling to survive 'just like the dispossessed of Thatcher's Britain' (ACGB, 1989, 41/15/8).

Companies, at times, appeared to adopt a political identity even when their work seemed absent of any direct content of this kind. Red Shift, a touring company formed by Jonathan Holloway in 1982, despite the name suggesting a left-wing focus, specialized in adaptations of classical work such as *The Duchess of Malfi* (1983), which incorporated elements of physical theatre. In 1984 the company paid lip-service, albeit in an unconvincing way, to the spirit of the times when it applied to the Arts Council's NAPS Committee for a show that took account of the Orwellian year. *Broken English*, subtitled *A Collage of Images – Britain in 1994*, was described as 'social statement', yet at the same time 'always entertaining', while under the application's Aims and Objectives criteria, the company stressed that its work will 'confront social issues and present a socialist perspective through the story telling process' (ACGB, 1984, 41/28/3). However, a year earlier, in his show report for *The Duchess of Malfi*, Jonathan Lamede had been unconvinced by Red Shift's 'half-hearted attempt to give it modern political overtones' (ACGB, 1983, 41/28/3). Red Shift is one of the few companies from the early 1980s still in existence today but, perhaps not surprisingly, it no longer highlights this particular strand of artistic policy on its website.

Jane Milling believes that in a response to what was seen by some as a weakening of purpose, a 'cry went up throughout the 1980s and beyond: what has happened to political theatre?' (Milling, 2012, 68). The reasons for this persistent lament have been many and various, but one thing was clear: the definitions and robust structures that constituted political theatre in the 1970s had started to unravel as the politics of the New Right and the free market began to do their work. The reassurance British political theatre felt about its own identity came out of a belief that revolution in Britain was not just likely, but imminent. This sense of belief also brought a resistance to contemplating new strategies to take account of how quickly things were changing following the election of Mrs Thatcher.

By the time of the Conservative's second decisive election victory in 1983, any certainty about the effectiveness of political theatre was now seriously called into question. The Arts Council archives also contain a number of memos, letters and show reports written by drama officers and advisers, drawn from fellow practitioners in theatre, who repeatedly criticize political companies for continuing to pursue a form of theatre that even in the early years of the Thatcher premiership already appeared moribund. An example is Counteract, who formed in 1977 and was described by its drama officer in 1981 as a group 'distinguished by a rare combination of stylistic ... approaches which ... improved on agitprop' (ACGB, 1981, 41/6/6). Elsewhere, in a report written about *Never Mind the Ballots*, a production based on the Thatcher government's 1980 Employment Act, which attempted to curb union power, Jill Davis, despite acknowledging that half the company was comprised of her former students, described the show as 'absolutely terrible' and 'like being taken back in a time capsule to, say 1973 and watching really crude and schematic political theatre' (ACGB, 1980, 41/6/6). In her report, drama officer Sian Eade, despite being a strong advocate for community and TIE companies, described Broadside Mobile Workers' Theatre's progress in 1980 as 'worthy, respectable and evangelical though artistically rather two-dimensional and not very impressive, if competent'. More ominously, Eade concludes, 'I remain convinced of more direct funding from the TUC' (ACGB, 1980a, 38/9/23), meaning presumably that the Arts Council should devolve responsibility for funding the company to the trade unions.

The policy of funding these companies was also questioned by the theatre critic Michael Coveney, who, in a letter to the Arts Council's Deputy Drama Director in March 1983, apologizes for being unable to attend the Drama Advisory Panel but offers suggestions for discussion at the all-day meeting. These include 'the state of the small touring companies: 7:84, Monstrous Regiment, Foco Novo etc [and] a need for a drastic review of the 1970s legacy of such groups against the needs of the time and indeed their contribution to it? On the basis of 7:84 England's recent work I would say there was' (ACGB, 1983a, 38/32/2). Coveney's proposal that the Arts Council cease supporting politically radical companies would prove prophetic: the following year, 7:84 England lost its funding.

One Big Blow or Trees in the Wind? – 7:84 in 1980

Despite the gloomy picture, it should also be recognized that the period between 1980 and 1994 did not simply mark the slow death of political companies. To give some sense of this, it is instructive to look at two 7:84 shows that took place in 1980. The first was a revival of the company's first production, *Trees in the Wind* (1971). Reviewers acting on behalf of the Arts Council's Drama Panel unanimously agreed that the play now looked out of touch with the times. For example, television producer Howard Gibbins described it as 'very dated, although Sue Timothy (7:84's drama officer) tried to persuade me that the issues were still as relevant as they were in 1971', but he remained unconvinced: 'I believe that socialist theatre companies still do not play to audiences they profess to play to and that the majority of these issues have been subsumed a long time ago.' While he does comment that 'the production was of the highest standard of its type and that 7:84 were on safe ground', he adds, 'They should be – they have been there before' (ACGG, 1979, 41/51/6).

With a new combative Conservative government and new decade ahead, 7:84 England did not get off to a good start in convincing either audiences or the Arts Council of its vibrancy and relevance by reviving an old show. However, its next production, *One Big Blow*, drew unanimous praise and did much to restore faith in the company. In effect, this was 7:84's first new work of 1980, as *Trees in the Wind* had started its tour in late 1979. In a plot that seemed to anticipate the film *Brassed Off* (1996), John Burrows play about a miners' brass band originated in devised workshops with students from the Rose Bruford College. Actor Robert Aldous's show report was typical in its praise for a production that 'rightly brought the house down' and further reassurance that 'in no way can the charge be made that 7:84 is preaching to the converted' (ACGB, 1980, 41/53/8).

However, even among the praise, some reservations were expressed that with the benefit of hindsight might be seen as portents of the eventual fate of 7:84 England. For example, in one report, despite describing *One Big Blow* as 'a gem of direction by John Burrows', the following questions were raised:

> whether it is in all respects the quality of work we should be expecting a company of the stature and subsidy level of 7:84 at this stage of its development may be another matter. Or do I really mean: what a (by and large) splendid and (surely) cheap way of doing popular theatre which should pull in good audiences, and do they really need the third largest subsidy on the touring companies list in order to achieve this?' (ACGB, 1980, 41/53/9)[4]

Yet, in an indication of just how far the company managed to provoke such divergent views, Nick Barter, a drama officer who saw *One Big Blow*, considered it a vindication of the company's development over the past ten years and concluded that 'it is good to know that 7:84 are maintaining such a vigorous policy and high standard of work' (ACGB, 1981, 41/51/6). However, many of the old criticisms had resurfaced by the time of *School for Emigrants* (1984): Yvonne Brewster, writing on behalf of Clive Perry (who at the time was Artistic Director of the Birmingham Repertory Theatre and, who submitted his show report by telephone), called it 'dreadful ... an improvisation gone totally wrong', and, while apologizing for sounding harsh, declared that the production made him recall his own early collaborations with the company in Scotland, but here he could find 'no trace of the sharpness of political stance or wit which used to mark those 7:84 early days' (ACGB, 1984, 41/53/9). While there were undoubted successes during the period, such as 7:84 Scotland's 1983 production of Ena Lamont Stewart's play *Men Should Weep* (1946), Yvonne Brewster still described this somewhat dismissively as a 'resurrection project' and while following others in her praise of Elizabeth Maclennan's central performance, ended her report by commenting, 'I keep reminding myself this is not 7:84 England – regrettably' (ACGB, 1983, 41/53/9).

It should also be said that 7:84 England itself recognized the changing situation as early as 1979/80 and decided to restrict operations by only touring to 40 venues in the north of the country – areas that included Cumbria, Merseyside, Teeside, Yorkshire, Corby, Northampton and Nottingham. An exception was made for a small enclave in north-west London (McGrath, 1990, 18; Timothy, 2014). In these areas, a positive reception could be assured, because they broadly mirrored geographical voting patterns and attitudes to the Thatcher government. However, this meant all but abandoning touring to the South of England, a move that was interpreted by some as a retrenchment. This left the company open to criticisms of abandoning its responsibilities as a national touring company and the perennial criticism of preaching to the converted.

Yet it would also be wrong to say that political companies immediately went into hibernation or had perished by the dawn of 1980. Touring companies, being relatively unencumbered by the bureaucratic and financial apparatus of mainstream theatre, which often necessitated planning seasons of work a year ahead, could respond quickly to a situation. An early example of this was 7:84 Scotland's *Joe's Drum*, a production conceived, rehearsed and produced in September 1979 that was able to respond almost immediately to both the failure of Scotland to win enough votes in the referendum to achieve devolution in March and Mrs Thatcher's election in May.

Black and Asian Theatre Companies

The association and grouping together of black and Asian companies, almost a default convention in theatre scholarship, has nevertheless always been a contentious one. Jatinder Verma, the Artistic Director of Tara Arts in their first application to the Arts Council in 1982 as a professional company for *The Lion's Raj* pointed out that using existing definitions and criteria applied to black theatre as a 'possible yardstick by which to judge Tara would be misleading' (ACGB, 1982d, 41/30/4). However, despite often having very different histories and approaches, the inclusion of black and Asian companies under a shared heading in this volume is deliberate, mainly because between 1980 and 1994 both groups were affected by many of the same issues.

(i) The Arts Britain begins to Recognize
On the one hand, the 1980s was a decade distinguished by growing success. Black companies, in particular, experienced a marked

improvement both in terms of their numbers, funding and visibility in London and regionally. In June 1981 the Arts Council had formerly recognized 'a prima facie case for some affirmative action in support of ethnic minorities' arts' (ACGB, 1984, 38/32/4), and an Ethnic Arts Working Group was set up in February 1982 to monitor progress. By 1984, Yvonne Brewster stated in a draft report on the subject to the Arts Council that 'ethnic minority arts rather than being the "Arts Britain Ignores" have become the "Arts Britain has just begun to notice"' (ACGB, 1984, 38/32/4). Brewster's report outlined how in 1979 Temba was the only black revenue-funded client, but by 1983/4 Temba had been joined by the Black Theatre Co-operative (BTC). The Black Theatre of Brixton was also in receipt of project finding and centres such Keskidee and The Drum had been allocated funds. By 1984 there were at least six new companies in existence, including Staunch Poets and Players, and Carib Theatre Productions. This improvement can also be seen in the annual funding Temba had received since its inception: in 1974/5, it had been awarded £4,150; by 1984/5, it was in receipt of £72,000 (ACGB, 1984, 38/32/4).

However, there was still a long way to go. Despite the generous award to BTC, who saw its budget rise from £19,000 to £61,380 in 1983 after it became a revenue client, the money itself was not new. In fact, it came out of the Arts Council's existing projects budget, rather than the larger drama allocation, which meant that BTC's rise came at the expense of other small-scale companies who relied on project funds. While this, at least, represented a commitment to black theatre on the Arts Council's behalf, Brewster's report also notes that in 1984 out of a total of £1.9 million allocated to non-building-based companies, black and Asian companies were in receipt of just 6.8 per cent of the overall drama budget (ACGB, 1984, 38/32/4).

In the same year in which *The Glory of the Garden* was written, Temba, one of the companies earmarked for closure, was in receipt of £70,000 annually. The contentious proposal to axe Temba when one of the central aims of *Glory* was to prioritize the funding of black theatre has always been difficult to reconcile. Briefing notes on the company for the 1987/8 Drama Budget Working Group suggest that concerns were less to do with artistic standards and more related to poor financial management. At the time Temba was running a deficit of £21,000 and was unwilling to take Arts Council advice on how to temper its ambitious programme of planned work (ACGB, 1987/8, 38/32/18).

These contradictions in policy against practice were recognised at the time by its Drama Director Dickon Reed, who outlined in a strategy paper that ' "Ethnic" provision would need to be strengthened particularly in view of the possible withdrawal of subsidy from the Temba Company' (ACGB, 1984, 38/32/1). Yet the proposed sum of £100,000 of extra money to enable this, even taking into account the £70,000 that would be saved from the proposed discontinuation of Temba's revenue funding, only left £30,000 of 'new' money available to fund the entire spectrum of black and Asian theatre in the UK. Put in a different context, the Arts Council was proposing to spend approximately the same amount of money in 1985/6 on the whole of black and Asian theatre that it spent on the annual costs of running the Yvonne Arnaud Theatre in Guildford (ACGB, 1984, 38/32/1).

Temba ultimately survived *Glory's* scythe, but it was a close-run thing. Even in a study of appeals by the threatened clients in July 1984, reference is made to Temba's 'dubious standards and little audience appeal' (ACGB, 1984, 28/32/5). At the same time it was also recognized that 'the company has obviously blazed a trail and filled a gap in theatrical provision', but the report concludes that even though Temba had responded to the threatened cut with an overhaul of its management, the best policy would be to find another company doing similar work to Temba rather than supporting the existing company (ACGB, 1984, 28/32/5). Yet, following its appeal, Temba was saved and its funding reinstated due to what Yvonne Brewster called 'impressive fundamental and welcome changes to its policies and administration' (ACGB, 1984, 38/32/4).

This probably referred to the appointment of Alby James as Temba's new artistic director, who introduced classical work into the company's repertoire together with the promotion of new work by black women including Trish Cooke's *Back Street Mammy* (1986) and Barbara Glouden's Jamaican pantomime *The Pirate Princess* (1986). While his appointment meant that the company still adhered to the existing new-writing policy, James justified the new artistic policy by arguing that 'black people's participation in classical work should be seen as a normal and expected activity' (Peacock, 1999, 181). This policy was later taken up with even more success by Talawa.

In 1985, the Arts Council's Deputy Secretary General, Anthony Everitt, while acknowledging some improvements in drama provision believed that, despite the resolution back in June 1981, collectively the organization had failed to provide the necessary support to black and Asian arts, with the result that 'in his view there were signs throughout the country, and particularly in London, that this issue was reaching explosion point, and … it would be timely for Council to take positive action' (ACGB, 1985, 99/46/1).

Part of the reason why Arts Council's initiatives lagged behind during the first half of the 1980s was simply that it found itself outpaced by metropolitan authorities such as the GLC. After hosting an ethnic arts conference in May 1982, the GLC set up an Ethnic Arts Sub-committee under the wider umbrella of its Arts and Recreational Committee. This sub-committee was an addition to the already newly formed Community Arts Sub-committee. In its first year alone, this body dispensed a budget of £30,000, rising substantially in 1984–5 to nearly £2 million. A significant number of its beneficiaries came from the first- and second-generation Afro-Caribbean and Asian communities who were resident in London.

This halcyon period proved all too brief, and after the abolition of the GLC in 1986, replacement funds granted by the Conservative government to the Arts Council to absorb former clients were simply not sufficient. In the case of theatre, during the financial year of 1986/7 drama projects were given an extra £100,000 to take on former GLC clients, but the following year this windfall was no longer available and, as a result, some harsh decisions were made. Because money was finite, it was assigned to priority companies. In the case of black and Asian theatre, decisions were made in favour of existing Arts Council clients BTC and Temba, while British Asian Theatre, Carib TIE, Carib Theatre, Double Edge, Hounslow Arts Co-operative, Staunch Poets and Players, Umoja and Zuriya, who had received the majority of their funding from the GLC, were listed as non-priorities (ACGB, 1985, 38/32/16).

However, the abolition of the GLC and the other metropolitan authorities did lead to a significant change of policy within the Arts Council, and it is likely that the levels of funding and attention the GLC had drawn to ethnic minority arts persuaded the Arts Council into pledging 4 per cent of its overall budget over the following two years to this area. Distribution was monitored, with all companies in receipt of funding being asked to outline their own employment policies. This was an important sea-change in thinking, and while the mid-1980s have widely been depicted as the time of Thatcherite values infiltrating the Arts Council, it also marked the first real evidence of policies aimed at promoting diversity, and it is instructive to see the term 'institutional racism' used as far back as 1986 in the same context we are familiar with today (ACGB, 1986, 99/36/4).

However, the Arts Council's decision to devote 4 per cent of its resources to black and Asian arts did not always meet with overwhelming support from some of its other funded clients. Michael Haynes, who at the time was the Arts Council's first black drama officer, reported that several companies questioned the necessity of producing work of this genre on the grounds that few, if any, black or Asian audiences existed in the regions they toured. Haynes's counter-argument to this was quite simply 'that since Britain is a multi-cultural society and theatre should reflect this ... white residents should be given the opportunity to share in the richness of the British culture' (ACGB, 1986a, 99/36/4). However, it is difficult to imagine how such a policy might have operated for groups such as The Medieval Players, or the Irish company Green Fields and Far Away, and it is easy to have sympathy with their position, especially given the implicit threat contained in Haynes' report, which states, 'we have also stressed that their willingness to reflect the multi-racial society will be part of our assessment of the company which naturally will reflect the level of subsidy the Arts Council allocated to the company' (ACGB, 1986a, 99/36/4).

Haynes also assumes that only black and Asian companies were exclusively producing work on multicultural issues, but this was not entirely the case. For example, in 1989 the community theatre group Major Road produced a devised show, *Daybreak*, using a professional writer and pupils from the Greenhead, Oakbark and Holy Family schools in Keighley, Yorkshire, that included commentary from the Asian communities living in the area. Drama officer Anthony Kearey's show report noted that out of the 45 performers, 'a quarter of the cast drawn from the three schools were Asian [and] saw the influence of their input in the content of the show ' (ACGB, 1989, 41/52/7).

(ii) Past and Present Identities
Many black and Asian companies during this period in one sense shared an agenda with the women's companies by attempting to produce work that sought to articulate a collective sense of past and present identity. However, the overwhelming majority of black theatre produced during the 1970s focused almost exclusively on a disaporic Caribbean experience, written by, and aimed at, the first generation who had settled in Britain, but rarely did this drama address day-to-day experiences of living in the UK. There were exceptions, most notably Trinidadian Mustapha Matura's 1979 play for BTC, *Welcome Home Jacko*. However, in his show report Gerald Chapman, then artistic director of the Royal Court's Young People's Theatre, argues that Matura had presented a 'fundamentally reactionary and middle class view of Black youth and of Rastas in particular', which he puts down to the playwright's background and age (ACGB, 1979, 41/45/1).

Yet by the 1980s some black artists started to take exception to how 'their' theatre companies chose to represent the wider community. This burden of representation fell particularly hard on larger companies such as BTC and Talawa, who were somehow expected to present work that would simultaneously represent both disaporic experience and contemporary life in Britain. Often this meant that they could please no one.

One such malcontent was the actor Norman Beaton. Hailing from Guyana, Beaton had co-founded the Black Theatre of Brixton in 1974 and had worked as an actor for companies such as Talawa and the RSC. Beaton was concerned at how unrepresentative this uneasy Caribbean/ British confluence was in much of the drama being produced in the 1980s. Beaton singles out BTC for especially harsh criticism, arguing that, whereas in the past white theatre culture depicted black people as 'Toms and Coons', BTC 'have fallen into the trap of ghettoizing every social issue [giving us] pimps, prostitutes, tired reluctant old West Indian men and their long suffering wives, sons on the dole or in prison, an entire society at war with the forces of law and order ... and therefore reinforces the white man's prejudice' (ACGB,1983, 41/9/13).

Some of Beaton's negative observations were echoed by feminists who saw patriarchal attitudes from the Caribbean finding their way into black British theatre through the nature of work presented and the organizational lines on which the companies were run. For example, Katerina Duncan, who had directed shows for Monstrous Regiment, in her show report for Temba's double bill *Mama Decemba* and *Streetwise* commented, 'I had problems with the politics of both pieces partly because I'm a white feminist' (ACGB, 1990b, 41/51/7), while Fiona Ellis, the regional drama officer for Southern Arts, in her show report on BTC's production of Edgar White's *Ritual* (1985) identifies some of the same features that so incensed Norman Beaton, including 'the unemployed Rasta-kids constantly in fear of police harassment' and even 'a one legged, grizzled West Indian ghost' in the form of a character called Uncle Charlie. However, Ellis singles out the central protagonist, a middle-aged youth worker called Basil, who re-establishes his masculinity through hitting his wife, as 'irremediable' (ACGB, 1985, 41/54/2).

To be fair to BTC, after 1985 a more diverse output of work emerged, including plays such as Yemi Ajibade's *Waiting for Hannibal* (1986), a play about the Punic wars, as well as revivals of classical work, such as its 1985 production of Lorraine Hansbury's *A Raisin in the Sun*. Temba, under Alby James in 1984, also started to commission new work by women. This commitment extended beyond writers, as in the 1989 production of *Mother Poem* by Edward Kamau Brathwaite for which the Arts Council show report notes, 'it is refreshing to see a company whose technical and acting team are all women, when the Company is not a Women's Group' (ACGB, 1989b, 41/56/6).

While Talawa and Tara are often cited as the two most prominent companies in bringing black and Asian theatre into the mainstream, often the impact of BTC is downplayed. For example, in 1988 BTC was a recipient, alongside Talawa and Tara, of the three-year Arts Council revenue funding scheme.

Originally set up in 1979 by the playwright Mustapha Matura and director Charlie Hanson as a way of securing a fringe venue interested in producing Matura's play *Welcome Home Jacko*, once established, BTC's ambitions clearly exceeded the values of the fringe. BTC also saw itself as providing a platform for black performers to gain access into mainstream theatre. Although D. Keith Peacock sees BTC's artistic policies as conservative when compared with other black companies (Peacock, 1999, 182), its unwillingness to be relegated to the margins of fringe or community theatre demonstrated admirable ambition and drive. For instance, in a set of 1988 briefing notes for the Drama Budget Working Party, whose task it was to assess future levels of subsidy for companies, Jean Bullwinkle notes that under its new Artistic Director, Malcolm Frederick, BTC's regional touring output had increased from the point of being non-existent to impressive and praises two new shows that have been well received by audiences (ACGB, 1988b, 38/32/13).

Many of these problems of representation can be identified as coming out of the histories of the companies themselves. The founding members of Talawa, for instance, hailed from the West Indies, so it is not surprising to see how its artistic policy privileged a disaporic past; yet it is true that many companies were slow in responding to changes in contemporary British culture. Writing in 1987, when she edited the first volume of plays by black British dramatists, Yvonne Brewster had warned, 'The work of those who live in this country must become more accessible: if not, then the work of playwrights living in the Caribbean and Africa will continue to dominate' (Brewster, 1987, 361). Despite Talawa's poor record of accomplishment in this area at that time, Brewster did at least seem aware of this problem, but her anthology not appearing until 1987 gives some indication of how far this problem reached.

In fact, even by 1990, there was little sign of change. For example, in his show report for Felix Cross's play *Glory*, produced by Temba,

Paul Ranger quite clearly identifies the company as West Indian rather than British when he comments, 'Only a Caribbean company could stage a show such as this, telling the story through dance, carnival, symbol and local customs' (ACGB, 1990, 41/56/6a). Cross's play, about a Catholic family living on an island in the West Indies on the eve of independence, was typical of the kind of work Temba produced. Yet Cross himself, who took over as artistic director of BTC in 1997 (when its name was changed to Nitro), commented: 'I'd say Nitro is probably a Black British company whereas perhaps Black Theatre Co-op reflected more its West Indian roots, its Caribbean roots. And most of its plays were in the early days certainly, set between the Caribbean and England, and you could absolutely see the links' (Cross, 2006, 225).

However, 1989 should be seen as the real moment when black British drama shifted from being exclusively defined through Caribbean traditions. This can be identified through a number of small developments that, when taken together, can be read as signs of definite change taking place. One of these is noted by Nicola Thorold, who at the time was working in the Arts Council's Finance department. In her show report for Talawa's *The Gods are Not to Blame*, she comments that in its programme the company had stated 'that they chose to perform this play in an attempt to redress the imbalance between Caribbean and African influences in Black theatre in England' (ACGB, 1989c, 41/56/6). The same year, Temba produced two short plays in a double bill: Nigel Moffat's *Mama Decemba* and Benjamin Zephaniah's *Streetwise*. While Moffat's play, originally written in 1985, was a familiar diaspora play, charting the eponymous character's journey from Jamaica to England, Zephaniah's play was set entirely in Britain and concerned a group of young black people who battle to maintain the independent spirit of the carnival from interference by the local authority. These two one-act plays marked a significant crossover point between an established generation of writers and an emerging new one. The double bill of *Mama Decemba* and *Streetwise* even provided a symbolic indication of the change to come in the actor Ian Roberts, who appeared in both plays; in his future incarnation as Kwame Kwei-Armah, he would emerge as one of Britain's most well-known black dramatists in the millennial decade. In her show report at the time, the director Claire Grove recognized this new development, whereby 'one [play] is contemporary and appeals to a young black audience, the other play looks backwards and appeals to an older black audience' (ACGB, 1989c, 41/56/6).

(iii) Avoiding the Ghetto: The Bid for Professionalism in Black Theatre Companies

A running theme in the history of black theatre in Britain has been the struggle not only for recognition and resources, but also against assumptions that its theatre is somehow second rate or worthy of special treatment simply because of ethnicity. It is possible to understand how far things have changed when looking back at the touring conditions a group such as Tara Arts had to endure in the early 1980s, when it attempted to take unfamiliar work to new audiences. Ian Kellgren provides a stark account of conditions in his Arts Council show report for *Ancestral Voices* in 1983. Even taking into account Tara's semi-professional status at the time, his observations are alarming:

> The performance was supposed to be in a residents' centre in the middle of Hyde Park flats, Sheffield. This was a monstrous, fearsome complex high on a hill, renowned for violence and people throwing things out of the windows. Someone must have tipped off Tara because there was a notice redirecting the audience to a Salvation Army hall a mile away ... There was no lighting and the set was three small moveable screens, two clumsily painted, one with coat hangers on ... There was an audience of 20+ with several small children with their lego and six Asian women. (ACGB, 1983, 41/30/4k)

Even with disappointing audiences and challenging conditions, such enterprises could be said to be justified in the long term by providing a visibility and presence that in time would become integrated into the artistic policies of many significant regional theatres.

Yet, there were some who questioned the whole project of deliberately seeking out black and Asian audiences. In 1983 Foco Novo toured *Sleeping Policeman*, the result of a collaboration between Howard Brenton and the black British dramatist Tunde Ikoli, which was deliberately set in Peckham, South London. Although generally well reviewed in the capital, when Philip Hedley, then Artistic Director of Stratford East, saw the production at the University Theatre in Colchester, Essex he was prompted to write in his show report, 'what on earth was this play about six random characters in Peckham doing playing to about 200 [for the total number of nights played at this venue] ... on an Essex campus? How heavily subsidised were each of those audience members for what tuned out to be an act of non-communication?' (ACGB, 1983b, 41/53/4).

Much the same story emerged after Temba's tour of Edward Brathwaite's *Mother Poem* (1989) left London. When it reached King Alfred's College in Hampshire, Southern Art's Drama Officer Fiona Ellis commented in her show report, 'regretfully this being Winchester most of us [the audience] were white [and that] as it was I found the mixture a bit too rich ... moreover I feel deeply inhibited that my response to it is that of a cultural tourist' (ACGB, 1989a, 41/56/6). This is not to say that all such touring failed to find an audience. For example, that same year, when Temba did a residency in Gloucester, which brought schools and the local community together, it not only managed to attract an almost exclusively black cast of 30 adults and the same number of children for the devised show *It's All in the Game*, but drew in 95 per cent of its audience from the surrounding West Indian community (ACGB, 1989, 41/51/7).

Nevertheless, Jane Milling argues that 'theatre did not trust that there was a large enough black audience, or one that they could attract, nor that their current audience constituency could find black playwrights' work "accessible", or a reflection of "universal" human experience' (Milling, 2012, 81). Moreover, in some assessors' reports for the Arts Council, low expectations can often be discerned when it came to reporting on the work of black companies.

At its worst, as in a report for Temba's *Teresa (The Modern Black Woman)*, a play written by Alton Kumalo, the anonymous reviewer commented, 'It was fun largely because he [Alton Kumalo] and Ellen Thomas were allowed to indulge with obvious relish – those very qualities that many black actors share – their love of mimicry, dancing and showing off' (ACGB, 1980, 42/57/7).[5] These same responses were identified three years later in a discussion paper, 'Black Theatre Policy', for the GLC's Ethnic Arts Sub-committee. This was produced by the black British writer, playwright and broadcaster Mike Philips and his findings agree with these attitudes when he concludes that black performers were still predominantly 'seen as mimics, musicians, dancers et cetera, but not as thinkers' (Greater London Council, 1984).

Expectations of lower standards were, at times, clearly assumed by some assessors working on behalf of the Arts Council. For instance, in his report on Staunch Poets' production *In Transit* (1981) the novelist and playwright John Bowen commented, 'It would be easy to put down much of the rest [of the production]; Kingsley Amis would have a ball. But with so little "for" the black community, Staunch probably have to be supported' (ACGB, 1981a, 41/30/2). Bowen's reference to the novelist Kingsley Amis's well-known public tirades against the Arts

Council's support for community and minority projects, while meant to show his own more enlightened position, still succeeds in relegating black theatre to a subsidiary position by assuming that the work will be of a lower artistic standard.

As already mentioned, concerns over low expectations and artistic standards were raised in Mike Philips' discussion paper for the GLC's Ethnic Arts Sub-committee, where he had written that for most black British audiences:

> Even at its most successful, the workshop companies tend to produce a narrow, partisan view which offers a definition of black life which is practically unrecognisable to anyone who doesn't actually belong to any of these groups [and that these same companies have] failed to produce any memorable plays – most of the plays are best seen as exercises for the skills of actors. (Greater London Council, 1984)

These sentiments were echoed when the theatre director Nicholas Kent, in a show report for Frank Mcfield's *No Place to be Nice*, commented that BTC 'should be producing better plays than this' and that 'it can only have some kind of half-hearted appeal to a theatrically literate black audience' (ACGB, 1984, 41/56/1).

However, there were a number of committed individuals who set themselves the task during the 1980s of raising ambitions and expectations. Yvonne Brewster, during her time as an Arts Council Drama Officer and later as one of the artistic directors of Talawa, was always insistent on the need for professional standards. This becomes a recurring issue in many of her Arts Council show reports. For instance, in 1980, reporting on Staunch Poets (a newly formed company set up by the writer and director Don Kinch) *Downside Up*, Brewster commented, 'The actors knew their lines, the drummers drummed well and the play was mercifully, quite short. *Downside Up* is neither entertaining, thought provoking, nor is it controversial. It is dull and mannered' (ACGB, 1982b, 41/30/2). While such an assessment might seem harsh, Brewster's comments should be gauged by her resistance to patronizing allowances being made for lower standards that resulted in black theatre being regarded as a special case rather than rightfully taking a full part in mainstream British culture.

Another prominent figure during this time was Norman Beaton. In 1981, Beaton approached the Arts Council with a proposal to set up what he called The Ira Aldridge Memorial Theatre Company with the director Michael McCaffery. Beaton saw this new enterprise as multi-racial and was critical of others who based themselves exclusively around a black identity. In the same vein, Beaton was sceptical of the practice of integrated casting that was just beginning to be adopted by major companies such as the RSC, seeing it as 'reduc[ing] plays to a series of individual performances' (ACGB, 1981, 41/9/13).

The idea for forming the company had come during Beaton's time working at the National Theatre in 1981 as an actor in Shakespeare's *Measure for Measure* and Harold Pinter's *The Caretaker*. As Talawa was later to do, Beaton envisaged his company providing an opportunity for black actors to perform in classical work ranging from Shakespeare's *King Lear*, Molière's *Amphityron* and Brecht's *The Threepenny Opera*. At the same time, he wanted the company to produce contemporary work by writers such as Michael Abbensetts, Wole Soyinka and Alton Kumalo (ACGB, 1981, 41/9/13).

Beaton was also insistent that black theatre should be led by the values of the mainstream rather than allowing it to be marginalized by Arts Council project funding and community initiatives. To this end, his proposal called not only for a permanent company of 15 actors, but also for a building in which the company could be based. Whereas Talawa was fortunate in securing generous initial funding from the GLC, Beaton was less fortunate in his dealings with the Arts Council. Despite anticipating that work produced by the company would be sold to Channel 4 when it started broadcasting, once in receipt of Beaton's application Jonathan Lamede estimated that it would cost £60,000 each year to fund the company. In a resubmission to the GLC two years later, both the ambitions and costs for the company were, if anything, even higher, with a request made for £500,000 over three years (ACGB, 1983, 41/9/13).

(iv) Black and Asian Flagships: Talawa and Tara Arts

Baz Kershaw has observed that the entrepreneurial spirit of alternative theatre combined with radical politics were the catalysts responsible for enervating this sector in the 1970s, whereas in the 1980s the entrepreneurial spirit remained but the politics had evaporated (Kershaw, 2004, 365). If anything can exemplify this argument, it would be the rise of Talawa and Tara Arts.

Talawa's inaugural production, *The Black Jacobins*, has already been discussed in respect to the auspicious start it made through generous funding by the GLC. It also had another effect – that of embarrassing the Arts Council into trying to match this support following the GLC's abolition. This resulted in Talawa becoming the Arts Council's first flagship black theatre company. At the same time, the Arts Council sensed it was backing a winner. *The Black Jacobins* had earned a £20,000 surplus with audiences, members of which were, on average, 82 per cent black. In the production's last week houses were sold out (ACGB, 1986, 92/1/1). Talawa held the promise of not only being able to attract new audiences, but also demonstrated financial acumen.

Talawa also proved its worth on artistic grounds remarkably quickly. Just three years after *The Black Jacobins*, Alastair Niven, the Arts Council's Literature Director, wrote in his report on its production of African playwright Ola Rotimi's *The Gods are Not to Blame* that the 'Company has surely become one of the leading companies in Britain' and adds, 'There is no need to add the word "black" in the sentence' (ACGB, 1989d, 41/56/6).

The Arts Council's faith in Talawa can be discerned in a report of a meeting between the Council and Talawa in which Ian Brown as Drama Director recommended that 'Talawa should look to regional reps and middle-scale touring houses rather than reduce the size of its productions to fit the small-scale touring circuit' (ACGB, 1989c, 38/32/13). Making it clear that Talawa was not meant for this sector is an important indication of the company's importance, especially so when small-scale was often the default destination for the majority of other black touring companies. Talawa was clearly being groomed for greater things. In the financial year 1988/9, it had reported a surplus of £6,911. That year, it was also announced that Talawa and Tara Arts would be among the beneficiaries of a move from project status to three-year funding, even though their promotion was seen at the time to benefit from the relegation of Foco Novo and Joint Stock. For Talawa, this meant more than just an increase of its annual budget from £30,000 to £70,000. Although far less than it had received under the GLC, the money enabled the company to tour outside London (ACGB, 1989c, 38/32/13). Victor Ukaegbu also observes that while Talawa's ambitions were evident it did so 'without losing its ideological and cultural status' (Ukaebu, 2006, 130).

It should be remembered that one of Talawa's artistic directors was Yvonne Brewster, who between 1982 and 1984 had worked as an Arts Council drama officer. This former gamekeeper (although gatekeeper would be a more accurate term) turned poacher would also have provided further reassurance that Talawa could become the flagship company by which the Arts Council could visibly demonstrate evidence of its commitment to ethnic minority arts.

Brewster, on her part, had clearly learnt from her time at the Arts Council about the kind of work that received optimum funding, and

– more crucially – how to secure it. This became the likely reason why Talawa began its long-running policy of reinterpreting well-known classical plays from Western theatre, such as *Anthony and Cleopatra* (1992) and *King Lear* (1994). With the exception of Dennis Scott's *An Echo in the Bone* (1986), it was not until 1992 with the African–American installation artist Ntozake Shange's *The Love Space Demands* that Talawa first started producing contemporary work. Brewster herself readily admits that the early policy of adapting the classics was 'part political and not purely artistic' and also points out that 'this truth should be more honestly acknowledged by those who grant the funds' (Brewster, 2006, 395).

While the entrepreneurial spirit of groups such as Talawa and Tara Arts allowed them to thrive in the 1980s, Gillian Hanna of Monstrous Regiment, writing in 1990, argues that their success only came by pursuing what she sees as a conservative policy of reinterpreting the classics rather than concentrating on the more risky venture of producing new writing and devised work (Hanna, 1990, 47). There is something to Hanna's argument and in an interesting, if troubling, justification of Talawa's decision not to stage any new women's writing during the 1980s, Yvonne Brewster employs an argument often made with a weary regularity by other artistic directors: namely, that new work by women cannot provide the epic scope of the classics (Brewster, 1991, 363). Although this view might appear to have made her an unlikely choice of editor for the first anthology of black British plays, Brewster's comments should be seen in the context of the importance she placed on black theatre being judged by the same professional standards as the mainstream. Brewster is not really referring to new writing being somehow inferior to the classics, but more about how the classics, by virtue of their canonicity, become the yardstick by which to judge artistic standards.

It should also be remembered that Talawa did not dominate to the exclusion of other companies. In fact, by the end of the 1980s, older companies such BTC and Temba were not only funded at higher levels than Talawa (ACGB, 1988c, 38/32/13) but also eclipsed Shared Experience and Cheek by Jowl, companies who had always appeared to be funding priorities for the Arts Council (ACGB, 1988b, 38/32/13).

(v) Tara Arts

Another company who chose the route of adapting the classics as a way of entering mainstream British theatre culture was the Asian company Tara Arts. Their rise to prominence, while less meteoric than Talawa's, was no less impressive. Formed in 1976 as a response to attacks on Asians in Southall, Tara Arts began as an amateur touring company and until 1984 had both an amateur and professional wing. Tara's artistic director Jatinder Verma has commented that establishing a reputation for itself on the touring circuit was important, as Asian audiences living in Britain were not familiar with established forms of theatre (Hingorani, 2010, 19).

Intimations about Tara Art's future can be traced back to the time when Gerald Chapman recommended the group to the Arts Council for funding in April 1981. Despite Tara being designated as an amateur company, Chapman had noted traits that were dear to the Arts Council's heart: namely Tara's 'administrative sense and care about detail'. Chapman also presciently identified the need for a major Asian company in 'comparison to ... the West Indian theatre groups whose rich acting talent may currently be seen all over Britain in every media and on every stage – not least the National [Theatre]' (ACGB, 1981a, 41/30/4). In fact, Tara had already been in receipt of small sums of money from the Arts Council's Community Arts Panel to pay for training sessions, the intention being, as Jonathan Lamede explains in his reply to Gerald Chapman, that 'once they have pulled themselves up by their bootlaces, the Drama Department might look at the possibility of helping them further' (ACGB, 1981b, 41/30/4).

By this, Lamede meant professionalization, which Tara set out to do, most controversially, by anglicizing themselves. This, in fact, can be seen very early on in Jatinder Verma's decision to use English as the group's performing language. At the time of Tara's formation in 1977, there were several Asian companies, including Leicester's Literary Arts and Lights, Birmingham's L & P Enterprises and London's Indian National Theatre who performed in Indian and Pakistani languages, a practice that Verma significantly felt to be backward looking (Verma, 1996). Although Dominic Hingorani argues that the exclusive use of English by Tara restricted the range of its expression in different cultural identities (Hingorani, 2010, 23), it is undeniable that the decision to perform in English was crucial in securing funding. Later shows such as *Meet Me* (1984) also found ingenious ways of incorporating both Urdu and English for multicultural audiences, who by this time started to comprise a growing second generation of British-born Asians who in everyday life navigated between the two languages.[6]

Chapman's comment about the lack of other Asian companies was brought to wider attention by Tara itself two months afterwards when in an open letter (and clearly prompted by the group's non-inclusion) they complained about an Asian Arts Festival organized by the National Association of Asian Youth: the fact that Joint Stock was producing a new play (*Borderline* by Hanif Kureshi) by an Asian writer and the actor Nigel Hawthorne directing a Chekhov play set in India led Tara to assume 'the indisputable implication ... that Asian artists on the whole are not good enough for inclusion in an Asian festival' (ACGB, 1981c, 41/30/4).[7]

Tara's outraged letter and Chapman's final rallying cry in his letter of recommendation – 'let's salvage some vestiges of new growth in amongst the jungle of cuts!' (ACGB, 1981a, 41/30/4) – seems to have had some effect. Jonathan Lamede encountered Tara's work for the first time that year and he decided to support the company after seeing *Vilayat* (*England Your England*), a play by Jatinder Verma that looked at Indian's historical presence in Britain alongside the current political situation in 1981. While Lamede's show report maintains that the company's amateur status precluded it from receiving Arts Council project funding, an after-show discussion between the company and its audience of around 50 seems to have made him think differently about supporting Tara:

> The one or two individuals who took the lead ... took the line 'well, you Asians / immigrants are obviously different; you have to work hard to prove yourselves; you can't blame English people if they have strong reactions to you; after all, think of the inequities of the caste system in India ... ' and so on. Throughout, the group responded politely and with civilized arguments, despite being confronted repeatedly with the sort of prejudices they had meant to counter with their play. And the people expressing this were middle class Hammersmith burghers, not a skinhead NF member amongst them ... A depressing if not shocking evening. (ACGB, 1981c, 41/30/4)

While there is no definitive evidence in the Arts Council's files that Lamede's account of the racism he witnessed that night produced any direct effect on supporting Tara, in the following year the company staged its first professional production, *The Lion's Raj*, for which it appointed the white English director Anthony Clark.[8] This decision had not been at Tara's behest, but at the Arts Council's, who made funding conditional on employing a professional director. This transition from amateur to professional status was quick to show itself: in his report for Tara's previous show that year entitled *Scenes in the Life*, Jonathan Lamede had noted that despite the company benefiting from training sessions and the use of David Sulkin from the Royal Court's Young People's Theatre as an outside director, 'this was still the amateur Tara group, not the new professional company' (ACGB, 1982c, 41/30/4). However, less than a month later, Lamede was able to enthusiastically declare that *The Lion's Raj* 'amounted to a new phase in the company's development' and 'showed the benefits of working with an outside director' (ACGB, 1982d, 41/30/4). By the following year, Philip Hedley's show report for *The Passage* (1983) not only alludes positively to the Arts Council's insistence on bringing in an outside director, but also notes that although 'the company has a lot to learn [if] they continue searching-out outside influences and training opportunities ... they are worth supporting' (ACGB, 1983, 41/30/4l). Yet the impression that Tara Arts was somehow forced by the Arts Council towards becoming a professional company is misleading. From its earliest days, Jatinder Verma had looked towards establishing contacts within mainstream theatre, such as Tara's involvement with the Royal Court's Young People's Theatre in 1978 on work such as *Fuse* (1978) and *Playing the Flame* (1979).

By 1983, despite being designated a touring company, Tara had managed to secure a permanent rehearsal/theatre space in Earlsfield, London and by the following year had a regular ensemble of seven actors as well as a full-time administrator and director. In 1984 the company's building was expanded to become an arts centre that could receive touring productions from other companies and visiting artists, and by 1986 the Arts Council's Chair of the Drama Panel, Sir Brian Rix, was recommending that Tara be moved on to revenue funding (Brown and Brannen, 1996, 375). In fact, evidence of this rapid promotion had been circulating in the higher echelons of the Arts Council during the previous year. Minutes of a NAPS committee meeting held in September 1985 reveal that the decision to move Tara to revenue funding had already been taken and approved by the directorate (ACGB, 1985, 99/36/2). This indicates the importance the Arts Council accorded to Tara and the company's ability to demonstrate visibly its commitment to supporting black and Asian arts.

According to Dominic Hingorani, between 1977 and 1984 there were three clear strands to Tara's artistic practice: first, there was work such as *Inkalaab 1919* (1980) that explored postcolonial histories; secondly, there were plays such as *The Lion's Raj* that explored histories of the Asian presence in Britain; while thirdly, work such as *Diwaali* (1977) looked at contemporary Asian life in Britain (Hingorani, 2010, 19–20). The second phase, lasting from 1984 to 1996 (Hingorani, 2010,

45–70), started with the play *Miti Ki Gadi* (*The Little Clay Cart*) (1984). This began Jatinder Verma's development of what he called 'Binglish' methodologies, a fusing of praxis between Eastern and Western theatre in a series of classical adaptations that included Buchner's *Danton's Death* (1989), Brecht's *The Beggar* (1990) and Molière's *Tartuffe* (1990) which saw the company rise to national prominence.

Opinion has remained divided over Tara's adaptations. Dimple Godiwala claims that the practice was effective at '*displaying and displacing the authority of the texts of empire* ... [and] making them work for interstitial communities of the Asians in Britain' (Godiwala, 2006, 108), although this argument is less convincing when one considers that, with the exception of Shakespeare, most of these adaptations were drawn from French and German theatre. Admittedly, France, like Britain was once a major colonial power, but it is difficult to see Tara's adaptations as direct critiques on British imperialism.

Sometimes criticisms were voiced when Eastern and Western theatrical traditions came together in the adaptations. In his show report for a 1990 double bill of Brecht's *The Emperor* and *The Beggar* and Chekhov's *The Proposal*, Robert Adams, a director of the Old Town Hall Arts Centre, Hemel Hempstead, objects that 'the nuances and subtleties of text, seemed an alien product in the hands of Asian actors. This isn't the first time Tara have grasped a thoroughly European play and Asianised it, and I think it just doesn't work' (ACGB, 1990g, 41/56/6).

Tara's use of Asian characters has also produced a similar split in opinion. With one or two exceptions, the company had always pursued a policy of employing Asian casts rather than the widespread practice elsewhere in British theatre of colour-blind casting. Dominic Hingorani sees this as a deliberate policy, providing what he calls 'an ironic inversion of the historically racist portrayals of black and Asian characters by white actors' (Hingorani, 2010, 21). Dimple Godiwala also sees the use of 'rich regional Asian accents ... tone and gesture, voice and stance' as a deliberately subversive practice in 'dislocating the canon' (Godiwala, 2006, 108), However, for others, the use of all-Asian casts has been seen as pandering to the very stereotypes perpetuated by colonialism over subaltern peoples. Higorani acknowledges that in plays such as *Yes, Memsahib* (1979) the imprecise use of English spoken by Asian characters as a result of their subaltern position had not been mastered theatrically where 'Tara were unable to meet the demands of performing the Asian voice and therefore descended into stereotype' (Hingorani, 2010, 28). Yet, these same stereotypes were still being commented upon as late as 1990 when in an anonymous report for East Midlands Arts, the assessor described Tara's adaptation of *The Government Inspector* as coming 'dangerously close to stepping over the barrier of stereotypical racism [and a] "Mind Your Language" type of approach which often re-enforces racist stereotypes of Asian community life'[9] (ACGB, 1990d, 41/56/6).

The appearance of such stereotypes might in some respects be seen as one of the more undesirable consequences of anglicization and with it Tara's quest for incorporation into mainstream theatre coming at the price of playing to the expectations of these audiences. The degree to which a black or Asian company anglicized itself was crucial: too little risked alarming its funders. For example, one of the regional drama officers, Fiona Ellis, expresses her gratitude to director Alby James and poet Edward Brathwaite before seeing Temba's *Mother Poem* (1989) for 'pinpoint[ing] various aspects of the work which might have been unfamiliar to a white audience', and she notes 'there were many parts in dialect and many parts which were elusively structured and which I would not have understood or appreciated at all' (ACGB, 1989a, 41/56/6). Conversely, too much anglicization raised questions by the funders that the work was no different from that of their white counterparts: a balance was needed whereby the companies could both draw in audiences from their own ethnic constituency, but at the same time appeal to white audiences.

However, it is an uncomfortable fact that despite concerted efforts by the Arts Council and the companies themselves Asian audiences were an elusive presence in the 1980s. Jacqueline Bolton's chapter on Joint Stock reveals that Asian audiences were notably absent for its production of Hanif Kureish's play *Borderline* (1981), and Arts Council show reports for Tara's *The Lion's Raj* noted predominantly white audiences in attendance throughout its tour.[10] This trait continued the following year with *The Passage*, where Philip Hedley commented that throughout its run at the Croydon Warehouse, neither the company nor the venue 'had been able to rally even the Asian contacts which both had from previous TARA visits to the venue', concluding, 'the purpose of presenting the show seemed somewhat defeated' (ACGB, 1983, 41/30/4l).

There is even some evidence to suggest that Asian audiences were alienated by Tara's use of Indian stereotypes, as with their adaptation of Gogol's *The Government Inspector*, which caused a number of concerns for the Arts Council. In one report for East Midlands Arts, the assessor expressed disquiet over the crude Indian stereotypes presented as well as the depiction of women 'as nymphomaniac materialists, subservient and chattel to the men in the play'. During a discussion afterwards with a member of the audience who worked with the Asian community, the assessor also reported that the kind of work Tara presented was not welcomed: 'This kind of reaction must raise questions about the effectiveness of links with Derby's Asian Community which this company is seeking to establish' (ACGB, 1990d, 41/56/6). Earlier during the same tour, in Manchester, Barbara Pemberton also commented in her report, 'there were very few Asian members in the audience, taking into account the large Asian community in Manchester', prompting her to conclude 'does this mean that they are harder to target or simply that they don't support Tara?' (ACGB, 1990b, 41/56/6).

In fairness, much of the hostility directed against Tara has come about not only through its status as a flagship company, but because for almost the entire 1980s it was the *only* high-profile Asian company. In a set of briefing notes as late as 1988, Jean Bullwinkle draws attention to Tara's predicament by noting that 'the general lack of significant Asian theatre work puts this organisation under the constant glare of the spotlight' (ACGB, 1988b, 38/32/13). At the same time, Tara's elevated position led some of its colleagues in theatre to question whether Tara's artistic abilities had been overestimated simply because there was no comparable competition. For example, the director Tony Lidington, in a show report on Tara's adaptation of *The Government Inspector*, commented '(I've now seen Bhavni Bhavi, Danton and The Government Inspector in the last two years), and cannot help but feel that we positively discriminate in our artistic assessment of their work because of their Asian connections ... either I am missing the point of their endeavours or there needs to be a declaration of "the emperor's new clothes"' (ACGB, 1981, 41/56/6).

(vi) Actors Unlimited and the Pitfalls of Anglicization

Tara Arts were not the only Asian company in existence. While almost forgotten today, Actors Unlimited, formed by the actor Madhav Sharma, were contemporaries of Tara and also pursued similar policies of adapting Western classics from an Asian perspective, such as *Hedda in India* (1983), as well as performing new plays by Asian writers.

Actors Unlimited is a useful company to compare alongside Tara, as it illustrated a dilemma for the Arts Council in the 1980s: namely the need for black and Asian companies to undergo some degree of accommodation to white audiences in order not to alienate them, yet at the same time display visible markers of difference through ethnicity, in order to meet the requirement for funding. Actors Unlimited is a good example of how failing to accept these contradictory positions could terminate the life of a company.

Actors Unlimited had been in semi-existence since 1973, but was revived in 1980 when Madhav Sharma started working for the Association of Asian Youth, a scheme funded by the government's Youth Services. His first project was to organize the same Asian festival in 1980 that Tara had taken such exception to. During its life, Actors Unlimited received funding from a number of sources including the Arts Council and the GLC, who, in 1982, gave the company £15,000 to put on a season of three plays (including Karim Alrawi's *Aliens* and Dilip Hero's *Apply, Apply, No Reply* in 1983). Yet it soon becomes clear that one of the principal reasons why Tara is still in existence today and Actors Unlimited no more, came from Sharma's stand against ghettoization, with his insistence on multiracial casting. In essence, as far as the Arts Council were concerned, Actors Unlimited were simply not Asian enough.

For example, in one project application entitled 'British Asians & Theatre in English', Sharma states that the company's artistic policy would be to demonstrate 'that "blacks" or "Asians" are not a homogenous group but are as disparate in their hopes and aspirations as any other groups or artists' (ACGB, 1983, 41/13/1), while in a letter to the GLC's Ethnic Minorities Unit Sharma even accuses the body of inherent racism through a funding policy that encouraged marginalization:

> While you will, I hope, have noted that I have never opposed support for ethnic artists, even when non-unionised, I am tired of the attacks on those professionals who are aware of where they live without necessarily forgetting where they come from. Racial discrimination works in strange ways and one of the worst to combat is the limitation of their artistic imagination to racial or cultural separatism. We don't have to import Italians to play Pirandello, Scandinavians for Ibsen, or Russians for Chekhov because, if we are white, we are allowed to explore universal concerns. Why must I be restricted to traditional Indian arts or art forms because they are my origins? … Am I not allowed the freedom to choose? … I cannot pretend to the belief that separatism is the only route to equality of opportunity. (ACGB, 1983, 41/13/12)

The sentiments expressed in Sharma's letter also echoed Kwesi Owusu's observation that the Arts Council was all too ready to accept the term 'ethnic arts' following The *Arts Britain Ignores*, which allowed for the separation of black and Asian theatre from the mainstream (Owusu, 1986, 5). Naseem Khan herself also acknowledged that her report enabled the Arts Council to make an association with the ethnic arts being 'colourful, exciting [and so] ... seen as the acceptable face of immigration' (Khan, undated). This prevailing attitude turned out to be the undoing for a multiracial company like Actors Unlimited, which was not prepared to accept its place in the ethnic ghetto.

Kwesi Owusu goes further, believing that the Arts Council was operating a quasi-colonial policy with its body of 'drama officers' (and here even the term is significant), and who, when it came to black and Asian drama, saw itself as responsible for what he calls 'native affairs', and who in a well-meaning but patronizing way saw it as a 'duty to help them [black and Asian artists] preserve their cultural identities' (Owusu, 1986, 29). By the same token, senior figures within the Arts Council also recognized that their policies for promoting black and Asian work might be perceived in exactly these ways. For example, in a memo written the same year that Owusu's book was published, Hugh Shaw, a former secretary general, spoke about trying to discourage an outlook that cast 'the ACGB as the Great White Mother Goddess surrounded by her adoring (but utterly dependent) piccaninnies, which obviously is deplorable' (ACGB, 1986c, 99/36/4). While Shaw's choice of language is somewhat unfortunate, his concerns seem genuine: for instance, he talks about the need 'to raise our own consciousness a little about how easy it is for whites and blacks alike to make mistakes which reinforce *institutional racism*' [my italics] – a term that Shaw uses in a context that did not enter common language until the late 1990s. Shaw even gives an example of a wider separatism in a theatre that he sees operating along ethnic lines when he spots 'a Rasta – or at least a black with locks – at [a] Tara [Arts] event. Only the second black I have ever seen at a mainly Indian event in the forty years of my involvement in this area' (ACGB, 1986c, 99/36/4).

In retrospect, Actors Unlimited practised a policy, based around multicultural casting, that was considerably ahead of the funding policies in operation at the time. This practice can best be seen in its production of *Hamlet* in 1984, whose cast included Chinese, Indian and English actors, following director Peter Brook's long-established inter-nationalist policy, and which he later realized in his own production of *Hamlet* in 2000.

David Edgar, whose play *Our Own People* (1977) had been revived by Actors Unlimited in 1981, wrote a letter to the Arts Council the following year in support of the company, whom he saw as resisting the prevailing trend to marginalize. Edgar took two current examples to illustrate his point, comparing the multicultural approach of Actors Unlimited to what he calls acerbically '[the] traps of either the National's one-off, Measure for Measure gimmickry [sic] on the one hand, and the RSC's token black Puckery on the other' (ACGB, 1982, 41/13/14).[11]

However, Edgar's intervention as well as other letters of support failed to save the company, nor should this come as a surprise. Sharma's provocations to the Arts Council and the GLC where ethnicity and difference became principal funding criteria was always likely to make the future of Actors Unlimited – extremely limited. Despite receiving Arts Council project funding in February 1983 amounting to £5,000 (ACGB, 1984, 38/32/4), a number of later projects were turned down, including another revival of David Edgar's *Our Own People*. In a letter to the playwright, the Arts Council's Drama Director John Faulkner explained that despite Edgar's advocacy of this production the three drama officers who saw it 'were unanimously of the view that Actors Unlimited had not done justice to the play', while Sharma's 'intentions regarding the employment of Asian performers ... cannot of themselves justify Arts Council subsidy' (ACGB, 1982, 41/13/12). Ironically, Faulkner's last comment associated Sharma with the very practice he condemned.

(vii) Touring Black and Asian Theatre
Talawa was never really a touring company in the same way as Temba or BTC. Talawa was essentially London-based and rarely visited other venues: for example, its production of Oscar Wilde's *The Importance of Being Earnest* (1989) comprised only two dates – one in London and one in Newcastle upon Tyne. During her time at the Arts Council, in September 1984 Yvonne Brewster had written in a report on the future of black theatre, 'there are at present regrettably no building-based ethnic minority theatre companies in receipt of annual subsidy from the Council' (ACGB, 1984, 38/32/4). By 1991, Talawa had secured the Jeannetta Cochrane Theatre as a base for its operations, a move Victor Ukaegbu saw as one of 'tremendous symbolic significance (Ukaegbu, 2006, 30). In the case of Talawa as well as Tara Arts, a clear link can be demonstrated between longevity and building-based companies, in contrast to the itinerant touring groups, whose careers were often far more short-lived.

However, this confinement to London and lack of dissemination to the regions was not unique to Talawa. This had been identified by the Arts Council as a problem for several other black companies in receipt of project funding (ACGB, 1987b, 38/32/2). While demand for such work outside multicultural cites such as London, Birmingham and

Leicester might be expected to be lower, by not touring nationally these companies reinforced a sense of remaining outside the mainstream.

A year earlier, Graham Devlin, whose influential 1986 report on touring for the Arts Council, *Keeping the Show on the Road*, had just been published, wrote in a memo to the Director of Touring expressing his concern at the lack of provision for any middle- to large-scale black or Asian company, recommending £5,000 'challenge funding for regional theatres to book these companies' (ACGB, 1986a, 99/36/4). However, cuts made to touring budgets at this time made Devlin's proposal hard to achieve. In response to the memo, plans were set up in 1986 for a national tour by a black company, but these were thwarted after it was estimated that funding such a tour on anything less than £50,000 would be impossible. Significantly, there were also doubts about existing companies' abilities to undertake such a tour, although concerns over BTC and Temba were less to do with artistic standards, but rather lingering 'doubts about their current financial position and administrative and financial capabilities' (ACGB, 1986b, 99/36/4).

The situation for Asian touring companies was even more paradoxical. In one memo to the Drama Director in October 1987, drama officer Jenny Waldman pointed out the problems of Tara being the only touring company (ACGB, 1987b, 38/32/2).[12] Yet, while there was much wringing of hands over this, it had been the Arts Council itself who had decided to discontinue funding companies such as the British Asian Theatre, Actors Unlimited and Hounslow Arts Co-operative.

An ancillary danger that black and Asian theatre faced, was being seen as fashionable. Just as the Arts Council led a short-lived effort to promote physical theatre in the mid-1980s, the same risk also threatened the so-called minority arts. In an interview, Bernadine Evaristo from The Theatre of Black Women commented that following a disagreement with the GLC, after which the company lost its funding, the long-term sustainability for the company became increasingly difficult:

> It had become clear eventually that the funding of black arts in the eighties was a fad, and we were the flavour of the month. When the fad passed, most groups were cut. In 1985, there were approximately seventeen black theatre companies in London; ten years later, there are less than a handful. (Goodman, 1993, 133)

This sentiment had been echoed a year earlier by Naseem Khan who, in her report on the conference *The Arts Britain Still Ignores*, refuted poet

Linton Kwesi Johnson's assertion that 'black theatre … had come into its own', arguing that based on her own extensive work in the area there was in fact less activity than there had been in the 1970s (Khan, c.1983).

Community and Social Practice Companies

Since the mid-1970s, the Arts Council had recognized the existence of what it called 'Community Arts'. Seen as a response to pioneering late-1960s initiatives, such as Ed Berman's Interaction in London and Bill and Wendy Harpe's Great George's project in Liverpool, this saw the involvement of theatre practitioners working directly within a specific geographical area, or with a group of people.

However, it is also true to say that the history of this work has always been one of marginalization or outright dismissal. For the Arts Council, the reasons for this were closely bound up in the founding principles laid down by John Maynard Keynes; this stipulated that artistic standards would alone predicate what was considered deserving of support, and this hiving off of art from social practice remained central to the Arts Council's way of thinking until devolution in 1994.

Numerous examples of this attitude can be found. For example, when in 1989 Temba set up a residency in the town of Gloucester with the local West Indian community, despite the success of the devised show *It's All in the Game*, the regional Arts Council theatre panel who helped fund the project concluded: 'In strictly theatre terms, this kind of activity is of relatively small importance but as a social service, bringing together, practically involving and presenting issues back to the local community it is obviously of inestimable value' (ACGB, 1989, 41/51/7).

Nevertheless, from the late-1960s onwards a number of agitators, made up of both practitioners as well as individuals from within the ranks of the Arts Council itself, brought about concessions. A good example of this in the period covered by this volume can be found in the early history of the disabled group Graeae. Although one of the few companies formed in the 1980s still in existence today, Graeae's request for project funding was rejected by the Arts Council in 1981. Hampshire County Council had been providing the company with some financial assistance and, in a letter to Jonathan Lamede, Hampshire Arts Officer Christopher Gordon not only made a case for Graeae, but also demonstrated his awareness of the Arts Council's dilemma, which he summarized as 'not to be pro-Graeae is like being in favour of sin'. He also stressed 'above all, that they [Graeae] are different – there are no comparisons yet'. At the same time, Gordon also raised and questioned the fundamental assumptions that governed the Arts Council's central philosophy:

> for the sake of their confidence, commitment and credibility they must be treated (whether that requires positive discrimination or not) alongside able-bodied companies operating in the same field and not fobbed off in the direction of charity, social services or para-medical institutions...Whatever individuals may think of their purely theatrical standards or content, their power over audiences is nothing if not dramatic – and that surely is what it is all about. (ACGB, 1982, 42/20/3)

However, Jonathan Lamede, who oversaw the NAPS committee for drama, was more circumspect when the question of Graeae had arisen the previous year. In a series of memos between himself and Community Arts officer Georgiana Barrowcliffe, who like Christopher Gordon was a champion the group, Lamede raised concerns over Graeae being seen as a 'special case', and with it the ethical questions of artistic standards against social need and the precedent that funding Graeae would set for other disabled companies (ACGB, 1981b, 41/42/2). Barrowcliffe counters these reservations by arguing that 'the floodgates would [not] be opened', that few, if any other disabled companies existed and that, regardless of this, each company would be assessed on its own merits. More significantly, Barrowcliffe also challenged the adamantine protocol of artistic merit as the overriding criteria for any assessment and a call to focus on a more diverse range of criteria including 'attendance figures, administration, other sources of income, the proposed scripts, the proposed venues, the company's past record and its potential for development through funding' (ACGB, 1981c, 41/42/2).

Political considerations for supporting Graeae were also added to the deliberations. In a memo to the Drama Director, Rod Fisher, the Arts Council's Information Officer, concedes: 'I don't know how you can start to judge Graeae by "normal" Council criteria', but he makes a case for supporting the company as a public relations strategy to help 'to erase the public image of the Council, created by media treatment of its funding in the past of such things as Ray Richards's antics and Bob Law's canvases', before cynically concluding, 'But then we're not in the game of trying to influence public opinion are we, as is clearly evidenced by the withdrawal of funds to the National Youth Theatre and National Youth Orchestra?' (ACGB, 1981a, 41/42/2).

Barrowcliffe's advocacy for Graeae won the day and the group began to receive project funding from 1982 onwards (ACGB, 1983/4, 38/32/1). These exchanges are worth mentioning as they reveal that, throughout the 1980s, the Arts Council was slowly beginning to reassess its definitions of what stood for artistic practice. For example, by the financial year 1988/9, disability had become a new funding priority, alongside existing ones in black, Asian, young people's, gay and women's theatre (ACGB, 1988/9b, 38/32/2).

Theatre in Education (TIE) companies have been a neglected area of study, but as far back as 1964, when the Arts Council set up its Young People's Theatre Enquiry, there had been a recognition of the need to fund work in this area. By the late 1960s, groups such as Ed Berman's Interaction and Jennie Harris's Brighton Combination worked with young people through drama projects. These companies also coincided with the TIE movement and a commitment (albeit sometimes a reluctant one) by the Arts Council to fund work of this genre. TIE companies were also relatively expensive to support and produced little or nothing in terms of revenue generated from paying audiences. There was also a feeling by the Arts Council that, due to the often regional locus of operations, the bulk of their work should be supported by the RAAs, who were more likely to have better relations with local education authorities. Although there were people who felt 'it could be damaging if the Arts Council were to turn its back on the work completely' by preventing new national companies emerging, it was still agreed that RAAs should be the first port of call for TIE companies (ACGB, 1985, 99/36/2).

Nicholas Whybrow argues that the 1988 Education Act finally put an end to many TIE companies when it allowed power to be devolved from Local Education Authorities to the schools themselves. This meant the removal of a centralized fund for supporting companies as well as the removal of drama as a foundation subject within the curriculum. The funding of companies was also increasingly being made dependent on their work conforming to narrower social concerns such as drug misuse or bullying, whereby the company's work could be justified on a pedagogical level (Whybrow, 1994, 277–8).

Documentary techniques also became a feature of the work of some theatre companies within their own community or associated institution. Many took their inspiration from the pioneering work done by Peter Cheesman, who staged documentary-style plays based on local issues, at the Victoria Theatre in Stroke-on-Trent in the 1960s. The Hull-based Remould Theatre, formed by Rupert Creed and Averil Coult in 1984, used similar methodologies: these involved extensive research to look at issues affecting the local community in Humberside. Creed and Coult fashioned these materials into plays that included *The Northern Trawl* (1986) about deep-sea fishing and *Steeltown* (1990), another work-based documentary play about the local steel industry.

Remould's identification with its community often meant that its main sources of support came locally, and while still an Arts Council client (the company eventually became recipients of the three-year franchise scheme in 1990), projects such as *Streetbeat* (1990), on policing, or *The Caretakers* (1989), about social workers, were partly funded by Humberside police and social services respectively. Occasionally, funding also came through business sponsorship, such as Sheila Yaegar's community play *A Day by the Sea* (1990), which was commissioned to celebrate the centenary of the parish church of Easington, a small village in the rural district of Holderness, Yorkshire; its proximity to a major off-shore gas refinery attracted the attention of British Gas, who partially funded the production.

As mentioned, the changing economic and political conditions of the 1980s caused problems for older companies with a clear socialist/Marxist mission. Some acclimatized to the changing political conditions by focusing their work on community and education initiatives. One such group were North West Spanner: formed in 1971, this group produced work such as *Just a Cog* (1976) and *Partisans* (1978). Ten years later it was producing work such as *The Shape Project* (1981), a show that through dramatic enactment enabled immigrants to do things such as apply for a job. Although North West Spanner still managed to tour, albeit sporadically, the enforced shift in direction away from its core identity weakened the company's sense of purpose and artistic direction. It is telling that Ian Brown's assessment of the company in 1981 advised the Arts Council that its funding for community projects should cease, together with a demotion from revenue to one-off project funding (ACGB, 1981, 41/19/5).

Adaptation and Classical Revival

One trend that marked the period between 1980 and 1994 was the number of companies who included adaptation and revivals of classical work as part of their repertoire, or made it a strand of their artistic policy.

For example, Monstrous Regiment, who had specialized in devised work in the 1970s, often in collaboration with a playwright, produced a number of adaptations during the 1980s. These included Debbie Shewell's *More Than an Antoinette* (1990), based on Charlotte Bronte's novel *Jane Eyre* and Marivaux's eighteenth-century comedy *The Colony*, paired in 1990 with a modern play (Robyn Archer's *Comes a Cropper*), with the aim of commenting on the original (a practice that Max Stafford-Clark's company Out of Joint would continue in the 1990s).

One offshoot of feminist theatre was an exploration of histories of women. By the late 1970s, independent publishing houses such as Virago, and courses and degrees in Women's Studies at polytechnics and universities, began the task of accessing and reassessing women's writing from the past. In 1981, the formation of the Women's Playwright Trust promoted the revival of neglected plays by women, while feminist theatre companies including Monstrous Regiment and WTG began to commission new plays that set out to recount stories of women in history. For example, in 1982, WTG produced Timberlake Wertenbaker's *New Anatomies* about the explorer Isabelle Eberhard. In a similar vein, Gay Sweatshop reclaimed events from gay history in plays such as Noël Greig's *Dear Love of Comrades* (1979), about the life of the Victorian socialist Edward Carpenter.

Ever since its inception the Arts Council had recognized the importance of reviving neglected plays through measures such as providing bursaries and guarantees against loss for theatres to produce these works. This produced an instance where the long established traditions of the Arts Council fortuitously met with the aims of feminist groups such as Mrs Worthington's Daughters. In a 1979 letter to the Arts Council introducing themselves, the company claim that in their preliminary search from 1900–1920 revealed over 500 women playwrights. They also talk about the need for a new translation of work by European women dramatists, and while conceding that many British plays of the past 'are theatrically crude, a few are worthy of revival' (ACGB, 1979, 41/25/1). They also talked about the need for a new translation of work by European women dramatists. While the Arts Council's support for reviving past work was never in dispute, sometimes the choices made by Mrs Worthington's Daughters attracted negative comment. The playwright Olwen Wymark, an assessor on the Drama Panel, wrote of her lack of enthusiasm about 'the idea of unearthing now unknown plays' (ACGB, 1981, 45/25/1) after seeing the revival of Muriel Box's 1935 *Angels of War*, about First World War female ambulance drivers. Drama officer Clive Tempest summed up the general critical response by advising that unless the company stopped 'digging up shards and not jewels, the whole strategy must rebound on them' (ACGB, 1981, 45/25/1). Wymark even makes the unsisterly observation that the company's decision to recover work by female dramatists was 'a bit restricting considering that in the main there weren't very many really first rate plays written by women in those days' (ACGB, 1981, 45/25/1).

For Stephen Lacey, the widespread practice of adaptation and revival during this period was symptomatic of a growing financial insecurity, both within the companies and British theatre in general; consequently, he sees this as a panacea and 'the perfect vehicle for a theatre nervously in search of a secure audience' (Lacey, 2004, 435). Jane Milling also points out that the 1980s penchant for heritage and nostalgia saw a renewed interest in Shakespeare (Milling, 2012, 56). The RSC was one of the few companies to flourish in the 1980s, with a series of seemingly evermore lavish productions, while elsewhere a number of new touring companies formed, such as Deborah Warner's Kick in 1980, Declan Donnellan and Nick Ormerod's Cheek by Jowl in 1981, Michael Pennington and Michael Bogdanov's English Shakespeare Company in 1986 and Kenneth Branagh's Renaissance Theatre Company in 1987. All these companies produced work that not only toured the traditional Shakespeare sites of Stratford and London but, due to their success, also became regulars on the British Council touring circuit abroad.

Popular Theatre Companies

While the majority of companies discussed in this volume would no doubt claim they were producing popular theatre, often this term is understood in its Brechtian sense where popular theatrical forms were yoked for the purposes of political education. As far as British companies were concerned, John McGrath's 7:84 was the company most associated with this practice through its incorporation of Scottish ceidlegh music and dance in shows such as *The Cheviot, the Stag and the Black, Black Oil* (1973).

However, companies in this section are defined as popular in the sense that their primary intention was to entertain. Baz Kershaw sees the rise of popular theatre companies during the 1980s as symptomatic of the corresponding weakening of their political counterparts (Kershaw, 2004, 367). Hull Truck provides an interesting example of this process. Based in East Yorkshire, this new-writing company, despite being in existence since 1971, only started to achieve national prominence after

1984 when John Godber was appointed its new artistic director. Godber started producing several of his own plays, such as *Up 'n' Under* (1984), *Shakers* (1985) and *Teechers* (1987), that not only proved popular with local audiences but also went on to achieve great national success. Yet, Godber did not subscribe to John McGrath's ideas of 'a good night out', and Hull Truck was not interested in giving its audiences a political education – its primary intention was to entertain.

Often the fervid politics of the 1980s meant that whether they really meant it or not, popular companies sometimes felt it was necessary to at least be perceived as politically motivated such as the National Theatre of Brent (NTB). Formed in 1980 by Patrick Barlow, NTB specialized in taking subjects from history, literature and myth and breaking them down into a series of comic sketches. However, no doubt thinking that highlighting a political dimension might further an application to the Arts Council for *Ben Hur* (1981), Barlow tried to argue that Bryony Lavery's principal aim in their previous production, *Zulu!* (1981), was to send up British imperial history in order to gain a perspective on what he calls 'political issues' (ACGB, 1981, 41/25/2). Ian Brown, in his report for the group's *The Black Hole of Calcutta* (1982), a show that condensed over 200 years of Indian history from 1756 to Mrs Ghandi's premiership in 1966, also detected a political undertone. While undoubtedly a comic treatment of historical events, Brown notes his own discomfort at being asked 'to be amused by the stories of atrocity I was hearing' and goes on to comment:

> [The] clarity of presentation ... leaves the audience to draw its own conclusions about the underlying issues involved, those concerning imperialism, without a sense of being propagandised ... I didn't want to be amused by their stories, but I was and my amusement was, in the end, turned on itself. (ACGB, 1982a, 41/25/2)

Patrick Barlow, like the eponymously named Ken Campbell Roadshow in the early 1970s, had an identity that was synonymous with the company he formed, as well as a shared fondness for working on epic material. Also, like Campbell, Barlow worked with a number of collaborators over the years, including Bob Goody, Barbara Thorn and Jim Broadbent. The company sometimes commissioned a writer, notably Bryony Lavery, who worked in collaboration on *Zulu!* and *Ben Hur*. The company also occasionally brought in outside directors such as Jude Kelly, who worked on the original stage version of *The Messiah* (1983).

The National Theatre of Brent was a popular company in every sense of the word. In one Arts Council show report of the company's parody of Wagner's *Ring Cycle*, *Gottendamerung: or Twilight of the Göds* (1982), Guy Slater commented, 'I can't think why they haven't got a TV series' (ACGB, 1982, 41/25/2) – and a feature of several of these companies was their cross-over from theatre to television. The National Theatre of Brent, for instance, produced adaptations of *Messiah* for Channel 4 in 1983 and *The French Revolution* for the BBC in 1989.

Another such theatre company were the Brighton based Cliffhanger, whose work was often based around comic pastiches of popular film genres such as 1950s science fiction, television soap opera and comic sketches. Their show *Gymslip Vicar*, nominated for the 1984 Olivier Award for Best Comedy, did a six week run at the Donmar Warehouse in London and when their show went up Edinburgh that August, it played to over six and a half thousand people in two weeks (ACGB, 1984, 44/92/2). Like the National Theatre of Brent, they also adapted their 1982 play *They Came From Somewhere Else* into a six part series for Channel 4 in 1984.

Physical Theatre Companies

Mixed fortunes defined the progress of physical theatre companies during this period. The 1986 Cork Report marked a shift in Arts Council policy by recommending that mime and physical theatre become funding priorities, with companies like Théâtre de Complicité and Trestle being among the first recipients of the new three-year revenue funding scheme in April 1989.

However, under its classification system, the Arts Council defined mime companies (as they were called at the time) as coming under the responsibility of the Dance Panel. These particular groups felt their natural home to be with the Drama Panel and considered themselves disadvantaged in regard to funding allocation. For example, in a 1986 letter to the Drama Director Ian Brown, Penny Mays, who worked as Trestle's administrator, while welcoming the recent publication of the Cork Report, points out that companies who specialized in physical theatre over text-based work had been 'pushed into a tight restricted corner by the Arts Council like a forlorn Cinderella – it is time we were allowed to go to the ball!' Mays goes on to say that six other funded mime companies, despite playing to 198,000 people in the previous year, had only received £70,000 collectively. Mays pointed out that this chronic underfunding had come about due to misunderstandings about their work not only by their colleagues in Dance, but also in Drama, and gives the example of a planned move by one company being thwarted once 'they discovered we did not speak and therefore should be Mime' (ACGB, 1986b, 41/45/7).

This had been a long-standing concern, and in an earlier response to the Cork Inquiry Trestle had pointed out 'this argument automatically collapses when 3 major "mime" companies [including] Theatre de Complicite use words throughout their pieces, as do many other so-called "mime" artists!' (ACGB, 1986a 41/45/7). Two years earlier in a letter to the Arts Council's Chairman William Rees-Mogg, in reaction to the failure of mime in the *Glory of the Garden* report, Mays wrote, 'it is obviously very depressing that the Arts Council still continues to dismiss Mime, hiding it within the Dance Department and hoping the (sic) it will go away' (ACGB, 1984, 41/45/7). The following year Trestle, Trickster and Théâtre de Complicité wrote collectively to the Secretary General, Luke Rittner, demonstrating how they were the poor relations in comparison to their drama colleagues by citing a series of statistics. They pointed out that less than 3 per cent of the Dance budget was allocated to mime and compared the 1984/5 funding allocations for Trestle (£2,500), Trickster (£10,000) and Complicite (£8,000) to the amounts given to the small-scale touring companies Paines Plough (£65,000) and Avon Touring (£73,000) (ACGB, 1985, 41/45/7). In its response to the Cork Inquiry, Trickster also brought to its attention that when it gave four performances in Japan as part of a British Council tour, the British taxpayer spent virtually the same sum on that as they did to support 86 performances in their own country (ACGB, 1986b, 41/45/6).

In a show report for Trickster's *Charavari* in January 1986, John Ashford, a figure who worked within both theatre and dance as a director, producer and manager, praised the production, and used his report as an appeal to the Drama Panel about the precarious financial state of the company. He raised concerns that its existing budget of £10,000 a year was inadequate and that it should be supported by at least six times that sum, 'given the achievement, popularity and willingness to tour the company will join the list of the lost', and for 'the Council to recognise and back a hit when they have one … even if the company happens to work in an area of Mime which was not even graced with an acknowledgement to its existence in the Glory of the Garden' (ACGB,1986b, 41/45/6).

Ironically, the sheer amount of touring undertaken as well as their commitment to the regions made these companies the very exemplars of what *The Glory of the Garden* sought to promote. This was confirmed by responses from the regional Arts Associations when called upon by the companies to support their case. In a letter to the Dance and Mime Officer Ruth Glick, Peter Stark, Director of Northern Arts and Susanne Burns, the Assistant Dance and Mime Officer, confirmed that 'we rely heavily on these companies for our touring product' (ACGB, 1985, 41/45/6). All this came to little avail and in June of the following year Trickster was forced to cancel the tour of *Memory Gate* when, after years of chronic underfunding, its technically ambitious new show could not be properly realized and the company disbanded (ACGB, 1986a, 41/45/6).

Live Art Companies

While the Arts Council had been funding companies engaged in what was then known as 'experimental performance' since 1968, its commitment and enthusiasm to this area had been halting (Saunders, 2012). Nevertheless, the 1980s witnessed a number of new companies, including Forced Entertainment and Dogs in Honey, who in turn were influenced by the work of older groups, such as Impact Theatre Co-operative, IOU and Hesitate and Demonstrate, groups who pioneered the use of visual media, immersive experiences and the dislocation of the physical performer.

A good example of the way in which many of these developments played out in the 1980s can be found in the work of Hesitate and Demonstrate. Formed in 1975 by Geraldine Pilgrim, the company was a pioneering forerunner of what is now termed 'Immersive Theatre' as well as work that incorporated objects and sound to evoke memory. Shows such as *Do Not Disturb* (1980) used these forms to make a nostalgic exploration of a lost Victorian England. Here, in an experience that uncannily resembles the work now produced by Punchdrunk, the audience moved between 'a series of tableaux performed on a ... set of a country-house hotel full of nooks and crannies and stuffed birds in glass boxes' with the audience encountering actors along the way such as 'a scantily clad lady standing in a bath with a cocktail and a toy yacht [who] catches the eye of the cigar smoking gent in the bedroom above' (Jackson, 1980, n.p). However, unlike Punchdrunk, who normally occupied a single site for the duration of a project, Hesitate and

Demonstrate was a touring company, adapting each performance to the space it was booked to play in.

Hesitate and Demonstrate also did much to bring live art to the attention of the Arts Council. For example, its long-standing and highly influential Financial Director Anthony Field in a brief but telling memo to the Drama Director, John Faulkner, simply writes 'Hesitate and Demonstrate's production of "Do not Disturb" is immaculate. What more can I say?' (ACGB, 1981, 41/20/7). Approval also came in a more discernible form two years later in NAPS minutes, when Hesitate and Demonstrate, together with fellow companies Impact Theatre Co-operative and Rational Theatre, was selected as ready to graduate on to revenue funding.[13]

Yet suspicions and misgivings directed towards live art continued to be raised periodically. One long-running sore was the company's rejection of the written play in favour of devising methodologies. This insistence on text being the definitive marker of authenticity and artistic quality can clearly be discerned when theatre director Mike Alfreds reported on Hesitate and Demonstrate's *Goodnight Ladies* (1982). He commented, 'I am bemused as ever about what I'm meant to be watching when I attend "performance" pieces and their ilk', and while recognizing that the show 'was executed with considerably more (apparent) care and finesse than a lot else I've seen', he concludes: 'My main feeling throughout was that it would have been wonderful if a play had been taking place inside all that "design" (décor and lighting)' and that, 'if its purpose is to create a sensuous delight in sounds and images, it's really doing no more than any well designed play achieves' (ACGB, 1982a, 41/20/7). This idea of the text having more intrinsic worth and permanence than a performance can also be discerned in Bradford Watson's show report. Watson attended on the same night as Alfreds, and, although his time spent as The People's Show administrator would presumably have made him more familiar with devised work, despite 'a clear recollection of deriving a lot of pleasure from this show [my] reservation is remarkably and annoyingly simple; for all that I felt at the time about the keen effec-tiveness of the collaging and editing ... and the haunting echoes of its imagery, I can now remember scarcely anything about it' (ACGB, 1982b, 41/20/7). Whereas Alfreds' report resembles that of the person who, when presented with a vegetarian meal, looks anxiously over the plate in search of meat, Watson's experience is reminiscent of apocryphal tales of Chinese food producing only ephemeral satisfaction.

In a period when politics often constituted an integral sense of a company's identity, live art, with its emphasis on aesthetics, attracted the same mixed responses that it continues to attract today. When for example Hesitate and Demonstrate visited Poland in October 1981 for six performances of *Do Not Disturb* at the Kalamboor Festival, it was at a time when the country was under martial law after protests led by the independent trade union Solidarity. The British Council, who was sponsoring the visit, reported back to the Arts Council that in the audience of 300 young people, 'applause was polite but the reactions were non-committal or puzzled'. In one review entitled 'Charm is not Enough' by someone simply known as 'D.D.' for the Kalamboor Festival, the Magazine commented, 'the performance is full of charm, there is charm in the carefully constructed set, in acting and music. Charm is a wonderful complement to art, but not if it becomes its sole justification' (ACGB, 1981, 41/20/7).

Chapter 3

JOINT STOCK THEATRE COMPANY

Jacqueline Bolton

I should like to correct the impression given in the *TV Times* interview with Paul Freeman – star of the recent ITV series *Yesterday's Dreams* – that the Joint Stock Theatre Group (referred by him as 'a Seventies *avant garde* theatre group') no longer exists. Last year we toured the country playing in 13 towns and cities from Wakefield, West Yorkshire, to Brighton, East Sussex, with *A Mouthful of Birds* by Caryl Churchill. This autumn we shall be touring nationally with another play. Twelve years after Paul's first production with Joint Stock, we are still producing new, exciting and enthralling theatre! (Dawson, 1987)

BILL GASKILL: Well, [Joint Stock] didn't have life after [1985]. I don't know whether there was a show after that.

SARA FREEMAN: There were … there were five shows after that. I think.

BILL GASKILL: Really? Really? You amaze me. (Freeman, 2006, 53)

In her 2006 article on Joint Stock, Sara Freeman rightly describes the final years of the company as 'startlingly unremembered' (Freeman, 2006, 53). As the implicit exasperation of Jane Dawson's letter indeed suggests, the company formerly heralded as 'the National Theatre of the Fringe' (Tinker, 1977, n.p.) was in the process of being 'unremembered' even as it continued to produce and tour new work. The only readily available full-length resource on the company, Rob Ritchie's *The Joint Stock Book: The Making of a Theatre Collective* (1987), neatly enacts this process, providing a retrospective view of the company's work to 1985 – the tenth anniversary of Joint Stock's critical and box-office success,

Fanshen (1975). Ritchie's ambivalent assessment of the company's future, together with the collection of personal reminiscences that concludes the book, compounds the suggestion that it was not merely a summation but a *commemoration* of the company's working life, an impression unfortunately reinforced by the book's inauguration and attendant publicity. Officially launched at the National Theatre – curiously, as Joint Stock never performed there – it was promoted by an evening of readings at the Royal Court, to which, as company minutes record, current members of Joint Stock were not invited to contribute (JSA, 27/4, 1986j).

A turbulent decade for all involved in subsidized theatre, the 1980s saw many fringe companies engage in protracted struggles between sustaining progressive ideals and enduring financial instability. Drawing upon Joint Stock's own company archives (held at the University of California, Davis) as well as the Arts Council of Great Britain's archives (ACGB) (held at the Victoria and Albert Museum, London), this chapter attempts to counter the undeserved 'unremembering' of Joint Stock by adding the company's experiences of political engagement and economic crisis to existing narratives of alternative theatre in the 1980s.[1]

Introduction

Founded in 1974 by Max Stafford-Clark, David Hare and David Aukin, in close association with William Gaskill, Joint Stock swiftly established a reputation for pioneering new writing through a series of critically acclaimed productions, including *Fanshen, Epsom Downs* (1977) and *Cloud Nine* (1979). Each one of these productions was created by what became known as the 'Joint Stock method', which, despite financial pressures, the company more or less managed to sustain throughout the 1980s.[2] This process began with a three- to four-week workshop where the company explored an idea through a mixture of research, improvisation, acting exercises and discussion. After this initial period of creative fermentation, the playwright was given ten weeks in which to write the play. Once a script was arrived at, a further five weeks of rehearsal would workshop and revise the text for production. Intended to 'fertiliz[e] the writer's imagination' (Stafford-Clark, quoted in Dunn, 1985, 16), this extended workshop process also invited and enabled actors to contribute to the *making*, not just the *performing*, of a play-text, a creative intervention common enough among fringe companies but not usually extended to actors working within established theatre. The centrality of the performer within 'the Joint Stock Method' attracted talents such as Simon Callow, Philip (Pip) Donaghy, Tony Rohr, David Rintoul, Jennie Stoller, Cecily Hobbs, Julie Covington and Miriam Margolyes, and the company quickly became celebrated for a standard of ensemble playing 'rare outside the major subsidised companies (or even within them, come to that)' (Woddis, 1983, 18).

The successes of the 1970s, however, dulled briefly at the turn of the 1980s. Of the first four productions presented – *An Optimistic Thrust* (devised by the company, 1980) *Say Your Prayers* (Nick Darke, 1980), *Borderline* (Hanif Kureishi, 1981) and *Real Time* (devised by the company, 1982) – only Kureishi's play received critical plaudits (although not, significantly, from the Asian audiences to which it was expensively marketed). Joint Stock's next seven productions, however, were important successes for the company: Caryl Churchill's *Fen* (1983) transferred to The Public in New York; Howard Barker's *Victory* (1983) and *The Power of the Dog* (1984) initiated a relationship between Barker and actor/director Kenny Ireland, which led to the founding of the Wrestling School, a company committed to the staging of Barker's plays. Nicholas Wright's *Crimes of Vautrin* (1983), an adaptation of Balzac's celebrated collection of novels *La Comedie Humaine* (1815–48), was at that point Joint Stock's most technically ambitious production. Sue Townsend's *The Great Celestial Cow* (1984), a carnivalesque depiction of Asian women in Leicester, and Stephen Wakelam's *Deadlines* (1985), a satirical account of tabloid journalism, sold out their three-week runs at Leicester Haymarket and the Royal Court, and Jane Thornton's *Amid The Standing Corn* (1985), a celebration of the 1984 Women Against Pit Closures movement in Barnsley, earned rave reviews both on tour and in London, prompting the Sheffield Crucible to offer a co-production on a sequel (this was never realized). Until 1985, Joint Stock maintained an average output of two new shows a year, sustained cast sizes of six to eight actors, introduced talent such as Vincent Ebrahim, Rita Wolf and Meera Syal, and maintained good relationships with theatres including the Sheffield Crucible, the Sherman Theatre, Cardiff, the ICA and, in particular, the Royal Court.

Crisis hit Joint Stock, however, in May 1985 when a staggering £60,000 deficit in the company's finances was discovered. To the disbelief of its own accountant, Joint Stock recovered this deficit in just four years; the cost, however, took its toll. From 1985 onwards, with the exception of Caryl Churchill and David Lan's spectacular *A Mouthful of Birds* (1986), cast sizes dwindled, wage levels stagnated and production budgets were slashed. Touring programmes became erratic and venues less prestigious: despite winning a Fringe First with Karim Alrawi's *Fire in the Lake* (1985), as well as the Samuel Beckett Award for Best New Play with Ralph Brown's *Sanctuary* (1987), by the late 1980s Joint Stock was barely visible as a producing company. As minutes from a meeting held November 1987 ruefully record, the company had by then 'lost recognition ... to the point of receiving actual censure and disapproval from past members. In brief, Joint Stock has lost respect and its profile has become murky' (JSA, 1987b).

The deficit crisis was not the only flashpoint of the decade. In July 1986 Joint Stock voted in favour of a '50:50 policy' of positive discrimination. This policy stipulated that no less than 50 per cent of Joint Stock's future production teams – to include 'writers, directors, actors, designers [and] stage management' – should be, in the company's own vocabulary, 'non-white' (JSA, 1986g). While many fringe companies were at this time making similar commitments to multiracial work, the resolution proved to be critically divisive, prompting many of Joint Stock's 'old guard' of actors and directors to discontinue their association with the company (Devlin, 1992; Freeman, 2006). With a profile compromised by the recent financial crisis, Joint Stock was unable to attract enough writers, directors and actors to renew and reinvigorate a by-now conflicted and diminished organization. Demoted from revenue to annual funding in 1988, Joint Stock's bid for three-year franchise subsidy was rejected by the Arts Council that same year. In September 1989 it was agreed that Joint Stock should 'go dormant and pursue no activities or incur any expenses until the artistic and funding climate changes (for the better)' (JSA, 1989b). Joint Stock was struck off the Companies House register in 1991.

Funding and Company Structure

Joint Stock evolved from Max Stafford-Clark and William Gaskill's dissatisfaction with conventional producing structures and their shared desire (inspired by the work of American and European ensembles) to experiment with new ways of working with actors. For its part, the Arts Council regarded Joint Stock as an important bridgehead between small and middle-scale theatre, described by drama officer Nicholas Barter in an internal memo to the Drama Panel as 'a water-tight kick-off for the old Fringe generation to make themselves really felt at a heavier level' (ACGB, 1973, 40/32). Joint Stock's initial subsidy catapulted from £14,400 in 1975/6 to £40,000 in 1976/7, rising to

£64,000 in 1979/80 and £89,000 in 1983/4, before cuts to the Arts Council's own grant from the government began to affect the budgets of its revenue-funded clients.

Of the 17 shows produced in the company's first five years, 13 were directed by either Stafford-Clark or Gaskill, or by the two in collaboration. As the company's acknowledged creative forces, it is tempting to divide the history of Joint Stock's development into 'before' and 'after' Stafford-Clark and Gaskill. Indeed, Stafford-Clark offers this view:

> The driving forces behind Joint Stock were Bill Gaskill and me ... And although the company experimented with becoming a cooperative, taking decisions in a cooperative manner, nonetheless, I think, we were the forces behind it. *When we left, it changed.* (Freeman, 2006, 54, my italics)

Certainly, the company founded in 1974 did not share the same complexion – aesthetically, politically and literally, in terms of skin colour – as the one forced to cease operations in 1989. The reasons behind Joint Stock's halting decline – or, from another perspective, dogged survival – are, however, both more complex and more interesting than Stafford-Clark submits, and are tied directly to the company's sustained commitment, from 1975/6 onwards, to operating as a *theatre collective*. The term 'collective' is used advisedly, and without the qualifier 'socialist': while some critics have sought to exhort Joint Stock's socialist principles (Itzin, 1980), the company's *lack* of a unified political stance is well documented (Ritchie, 1987; Bradby, James and Sharratt 1980; Roberts and Stafford-Clark, 2007; Devlin, 1992; Freeman, 2006). While vested in operational, rather than ideological structures, the company's commitment to upholding collective processes of decision-making nevertheless made a critical impact upon its artistic and political direction.

A formalized process of collective decision-making was first inaugurated by Gaskill and Stafford-Clark during the production of *Fanshen*, David Hare's adaptation of William Hinton's chronicle of Communist land reform in a small village in China during the 1940s. This method was initially adopted during the workshop period as a means of accessing and exploring the Marxist imperative that informed Hinton's account, and led to all decisions pertaining to the production being made through group discussion and consensus. It was enthusiastically endorsed by the *Fanshen* company and, subsequently, extended to the running of Joint

Stock itself. In 1977, Joint Stock formally abolished the post of artistic director, instituted a policy of pay parity, and reformulated itself as a collective constituted, at least initially, of anyone who was currently working, or had ever worked, for Joint Stock. From this sizable membership a Policy Committee – initially comprised of the creative team(s) currently working on a show, and later supplemented by elected representatives – was formed to source, select and programme productions, approve production budgets, plan touring schedules, guide major policy decisions and generally oversee the day-to-day running of the company. This Policy Committee, anchored by the company's General Manager, was (theoretically) answerable to the Joint Stock membership, who were kept briefed of the company's activities via a newsletter and whose views could be aired at Joint Stock's Annual General Meeting.

Joint Stock's credentials as a collective have lately been regarded with some scepticism, not least by Stafford-Clark and Gaskill themselves (Roberts and Stafford-Clark, 2007; Freeman, 2006; Callow, 1984). Separating the unrecorded dynamics of the rehearsal room from the core administrative workings of the company is problematic, but archival records attest that Joint Stock did not merely 'experiment' with collectivism. While the precise structure of the collective was necessarily modified as the company responded to internal and external pressures, the principle that it was run by the people who created the work, and/or were committed to making future work possible, underpinned the identity and operations of the company throughout the 1980s – for better and for worse. While likely that Stafford-Clark and Gaskill's working relationship came to a natural end around 1979/80, with the former's appointment as Artistic Director of the Royal Court, over time Joint Stock's collectivist model weakened the influence of its two directors. Without inverting Stafford-Clark's statement into another dubiously straightforward narrative – 'when Joint Stock changed, they left' – it is instructive to trace in company minutes and personal letters a palpable tension between the company's founding directors and the collective they inaugurated.

A History of the Company's Development 1980–9

Joint Stock suffered a loss of momentum at the beginning of the 1980s. Minutes from a Policy Committee meeting held in January identify 'a need to determine the direction of the company' (JSA, 1980a); the discussions that followed over the next few months, however, failed to reach a consensus on what this direction might be. Minutes from a Policy Committee Meeting in June record the suggestion that 'to have somebody fill the post of Artistic Director might [now] be appropriate' but this proposal is overruled by the committee (JSA/26/89, 1 June 1980). The minutes record Philip Donaghy cautioning against a loss of faith in the collective:

> ... the process within Joint Stock of democratisation and breaking down hierarchies was essential to continue with. It was part of the experience of working with Joint Stock, and though difficulties would be encountered, it was vital not to become demoralised and allow the process to stop. (JSA, 1980b)

This hiatus was not, however, immediately remedied and in September David Hare wrote to Joint Stock, advocating that the company be wound up. Again, minutes record that this proposition 'was strongly rejected by everyone present':

> The fact that Max Stafford-Clark and Bill Gaskill's other commitments would prevent them from directing for Joint Stock in the immediate future was more than compensated for, it was felt, by the creative energy within the group. The main issue was to increase productivity and it was RESOLVED to definitely do two shows in 1981/82. (JSA, 1980d)

Far from dissuading its members to disband, Hare's letter galvanized Joint Stock into action. Long-standing members Caryl Churchill and Tony Rohr, together with two new directors working with Stafford-Clark at the Royal Court – Les Waters and Danny Boyle – were co-opted on to the Policy Committee; a Finance Working Group was created to calculate the budget for 1981/2 and a Projects Committee inaugurated (JSA, 1980d).

At this point in the company's organization, the Policy Committee comprised at least one member from each area of work (acting, directing, writing, stage management) from previous shows, plus two 'representatives' from the last two shows, plus the current acting company or companies. At Joint Stock's AGM in June 1981, however, it was agreed that 'the Policy Committee was too large and had become cumbersome' (JSA, 1981b). A resolution was passed that any decisions pertaining to Joint Stock's activity in the financial year 1982/3 should be made only by those members who were free to work during this period; a resolution that ostensibly excluded Stafford-Clark from the Policy

Committee, as his priorities now lay with his appointment as Artistic Director of the Royal Court.

Stafford-Clark had directed at the Royal Court since the early 1970s and of the 17 productions Joint Stock produced in its first five years, over half were either co-produced or subsequently performed at the theatre. This closeness had led some within the Arts Council to query whether there was 'any justification for treating Joint Stock and the English Stage Company as two separately subsidized companies when Joint Stock is so clearly the touring arm of the ESC?' (ACGB, 1981) and, indeed, in spring 1983, after its successes with *Fen* and *Victory*, Joint Stock received a letter from Stafford-Clark 'regarding the possibility of setting up a relationship on a semi-permanent basis with the Royal Court for co-productions' (JSA, 1983a). The theatre offered a guaranteed weekly fee of £2,500, plus a percentage of the box office, plus use of its staff and facilities, in return for 'full status as co-producer' and six weeks of performance at the Royal Court (JSA, 1983b). This offer would formalize the relationship that existed between the two companies and effectively confine Joint Stock's choice of London venue to the Royal Court.

It had been clear to Joint Stock since 1980 that if the company was to continue producing two workshop productions a year, it would need to be reliant upon co-production with other theatres in order to meet the costs of this lengthy and expensive process. Despite this, however, it was resolved at the Joint Stock AGM to reject Stafford-Clark's offer (JSA, 1983).

Not all members of Joint Stock were happy with this decision; minutes from a Policy Committee meeting in August 1983 record actor Kenny Ireland asserting that the rejection of this offer 'was a mistake, especially as it was clear that the company would continue to need co-productions each year' (JSA, 1983e); indeed, of the next ten productions by Joint Stock, over half would be co-produced. The wisdom of this decision remains a matter for speculation; nevertheless, the collective had once again voted to maintain their autonomy, deciding against an offer that might have returned Stafford-Clark to a singular position of authority within the company.

Joint Stock had its tenth anniversary in 1984. Discussions as to how this should be marked had begun as early as July 1983, when it had been suggested that the company should mount three productions, playing two simultaneously at the Royal Court, both on its main stage and the smaller Theatre Upstairs. The necessary planning, however, did not occur, and as late as spring 1984 Joint Stock was still searching for a production to open its autumn season. In March, Gaskill opened a Policy Committee meeting by declaring that the company was 'in an emergency state both in its organisation and as regards future projects' (JSA, 1984b). By June, with still no productions planned, an Extraordinary Meeting (an emergency AGM to which the entire Joint Stock membership was invited) was called by Stafford-Clark to discuss his renewed proposal that Joint Stock should have a paid Artistic Director for at least one year. At this meeting, Stafford-Clark argued that this action was a 'practical solution' to the problem that 'there was no longer a continuing body of experience to carry the group' (JSA, 1984d).

Indeed, Joint Stock had rapidly expanded its membership over the past four years, introducing a 'second generation' of Joint Stock actors with no previous experience of how the company operated. Minutes from Policy Committee meetings over this period indicate that existing members overlooked the importance of initiating new recruits into the company and, specifically, of explaining the artistic and financial responsibilities of the Policy Committee on which these new members now sat. Minutes from a meeting held in May 1981, for example, state that when Stafford-Clark introduced the cast of *Borderline* – almost all of whom were new to the company – only 'the workings of the Policy Committee *were briefly discussed*' (JSA, 1981a, my italics). Similarly, at the June 1984 AGM it was noted by actress Souad Faress that 'an initial meeting before the workshops started, explaining how Joint Stock works, and the responsibilities of the company members, would have been very useful' (JSA, 1984c). By neglecting to properly induct new members into the collective, the operation of Joint Stock's Committees subsequently faltered, leading to the 'emergency state' in which the company now found itself.

At the Extraordinary Meeting in June, however, it was decided that to accept Stafford-Clark's proposal for an Artistic Director 'would be a backwards step for the company' (JSA, 1984d). 'Open workshops' for writers, directors and actors held earlier that month had, according to the minutes, 'generated energy, commitment and work', and the meeting considered that '*this* was the solution to the problems that had arisen over the last six months' (JSA, 1984d, my italics); indeed, these open workshops had resulted in two shows that were subsequently produced in 1985: *Deadlines* by Stephen Wakelam and *Amid the Standing Corn* by Jane Thornton. In order to address the lack of continuity that those attending the meeting agreed had arisen, it was resolved that 'company calls' to explain the responsibilities and working methods of the collective should be introduced for a new acting company *before* workshops began, and that it would be 'recommended to the writer and director when casting a Joint Stock production that [at least one or two existing] Joint Stock members should be within the new company' (JSA, 1984d). The matter did not, however, immediately end there. In July, Gaskill wrote to the Policy Committee, putting himself forward as a prospective Artistic Director. The Policy Committee independently decided that it could, and would, 'enthusiastically invite' Gaskill to become Artistic Director, in direct contradiction to the resolution passed by the membership at the Extraordinary Meeting (JSA, 1984e). Although Gaskill subsequently withdrew his offer due to other commitments, the decision of the Policy Committee to overrule the consensus reached by the membership indicated that Joint Stock's collective structure was by now under some strain. Just how damaging the consequences of mismanagement would be for the company became apparent in May 1985, when Joint Stock's financial crisis came to light.

In an ACGB internal memo dated 3 May 1985, Joint Stock's Drama Officer, Jonathan Lamede, reported to the Drama Panel:

... The situation is immensely complicated and extremely muddled, but the main points are as follows:

2.1 There are a number of hitherto undisclosed creditors ... These include National Insurance debts of over £22,000 dating from 1983/84 and 1984/85; sundry creditors of £16,500 and an overdraft of £4,500.

2.2 There seems to be an undisclosed accumulated deficit, originating in 1982/83, of £8,000.

2.3 Some months ago, the bank manager threatened to withdraw the overdraft facility completely and, to continue trading, Anne-Louise Wirgman [the company's then General Manager] put up her own flat as surety. (ACGB, 1985a)

The last of these points is underlined in ink with 'madness!' written next to it; 'One of these would be bad enough' the handwriting continues, 'but all three ... !' (ACGB, 1985a). Joint Stock swiftly reconvened its Finance Committee, which consisted of Kenny Ireland and Souad Faress (a qualified bookkeeper as well as an actress), Ralph Brown and Simon Curtis (*Deadlines*), and, later, Jennie Stoller and Karim Alrawi

(*Fire in the Lake*). A final audit of Joint Stock's accounts in August 1985 revealed that the company's total deficit stood at £61,526.

The Finance Committee lost no time in blaming the crisis on the alleged 'grossly incompetent' manner in which Joint Stock's then General Manager, Anne-Louise Wirgman, had handled the company's finances over the past year (JSA, 1985a). In a 'Finance Committee Statement' dated 15 June 1985, Wirgman is accused of failing to adhere to an established bookkeeping system, concealing information from the Policy Committee, unrealistic budgeting and lack of control over the company's expenditure. While the statement also acknowledges that the Policy Committee had 'been naïve' and 'shirked responsibility for actions performed in their name', the Finance Committee concluded that Wirgman was 'not suited to the tough job of relating to, and in some cases curtailing the enthusiasm of the Policy Committee' (JSA, 1985a). The report ended by inviting Wirgman to resign.

Reconstructing the total picture of events from minutes, reports and statements is obviously difficult. While Wirgman's negligence in respect of National Insurance payments and creditors' bills cannot be disputed, her written reply to the accusations levelled at her by the Finance Committee does provide a more nuanced account of the awkward functioning of the collective during this period. In 'A Response to the Finance Committee's Statement', dated 16 June 1985, Wirgman contended that when she was appointed in June 1983 the company's books for the previous quarter were not up to date (they were actually two shows behind); that in November 1983 she had requested the appointment of a bookkeeper but that this had been ignored; and, most significantly, that *all three* of the production budgets she had drawn up since joining the company had been approved by the Policy Committee. Wirgman further points out that:

> [Howard Barker's] 'Power of the Dog' went over [budget] by £11,424.67. Due to 'Power of the Dog' opening at the Lyceum Studio, Edinburgh, a choice made by Kenny Ireland without consultation with me and against the advice of the production manager, the deficit on the show [was] increased by a further £2,600 since the venue was technically totally unsuitable and brought in an income of £400 instead of £4,000. 'Power of the Dog' total deficit is therefore £14,024.67. 'Deadlines' production budget went over by £1,000 due to the technical nature of the show. Both of the directors now alleging that my budgeting is not realistic are of course members of the Finance Committee and Policy Committee. (JSA, 1985b)

Wirgman agreed that expenditure had been out of her control, but maintained that it had been *taken* out of her control 'by decisions made with and without the consent of the Policy Committee on the last two productions' (JSA, 1985b). Wirgman's relationship to the Policy Committee echoes that described by her predecessor, Lynda Farran, when in 1982 the company decided to approve a budget for *Victory*'s set design of £9,500 – twice the amount usually allocated.

> This kind of expenditure was unprecedented and would, I argued, put the company into deficit ... The increased expenditure would not penalise the immediate productions, as expenditure was committed, and therefore not the majority of those attending the meeting – but it would be detrimental to future projects, perhaps mean employing one less actor, or losing a further rehearsal week. But, the meeting was fully aware of the implications of the decisions. These were the rules, and I had to carry out the majority decision. (Ritchie, 1987, 153)

The inability of the General Manager to veto decisions made by the company – as well as the undesirability of this kind of executive power – is iterated by Wirgman in her conclusion:

> My understanding of the job as General Manager of Joint Stock is that I would run the company with the Policy Committee. It is not my position to 'curtail the enthusiasm of the Policy Committee' if within the collective my advice is not heard or listened to. I have not the power to have a block vote and overrule the Policy Committee decisions. The Finance Committee seem now to be suggesting that Joint Stock should be a collective in name only and that the General Manager should function as a benevolent dictator. (JSA, 1985b)

Wirgman resigned on 25 June 1985 and was replaced by Jane Dawson. In revealing the administrative chaos at the heart of Joint Stock, the financial crisis had exposed two key structural weaknesses within the collective: namely, the relationship between the 'short-term' members of the Policy Committee – the current acting company – and the 'long-term' elected members of the Policy Committee; and the relationship between the director of the current company – responsible for his or her production – and the General Manager/Policy Committee – responsible for the company as a whole. It was clear to Joint Stock that the function and composition of the Policy Committee needed to be revised, and the company addressed itself to this issue at the August

AGM. Lamede attended the AGM and it is instructive to compare his notes with the minutes recorded by Kathryn Pogson. According to Lamede, at this meeting Stafford-Clark

> ... made an impassioned plea for the power to be returned to those who did the work. He also joined Danny Boyle (or did Danny Boyle join him?) in the suggestion that the company might appoint an Artistic Director, at least for the coming year. *But there is quite powerful resistance to Max in the company and the proposal in principle never had a chance.* (ACGB, 1985d, my italics)

Indeed, the official AGM minutes make no reference to Stafford-Clark's 'impassioned plea'. Instead, the collective regrouped and reconfigured the Policy Committee to include members of the current working company, six people elected at the AGM, the General Manager *and* the writer and director preparing the next project – a crucial addition designed to encourage Joint Stock to move from short-term to long-term planning as well as prevent the kind of short-sighted decision-making by directors and companies highlighted above. In an effort to restore power to the artists making the work it was furthermore agreed that, once the working company was on tour, the Policy Committee 'would be deemed to consist of the working company plus two representatives of the elected members whose fares will be paid to attend that meeting' (JSA, 1985d). Finally, in order to 'put a stop to the unbridled growth of membership', this would now be conditional upon an annual subscription fee of £10 (ACGB, 1985b). According to Lamede, the new structure seemed 'cumbersome', but was 'workable ... they do realise that the remaining problems are horrendous, but at least there is a basis for progress' (ACGB, 1985b). A year later, the new General Manager, Jane Dawson, would comment in her report written for the 1986 AGM that this restructuring of Joint Stock 'served to strengthen a group which, until the rescue attempt, had been at best nebulous for some time' (JSA, 1986e).

Before these measures could be put in place, however, Karim Alrawi's *Fire in the Lake* premiered at the Edinburgh Festival Fringe in August 1985. When the deficit crisis struck, the *Fire in the Lake* company was weeks away from starting rehearsals in Liverpool. One week before rehearsals were due to begin, the director Jules Wright withdrew from the project and was followed by three of the six actors. The *Fire in the Lake* company interviewed for a replacement director and, after Jane Howell had accepted the post but subsequently withdrawn, Les Waters agreed to take on the project. After being persuaded by Waters to continue, Alrawi rewrote the play for a cast of five and Waters cast two new actors. Despite having lost two rehearsal weeks, *Fire in the Lake* opened on time and won a Fringe First.

The confusion and frustration, however, led Alrawi to tender his resignation from Joint Stock just five days after the premiere. In a letter dated 25 August 1985, Alrawi highlights the mishandling of information between the *Fire in the Lake* company and the Policy Committee, citing lack of consultation on poster design and copy, cancellation of the script's publication and the appointment of Jane Dawson as the new General Manager (JSA, 1985e). Negotiation of a co-production with Liverpool Playhouse, as well as the organization of the show's subsequent tour, had also been taken out of the hands of the *Fire in the Lake* company and (haphazardly) administrated by the Policy and Finance Committees, whose first priority had been to remedy Joint Stock's financial problems. In response to their grievances, presented in a report at the 1986 AGM, Kenny Ireland admitted that at the time of the financial crisis 'decisions had to be taken on a day to day basis and so normal democratic processes had broken down', but he maintained that the decision-making process had been 'handed back to the company at the earliest opportunity' (JSA, 1986g). Other members attending the AGM, however, recognized that while *Fire in the Lake* was the 'victim of unique circumstances', the situation had nevertheless demonstrated 'the peculiar attitude of Joint Stock concerning the role of management and company' (JSA, 1986g). For the first time in the company's history, a proposal to issue actors and directors with legal contracts was advanced and a Contracts Working Party formed to investigate this proposal. After a considerable period of evaluation, the use of legal contracts was finally rejected, on the grounds that it would undermine the principle that Joint Stock members were 'simultaneously employer and employee', temporary custodians collectively responsible for the company (Ritchie, 1987, 153).

Indeed, despite evident tensions, a palpable sense of 'collective responsibility' enabled Joint Stock to make remarkable progress in reducing its deficit between June 1985/6 and March 1986/7 (JSA, 1986e). Led by the Policy and Finance Committees, the company changed banks, securing a £5,000 overdraft and releasing Wirgman's flat from surety; demanded and received a reduction of £3,200 from accountancy fees; changed accountants, saving the company £2,000 in annual fees; paid off a number of creditors; and negotiated with the Inland Revenue a schedule of National Insurance repayments, thereby removing the threat of prosecution. A Fundraising Committee was also formed and raised a substantial amount of money through donations. By March 1986, the deficit was reduced to £28,323. Minutes from the July 1986 AGM record a vote of thanks to the Finance Committee, Jane Dawson and the new accountant Jon Catty, who 'congratulated the company and admitted that he was surprised that Joint Stock had indeed survived' (JSA, 1986g).

In common with many fringe companies, the racial composition of Joint Stock's collective was a conversation that recurred during the 1980s. After the company's production of Sue Townsend's *The Great Celestial Cow* in 1984, the Policy Committee had minuted that it would like to 'try and get rid of the term "ethnic considerations" and implement a real policy of integrated casting' (JSA, 1984f); a directive had consequently been issued urging directors of future projects to employ black actors. Irrespective of these pronouncements, however, Joint Stock's next three shows (*The Power of the Dog, Deadlines* and *Amid the Standing Corn*) had featured all-white casts. In spring 1986 Joint Stock's patchy discussion of, and fitful adherence to, a policy of integrated casting assumed a new significance, prompted by the Arts Council's own implementation of an 'Arts and Ethnic Minorities' policy. As outlined in a letter sent in February to all its theatre clients in receipt of revenue funding, the ACGB was seeking to encourage 'the employment of people from Britain's ethnic minority communities' and the 'development of opportunities for ethnic minority art forms, artists and audiences' (JSA, 1986a). The ACGB accordingly expected its clients to 'adopt parallel plans for their own operations' – specifically, to ensure that not less than 4 per cent of a company's turnover would be spent on 'the employment of Afro-Caribbean and Asian people, the promotion of Afro-Caribbean and Asian Art forms and the encouragement, through marketing, of audiences from these communities' (JSA,1986a).

This letter re-ignited the debate on integrated casting within Joint Stock and, in March, actor Ralph Brown proposed that the company resolve to 'employ at least one non-white performer in all future productions' (JSA, 1986b). Brown's proposal initially met with resistance: some members were concerned about the loss of 'artistic freedom' that a policy of positive discrimination might impose, others more pertinently argued that 'employing a "token black" would do little to improve the situation overall or the work itself' (JSA, 1986b). At a meeting in April, the Policy Committee passed a diluted version of Brown's proposal, resolving that 'Joint Stock commits itself to a policy of racially integrated casting ... with a view to creating a more multi-racial company with a greater diversity of work' (JSA, 1986c).

The broader Joint Stock membership were informed of the Arts Council's new policy and the Policy Committee's response to it at the 1986 AGM, at which point more assertive arguments were advanced for 'some form of legislation' to be implemented within the company (JSA, 1986g). Actor Nizwar Karanj felt that in terms of racial policy Joint Stock had not moved on since *Borderline* and requested a full and precise definition of 'integrated casting'; the minutes record that 'answers were varied but in general favoured the view that black and white performers would be cast to perform parts according to their versatility and not colour or creed' (JSA, 1986g). Concerns about tokenism were countered by Ralph Brown's suggestion that 50 per cent of any cast should be non-white; Karanj pointed out that it was not just casting that should be addressed, but the entire creative team and stage management – Joint Stock should be inviting black directors, writers and companies to submit projects to the company. Choreographer Ian Spink agreed with Karanj and suggested that 'to make a better, more solid start, a resolution should be framed to include integration on every level – fifty per cent of those involved in a project should not be white' (JSA, 1986g).

Thirty-one members attended the July AGM, including Stafford-Clark. The minutes record that while he 'felt it was time to take some positive step'; his feeling was that casting was 'often determined by the writer' and so 'cannot always be open ... the work should be determined by those involved in it' (JSA, 1986g). The minutes continue: 'the AGM dictates policy but he [Stafford-Clark] could not endorse policy dictating the work' (JSA, 1986g). Three key resolutions were, however, eventually passed. These were:

> Joint Stock commits itself to a policy of racial integration. To facilitate this, the company (to include writers, directors, actors, designers, stage management) should be 50% non-white.

> At least 50% of the elected members on the Policy Committee should not be white and at least 50% should not be men.

> Within the next four shows, one will encompass the black experience. Both the writer and the director must be black and in this case the 50% ruling on the company should mean at least 50%. (JSA, 1986g, original emphasis)

Following the AGM, a substantial number of Joint Stock members ended their relationship with the company. Interestingly however, given his reservations, Stafford-Clark did not immediately withdraw. In autumn 1986 he proposed a project about the Grenadian People's Revolution (1979–83), which, together with Ralph Brown's *Sanctuary*, was accepted by the Projects and Policy Committee for production in 1987/8. However, when the Finance and Policy Committees convened to consider the finances for the year, they discovered Joint Stock was not able to produce both shows without an extra £70,000 from the Arts Council. Staggeringly, given the ongoing financial crisis, 'budgets had not really been discussed' by the Projects Committee and the Policy Committee had accepted its recommendations without consulting with the Finance Committee (JSA, 1986i). An Extraordinary Meeting was immediately called; in contrast to the 31 members at the AGM in July, only 18 attended. Adamant that the company be seen to produce two shows in 1987/8, it was decided that Joint Stock would produce Brown's *Sanctuary*, workshop a smaller-scale production (Alrawi's *Child in the Heart*) and pay off the remaining deficit (£13,000). The Grenada project would be pushed back into 1988/9; in the event, however, Stafford-Clark failed to find a suitable writer and subsequently withdrew the project.

Though Joint Stock successfully premiered the two productions in 1987/8, together with a third play, *A Promised Land* in autumn 1988, morale and commitment were at low ebb. Attendance at meetings dwindled; minutes from July 1987 noted 'that many people unable to attend meetings were omitting to give their apologies' (JSA, 1987a) and minutes from an Extraordinary Meeting held in November, attended by only 14 members, observed that 'within the last 18 months or so there has been a noticeable drifting away and a lack of solidarity' (JSA, 1987b). In a final effort to regroup and re-energize Joint Stock it was agreed, over a series of meetings, to dissolve all existing committees and replace them with one Council of Management. This Council would consist of Souad Faress, Karim Alrawi and Nick Broadhurst and would undertake responsibility 'for all actions and decisions taken by the company or individuals in the company' (JSA, 1987c). Its three members would be paid 'for attendance and contractual obligations' and they would commit themselves to the company for a period of three years (JSA, 1987c). This decision ended Joint Stock's decade of working as a theatre collective.

This radical restructuring came too late. In January 1988, the Arts Council wrote to the company to express its concerns about what it regarded as 'the diminishing ability of the company ... to form and implement a coherent touring policy at a level of achievement that the profession and the Arts Council expect from Joint Stock' (ACGB, 1988a). Subsequently they received a cut of £23,000. In February, the company received another letter informing them that they were one of seven companies who had been demoted from revenue to annual funding; in April, they were invited to submit a three-year plan in a bid to regain revenue funding on a three-year cycle. A programme was swiftly drawn up by Faress, Alrawi and Broadhurst and was favourably received by the Arts Council as 'ambitious', 'imaginative' and 'a welcome change in the Company's aspirations and attitudes' (ACGB, 1988c). Reservations over company personnel persisted, however, as an internal memo dated July 1988 from drama officer Jonathan Pope to drama director Ian Brown, evidences:

> The new structure is fundamental to the success of the three year plan as you will see when you have read it. It's therefore essential that we genuinely believe in their ability to implement this new structure and make it work. Do we? (ACGB, 1988c)

Pope answers his own question later that month:

> This was my first Joint Stock formal meeting and it confirmed my worst suspicions. Plenty of willy [sic] thinking, rambling discussion, all at a very slow pace. I saw nothing in this meeting to suggest that the company have the dynamic management or realism to enable them to achieve their three year bid. (ACGB, 1988d)

An application for project funding in May 1989 was rejected by the Arts Council and, though the Thorndike Theatre in Leatherhead offered to pay all costs for the production, the director–writer team, Sian Evans and Paulette Randall, pulled out and the project collapsed. The idea of reviving an existing Joint Stock play was discussed but decided against 'due to a general feeling that there didn't exist an artistic energy within Joint Stock' (JSA, 1989a). 'If we can allow a situation to arise which forces us to turn down an offer of £25,000', the minutes of a Board Meeting read, 'then perhaps we don't deserve it' (JSA, 1989a). The decision to wind up Joint Stock was taken in September 1989.

Key Works and Critical Reception

While the decision in 1986 to legislate for a 50:50 policy of racial integration was an act many company members felt they could not support, during the course of the 1980s Joint Stock nevertheless transformed from what Joyce Devlin describes as a 'Caucasian company' into a 'multi-racial collective' (Devlin, 1992, 63). Four productions in particular were instrumental in this transformation: *Borderline* (1981), *The Great Celestial Cow* (1984), *Fire in the Lake* (1985) and *A Mouthful of Birds* – the latter regarded today as a seminal work of theatrical experimentation. While the immediate critical reception of these shows was decidedly mixed (a measure, perhaps, of the complexities of representing different cultures to audiences experiencing racial tensions within broader society), these productions represent significant attempts to engage with black and Asian issues, subjects and stories - despite occurring during somewhat fractious moments in the evolution of Joint Stock's social and artistic consciousness.

Borderline (1981)

Initially referred to as simply 'The Asian Project', *Borderline* would subsequently be recognized by Joint Stock as the production that not only led the company to 'an appreciation of the particular problems black[3] actors and their communities face in this country' but also presented 'a challenge to the way the company was constituted and, in particular, to its choice of projects' (ACGB, 1988b, 34/54/3).

An investigation by Stafford-Clark and writer Hanif Kureishi into 'patterns of social adjustment for Asian immigrants to this country' (JSA, 1980c), *Borderline* was Joint Stock's nineteenth production but the first to use a racially mixed cast. Researched for four weeks among Pakistani communities resident in Southall, London, the play's examination of tensions between and within English and Asian cultures, generations and classes was generally applauded by broadsheet theatre critics who praised its subtly drawn characters and avoidance of polemic. The Asian audiences to whom the play was ostensibly directed, however, did not accept the invitation. Minutes from a Policy Committee meeting in November 1981 (five weeks after the play had opened in London) record Shreela Ghosh, a freelance publicity officer employed on the production, reporting that 'it had proven impossible so far to draw Asian audiences'; 'after talking to numerous Asian groups and contacts', the minutes continue, '[Shreela] had come to the conclusion that the show was unlikely to be suitable or suited to their entertainment tastes' (JSA, 1981d).

Borderline drew direct criticism, moreover, for the decision to cast Caucasian actors, David Beames and Deborah Findlay, as Asian characters. In February 1982, the *Guardian* printed a letter written by Madhav Sharma, founding director of the multiracial company Actors Unlimited and also Artistic Director of an Asian Festival held annually by the National Association for Asian Youth (itself based in Southall):[4]

> The Tricycle theatre is currently employing white actors to portray the historical characters of Mahatma Ghandi (revered by Hindus as something of a saint) and Mr Jinnah (admired by Muslims as the founder of Pakistan). Recently, the Joint Stock Company at the Royal Court Theatre employed white actors to portray Asians in a contemporary piece set in Southall. If these were examples of progressive theatres employing people irrespective of race, colour or creed, it is strange that no actors of Indian or Pakistani origin were employed in either production (or in other productions at these theatres) to portray white characters and that the directors, designers and members of stage-management, in both instances, were all whites. (Sharma, 1982)

Policy Committee minutes, however, show that the *Borderline* company had anticipated these criticisms and requested before the production opened that Kureishi write a programme note 'to explain how the play was made and to justify white actors playing Asian roles' (JSA, 1981c). In earlier plays such as *Epsom Downs* and *Cloud Nine* Joint Stock had established a credo whereby an actor's sex, age and colour were irrelevant to the role in which he or she was cast – though in fact, no black or Asian actor had ever played a white character in Joint Stock's history up to that date. According to Stafford-Clark, the intention had been that Asian actors would play white roles and vice versa; this had not, however, been upheld during the workshopping and writing of the play, as Kureishi's programme note explains:

> From the outset Max Stafford-Clark and I decided to have a racially mixed cast: three white actors and three Asian ones and in Joint Stock tradition everyone would play everything … The idea of the play in my mind was still the picaresque journey of an immigrant through a foreign and possibly hostile land. A strand of this idea remains, but when I sat down to write, a more domestic epic emerged with eight

main parts; seven of these were Asian and one was white. This is why you would see whites playing Asians but not vice versa tonight. This is in no sense an apology but an explanation, for the group's diversity of experience has been as stimulating throughout the whole period of work as were the people we met during the workshop. In a loose way the play has been fed by all these lives. (ACGB, 96/90, n.d)

According to Rita Wolf, the fact that none of *Borderline*'s three Asian actors would play white characters was regarded at the time as 'something [Joint Stock] would doubtless rectify next season' (Ritchie, 1987, 147). This did not, as Wolf notes with some bitterness, turn out to be the case (Ritchie, 1987, 147–8). It would be another three years and four more shows before Asian actors were again employed by Joint Stock.

The Great Celestial Cow (1984)

The next Joint Stock show to employ non-white actors was also the first to be directed by a woman. Proposed in the summer of 1983 by director Carole Hayman and writer Sue Townsend – author of the successful Adrian Mole novels – *The Great Celestial Cow* was envisaged as a 'fantastical extravaganza', a celebration with music and dance of the humour and resilience of Asian women relocated to an unfamiliar culture (JSA, 21/1, n.d.). Three weeks of workshops involving the director, writer and cast were held during October in Leicester, where Townsend lived and the play was set.

The cast comprised six Asian actors and one white actor and yet, once again, Joint Stock failed to convincingly uphold its alleged commitment to integrated casting: Asian actors played only very minor (walk-on) white roles, while white actress Lou Wakefield was cast as Prem, the son of the play's protagonist, Sita. While *Celestial Cow* enjoyed an extremely successful run at Leicester Playhouse, with extra performances added to satisfy demand, reviews for the production were mixed. Some critics were happy to accept the play as a funny, touching and perceptive parable of an 'East-meets-West' culture clash, but others were alarmed by the caricatures they perceived onstage. Barney Bardsley provides a forceful articulation of this unease in her review for the *Tribune*:

Joint Stock have gone badly wrong in their latest venture ... The aim behind the play is admirable enough – to depict Asian family life in Britain without resorting to stereotyped categories of 'hardworking', 'submissive' and 'humourless' usually attributed to Asians. Unfortunately the play errs in the other direction. The characters become coarsened, so willing to send themselves up that the whole thing becomes one big joke – at the expense of the Asian community it purports to represent ... Who was it aimed at? Not Asian people, certainly, for they would spot the over simplified distortions of their lives and be justifiably offended. No, this play is for whites only – and they will have their prejudices confirmed by it, rather than refuted. (Bardsley, 1984)

Bardsley's critique of the production echoes an anonymous pamphlet, distributed by an organization called 'Just Asian Voices' with addresses in Leicester and London, circulated in March 1984:

'The Great Celestial Cow' is a comedy; and comedy, as we all know, requires the ability to laugh. It is singularly arrogant of the writer and the director, however, to ask Asians and non-Asians to laugh at negative images of Asians ... 'The Great Celestial Cow' is, in intent and detail, an unashamedly white view of Asians. As such, this is not a comedy ... it is a political statement. (JSA, 1984a)

The pamphlet further alleges that:

if one is to believe the Asian cast in the company, they have had no say in the production of this play ... the writer and director alone decided what vision of Asians to offer the worthy public of Leicester, and the other towns to which this show is going. (JSA, 1984a)

It is not clear on what evidence this allegation is made; a company report submitted in June does include the statement that 'in the end, the play represented a broader feminism' than had been first anticipated' (JSA, 1984c), but the archives record no further criticism. Indeed, the significance of the cast's contribution was formally recognized by Townsend in December 1983 when she requested that 'in acknowledgement of the participation of the actors and director in creating the play' 10 per cent of any future royalties were to be shared with Hayman and the actors (JSA, 26/91, n.d.).

A Mouthful of Birds (*1986*)

With a cast comprised of three black and two white actors, in 1985 *Fire in the Lake* was the first Joint Stock play in which black actors played both black and white main characters, and vice versa. This was an important step for the company, but the wording of a post-production report implied that racial background remained a live and somewhat divisive issue for the company: 'the multi-racial company worked very well both in research and rehearsal and should be worked upon as much for the actors as for the product and audience. Both *sides* learnt much from each other' (JSA, 1986f, my italics). This statement suggests that race could yet divide the company into two implicitly opposed factions. In this respect, it seems significant to note that *A Mouthful of Birds* was the first – and only – Joint Stock production to cast black actors (two female dancers) in a piece that didn't situate at its core issues of race and ethnicity.

   In the knowledge that it was economically viable to produce only one show in 1986/7, Joint Stock decided in June 1985 to focus its energies on producing a large-scale, high-profile and hopefully high-earning show to tour the UK, Europe and the United States. The project chosen was a proposal from Caryl Churchill, David Lan and Les Waters to use *The Bacchae* as the basis for an investigation into religion, cultism, ecstasy, possession and female violence. Their interest was in 'challenging and extending acting styles' and the production would take inspiration from the work of Pina Bausch (JSA, 1985c). Caryl Churchill's version of Euripides's *The Bacchae* was an attractive prospect and, as a long-standing member of Joint Stock, Churchill was 'aware of and sympathetic to the company's need for an artistic and financial success' (JSA, 1985c). The desired scale of the show – eight dancers/actors, two writers, one director and one choreographer, Ian Spink, employed over a twelve-week continuous workshop/rehearsal period – demanded that Joint Stock co-produce with both a London and a regional theatre. They struck a box-office deal with the Royal Court but finding a regional co-producer proved more difficult. After six months of searching, the Birmingham Repertory Theatre agreed to co-produce, and programmed the (as yet unwritten) production into the main auditorium to open the autumn season.

   This, it transpired, was an unfortunate decision. Actress Tricia Kelly (*Fen*, *Deadlines*) remembers the first night at Birmingham in September 1986:

[It] was a wildly experimental, portmanteau piece … In the first story I played a woman having a breakdown, it was post-natal depression, really … And at the end of this little story – and this was only one story – I got this towel, and it was a baby, and I put it under the water in this sink and held it down. Well, on the first night, the seats were tipping up, when I put this towel under the water. It was like *Saved*, the seats were tipping up and people started shouting! And they carried on shouting. Because they all thought they'd come to see *The Bacchae*, you see! It was the first show of the season, so it was the great and the good there … nine hundred people. And people started leaving and shouting, 'this is not what I came to see!' It was like being in the eye of a storm. It was the most extraordinary night I've ever experienced in theatre. By the end of the evening we had about a third of the audience left. (Kelly, 2013)

Such was the reaction that Birmingham Rep wrote a letter to their subscription holders that, while endorsing the production, offered them the opportunity to see the Rep's studio piece instead (JSA, 1986h). On tour, *A Mouthful of Birds* continued to provoke extreme responses; while the majority of theatre critics wrote bewildered and often disparaging reviews, the Joint Stock archives also contain several letters from members of the public expressing how deeply they were moved by the production. An Arts Council internal memo from drama officer Ruth McKenzie titled 'Mouthful of Birds' and dated November 1986 reads: 'Although it is a muddle, there is no doubt of its high quality and possibly historic significance' (ACGB, 1986). The planned European and American tours, however, never transpired and even booking a UK tour proved difficult. The show's scale required a main auditorium, but its taboo content and experimental aesthetic constituted too much of a financial risk for most theatres. Joint Stock had hoped to make a profit on *A Mouthful of Birds*; in the event, this seminal production lost the company £2,800.

Joint Stock's organization as a collective required of its members an investment in time, energy, ideas and skills which, when provided, resulted in a creative, resilient and progressive theatre company, creating topical, successful and, in rare cases, seminal productions. The way in which the collective was organized in the 1980s, however, also directly engendered the artistic discontinuity and financial instability which ultimately led to the company's demise. Ralph Brown's observation in 1987 that the collective was something that 'worked in spasms, in much the same manner as a war' (JSA, 1987b) eloquently captures the company's rocky history, with both the deficit crisis *and* its recovery, together with the 50:50 policy *and* its ensuing problems, attributable to the (mis)firings of Joint Stock's ten-year stint as a functioning theatre collective.

Chapter 4

GAY SWEATSHOP

Sara Freeman

Introduction

In 1985, during its tenth anniversary, designer Kate Owen noted that the 'men who started up Gay Sweatshop didn't believe there would still be a need ten years later' (GS, n.d, 3/17/4). Owen overstates the certainty of Sweatshop's founders: in 1975, Roger Baker, Drew Griffiths, Alan Pope, Norman Coates, Alan Wakeman and Gerald Chapman may have fervently envisioned that at some point Britain's first openly gay and lesbian professional theatre company would be unnecessary, but they did not precisely put a timeline on this. Sweatshop's mission was to agitate for the social liberation of gay men and lesbian women and to revise biased representations of homosexuality in performance. Griffiths held that 'if the aims and objectives of Gay Sweatshop are ever achieved, we will have done ourselves out of a job', yet that dream still seemed very far off to actor, writer and director Philip Osment even as he wrote a company history for the group in 1989 (Osment,1989, lxvi).

Sweatshop's trajectory challenges the simple timeline of alternative theatre's decline across the 1980s, even while what happened to the company in the 1990s confirms how much the British theatre landscape changed between 1980 and 1994. The period markers of this volume break up Sweatshop's history and force a focus on the group's middle period, drawing attention to the company's programme after its first flush of activism and allowing an exploration of the group's longevity and attempts at institutionalization before the last three years leading up to its closure in 1997.

In 1980, Sweatshop received a number of negative evaluations from the Arts Council of Great Britain. At that point, the group was reckoning how to reintegrate its men's and women's companies and find a new mode to work in now that the project of 'coming-out plays' seemed exhausted and show creation divided by gender was causing as many problems as it had previously solved. Within a year, the Arts Council cut Sweatshop's funding entirely as part of the changes in public spending across the 1980s that immediately impacted upon the Arts Council at the start of the decade. The company went into hiatus. Yet a resurrection was immanent in the leadership of Noël Greig.

Osment records that actor Barry Jackson, who also served as an Arts Council drama adviser, conveyed to Greig that he was surprised at Sweatshop's fate. Jackson told Greig 'he would have imagined that by 1983 there should have been six state funded companies producing gay theatre' (Osment, 1989, lii). Sweatshop roused itself in the face of that absence, and, as detailed below, Arts Council reports of 1984 began to categorize it as a leading gay company and justify this as a legible category of alternative work. By contrast, in 1994, Sweatshop faced a number of conflicts between new writing and experimental performance resulting from its appointment of co-artistic directors Lois Weaver and James Neale-Kennerly and its reorganization after receiving a three-year cycle of Arts Council franchise funding in 1992. An unusual mid-cycle appraisal by the Arts Council scheduled for April/May 1994 and the pending application for another cycle of funding to the newly consti-tuted Arts Council England (ACE) shaped the discussion recorded in Sweatshop's board meeting minutes from 1994 and 1995. The group, having just enjoyed its most official period of institutional status, faced the hard reality that small-scale touring had changed so drastically from the early 1980s that the company could no longer carry it off and maintain the type of 'stature' expected of it (GS, 1994, 1/2/8b).

Sweatshop's placement into this second volume adopts a different approach to the company than has been taken by scholars so far. One of the assertions of this chapter is to argue that Sweatshop's work in the 1980s holds more importance than scholarship's existing focus on the company's origins and work in the 1970s has admitted. Because this group strengthened when others weakened, the work of the 1980s represents the company ethos far better than the work of the 1970s. Whether published in 1980, like Catherine Itzin's *Stages in the Revolution*, or 2012, like Stephen Greer's study *Contemporary British Queer Performance*, treatment of Sweatshop obsessively returns to the story of the company's origin. This includes close readings of *Mr X* and *Any Woman Can* (1975) along with discussion about the contrast between gay-male identity and activism and the need for lesbian subjectivity and liberation that resulted in Sweatshop splitting into separate men's and woman's companies between 1977 and 1980.

This repetition of focus means Sweatshop provides critics with both a place to start and a way to memorialize. As a starting point, Sweatshop provides the first case study in John Deeny's chapter on lesbian and gay theatre in *A Companion to Modern British and Irish Drama 1880–2005*; it is the subject of Greer's first chapter in his book, which uses *Mr X* and *Any Woman Can* as the foundation for questions about authenticity and legitimacy in relation to self-reflective queer performance in the 1990s and the first decade of the twenty-first century. Sweatshop is the company referred to when Brian Roberts begins his article by trying to answer the question 'Whatever happened to gay theatre?' (Roberts, 2000, 175). In fact, the question Roberts recounts as initiating his article was 'Whatever happened to Gay Sweatshop?' Meanwhile, Alan Sinfield and Nicholas de Jongh sounded alarm bells about Sweatshop's demise in the 1990s after the passage of Section 28 and funding cuts to the company that they attributed to anti-homosexual policy in that legislation; Helen Freshwater also erroneously claims that Sweatshop closed its doors entirely due to such censorship (Sinfield, 1999, 283; de Jongh, 1992, 178–9; Freshwater, 2009, 109).

When scholarship is not veering between origins or funereal concerns, it turns to the dynamics of AIDS plays and feminist theatre and rightly notes Sweatshop's contribution to both canons. Thus, there are three areas of critical orthodoxy about Sweatshop: first is the treatment of the company in relation to alternative theatre in general; then there is an assessment of them in terms of specifically gay and feminist theatre, and finally, there is orthodoxy about them in so far as they demonstrate the dynamics of theatre funding in the post-war and Thatcher periods. Sweatshop also forms a point of reference in overviews about British alternative theatre as scholars set up rubrics to organize this evolving field of production. For example, issues of oppositional and ideological praxis through theatre frame Baz Kershaw's references to Sweatshop in the *Cambridge History of British Theatre* (Kershaw, 2004, 343–4). In his 1980 collection *Dreams and Deconstructions: Alternative Theatre in Britain*, Sandy Craig likewise credits Sweatshop for the way in which its work married issues about socialism and the campaign for homosexual equality in the face of the 1970s 'tendency on the British left to ignore gay politics' (Craig, 1980, 34–5). Underneath the contrasts Craig sets up and in general discussions of Sweatshop in the context of alternative theatre, there were efforts to identify the way politics was played out and to assess when and how theatre companies succeeded or failed at creating controversy, social critique and change. Sweatshop served as an example of a seemingly direct circuit from identity and political commitment to aesthetic expression that created social impact, especially in its early years when performance interruptions, protesting letters to the editor and televised debates followed Sweatshop's productions and communities experienced an unprecedented degree of consciousness-raising through the work (Osment, 1989, xxvii–ixli; Itzin, 1980, 236).

More recent historical and theoretical approaches to alternative theatre recast utopian activist impulses and observe that the politics of theatre do not always or even primarily work directly. Deeny's chapter exemplifies recent questions about what it means to privilege the alternative and campaigning aspects of gay theatre because to do so relies on a 'narrative of exclusion' about what came before that particular political model and fosters a distorting focus on the 1968 generation (Deeny, 2006, 399). In other words, Sweatshop's artistry and attempts at institutionalization matter as much to the gay movement as its agitation and political formulations. Indeed, the degree to which Sweatshop is 'of' 1968 may be more complex than narrated by people like Catherine Itzin. Matthew Jones's reference to Sweatshop in his article 'Funding a Company of Identity', signals the way in which, in its last years, Sweatshop shifted to being positioned as more 'like' Tara Arts than 'like' the explicitly agitprop Red Ladder because of its concern with multifaceted issues concerning community, identity and representation as the mark of its politics and its modes of work in touring, new writing and Theatre in Education (TIE) (Jones, 1997, 370).

In scholarship, specifically regarding gay and feminist theatre (as overlapping and separate modes), Sweatshop receives sustained analysis far beyond the more notational references in alternative theatre overviews. Studies like Lizbeth Goodman's *Feminist Theatres: To Each Her Own* (1993), Sandra Freeman's *Putting Your Daughters on the Stage* (1997), Alan Sinfield's *Out on Stage* (1999) or John Clum's *Acting Gay* (1994) provide close reading and contextual analysis of *Care and Control* (1977), *As Time Goes By* (1977), *Dear Love of Comrades* (1979), *Compromised Immunity* (1986), *More* (1986), *This Island's Mine* (1988) and *Twice Over* (1988) especially. These productions provide critical touchstones and track Sweatshop's negotiation of devising and new-writing models, agitprop and mainstream aesthetics, and shifting theoretical and social preoccupations.

Across the 1980s, Sweatshop increasingly returned to and focused on its new-writing mission, in addition to its specifically gay and feminist commitments. Yet, the company continued to strive, especially through anniversary festivals, and to stimulate new writing from specific identity groups. In 1985, Sweatshop held a tenth-anniversary festival entitled Gay Sweatshop x10 that presented staged readings, writing workshops, performances from visiting artists, networking events and cabarets for three weeks at the Drill Hall, London. The writing workshops focused on different intersections of identity: for instance, race, sexuality, homosexuality, disability and gender. The programme succeeded in its aim of encouraging young writers, such as Jackie Kay, and bringing new plays into production by Sweatshop and other companies. In this way, borrowing from Alan Sinfield's terminology, Sweatshop did 'subcultural work' via 'dissident strategies' (Sinfield, 1999, 296, 330). On a smaller scale, in 1987 at the Ovalhouse, Sweatshop held a 'x12' anniversary festival and incubated *This Island's Mine* and *Twice Over*.

The valorization of Sweatshop's best productions in feminist and gay scholarship sits beside the tendency to treat the company as a victim of funding cuts that possibly reflected anti-homosexual prejudice or at least an attempt to curtail political theatre. However, the main funding problem after 1980, in terms of the company's relationship with grant-making bodies, came from the change in priority of types of companies that began to obtain funding in the 1990s. Companies were increasingly sorted by their focus on new writing, the identity groups they addressed or their formal preoccupation (dance or mime, for example). The way Helen Freshwater omits the company's trajectory after 1991 is particularly revealing of the desire to create the impression that Sweatshop completed a sacrificial journey at the hands of funding bureaucracies because of its politics. Freshwater abruptly ends her narrative about Sweatshop in 1991, as if the company ceased operations forever after *Kitchen Matters* due to Section 28 legislation. In fact, Sweatshop lost funding because the 1986 Local Government Act, to which Section 28 was appended, led to the elimination of the (GLC), one of Sweatshop's largest financial supporters; however, it later received its first round of three-year Arts Council franchise funding for 1992–5. Freshwater also fails to mention the way in which the solo performances and more experimental work Sweatshop pursued between 1992 and 1995 functioned essentially as another type of reaction to suppression and silencing, as the company tried and subsequently failed to reposition itself within funding streams that emphasized it as a gay new-writing company rather than an experimental performance group.

History of Company Development

Baz Kershaw identifies post-war alternative theatre as an 'ideological formation' that became an 'aesthetic movement' and turned into an 'industrial sector' (Kershaw, 2004, 351, 365). Sweatshop experienced each of these modalities in different combinations through three phases of company history. In 1975 and 1976 a group of artists gathered, called together by an advertisement proposing a season of lunchtime plays on gay themes at the Almost Free Theatre, whose initial aim was to 'change the media misrepresentation of homosexuals' and to 'present themes to liberate rather than oppress' (Itzin, 1980, 235). Incubated by Ed Berman's group Interaction, which ran the Almost Free, the project was modelled on the Women's Season of 1973 and came to be called the Homosexual Acts season. The group gathered plays depicting gay male life, some already written, some composed by members of the fledging company, all of which refused homosexual stereotypes. A socialist thread also wove through the company's mission because members' reading of Andrew Hodge's and David Hutter's *With Downcast Gays* (1974) and Richard Hoggart's *The Uses of Literacy* (1957) convinced them of the links between all forms of oppression and the vitality of a working-class position in defending against marginalization. The company name Sweatshop came about in part because, as Itzin reminds her readers, 'a major chapter in the history of political theatre in the seventies' was a 'history of organizational effort', rooted in the 'organization of workers at the grassroots in a Marxist sense' (Itzin, 1980, xiii). Sweatshop understood gay men and women to be oppressed workers in the theatre industry as well as oppressed subjects in the public sphere (GS, n.d., 1/2/1).

Sweatshop followed up the season at the Almost Free with tours of two coming-out plays that engaged the company in direct activism. With both *Mr X* and *Any Woman Can* on tour at the same time, each show's ensemble was self-administered but stayed in general communication with the overall collective. By 1977, core members had applied for an Arts Council project grant, and began setting up sustainable administrative structures for the group as a whole (Osment, 1989, xxix–xxx). The evolution of the company's artistic policies and working methodologies were both focused on becoming viable in the theatre scene while expressing gay political analysis through new work. This well-documented phase of Sweatshop's history most directly concerned the work of undoing self-oppression and wider forms of social bias against homosexuals by reclaiming gay history and addressing contemporary legal issues. After 1980, the company's artistic policy cohered around the development of gay voices and perspectives through new writing and touring. The difference between these phases of the company's work is apparent in the dominant company issues of the time: throughout the late 1970s, there were two difficult points of debate for Sweatshop. These have been well analyzed elsewhere, but concerned whether all the company members and performers needed to be both actually homosexual *and* out, and about the divergence in theatrical experience and political concerns between men and women in the company. The creative methods of this period focused on modes of workshopping, collaborative writing and author-led devising: these supported an authentic mediation of self and a shared authority over the created project.

The company also focused on a set of desiderata: reaching a broad audience while also speaking to its own 'constituency'; developing playwriting skills among gay writers, especially women working in other genres; encouraging young writers, Black and Asian and those with disabilities; putting the company on a secure footing both financially and in terms of artistic quality.

These institutionally focused threads surface in dialogue with the company's politics in the overview of Sweatshop's policy that Noël Greig included with the 1983 application for a project grant to stage *Poppies* that restarted the company after its closure in 1981. Greig put Sweatshop's combination of alterity and institutional organization into context, describing how 'growing out of the Gay and Feminist movements, Gay Sweatshop has always attempted to retain links with that movement and to be a feature of it, while also establishing itself on an equal footing with other professional theatre companies' (GS, 1983, 3/14/3). Greig asserted that *Poppies* 'is in a style that can draw together, in middle-scale auditoria, a broad audience, and relates the sexuality of the characters outwards into the events of the world' (GS, 1983, 3/14/3). Sweatshop sought to legitimize itself through *Poppies* and that meant drawing attention to questions of artistry and audience.

Sweatshop knew this terrain because of the way the devised shows of 1979 and 1980 – *I Like Me Like This* (women's company), *Who Knows?* (a youth project at the Royal Court) and *Blood Green* (mixed company) – met with limited critical success and were judged harshly by Arts Council evaluators. Sweatshop elected to cut short their tour of *Blood Green* because company members themselves were 'unsatisfied with the piece' on an artistic level (ACGB, 1981, 41/19/9). When the show reports came in on *Blood Green*, Gerald Chapman, himself one of Sweatshop's former members, despaired: Sweatshop, he commented 'seems to be isolating itself from the centre of what the Gay experience is in Britain … It should be trying to define this centrality: instead it comes up with an extremely ill-written, largely ill-acted, ill-designed piece of exotica – this show is a disaster and does great disservice to the "cause"' (ACGB, 1980, 41/19/9).

Blood Green was not the only play to receive harsh criticism. In his report on Angela Stewart-Park and Sharon Nassauer's rock musical *I Like Me Like This* on 5 September 1979, Drama Officer Jonathan Lamede rated the script as 'poor' and the performances as 'slack'. Lamede worried particularly that 'this is the first Sweatshop show I've seen which, to me at least, expressed a hatred of heterosexuality' (ACGB, 1979, 41/19/9). Sweatshop's membership also felt something amiss at this point. In the lead-up to *Blood Green*, a proposal circulated among the company to address a lack of continuity in administrative work, establish a stronger relationship between administration and artistic policy, and 'create a programme of work which will, hopefully, reflect consistent artistic and administrative development' (GS, n.d., 1/2/4).

Still, the company could not avoid the elimination of its funding in 1981. In the wake of this it resurrected itself and launched a decade of activity dominated by seeking legibility, influence and credibility as both a touring and as a gay company specializing in new writing. The Arts Council defence of *Poppies* shows that it succeeded. In early 1984, controversy created by school performances of *Poppies* and its alignment with the Campaign for Nuclear Disarmament (CND) caused the Arts Council to assess and defend the company both internally and to Members of Parliament. On 7 February, Jonathan Lamede submitted an internal memo to Secretary General Luke Rittner, giving an overview on the company's background and excellent 'reputation', justifying support for *Poppies* based on the group's 'substantial track record' and on the grounds that the play was 'one of the more interesting and artistically adventurous projects of 1983/84: it took artistic risks of a kind that unfortunately is quite rare nowadays' (ACGB, 1984, 41b).

This memo seems to have been created in response to a letter about Sweatshop from Tory MP Jerry Wiggan to the Arts Council's Chairman William Rees-Mogg, dated 1 February 1984: 'It looks as if this organisation has a very deliberate political objective and is unsuitable for subsidies from public funds. I would be most grateful if you could investigate this and let me have your comments' (ACGB, 1984, 41a). Rees-Mogg responded at length on 29 February, reiterating

Lamede's points and declaring, 'We do not base our funding on the political views expressed in political plays, of which this is plainly one, but on the panel's assessment of dramatic merit' (ACGB, 1984, 41c). This emphasis on Sweatshop's artistic achievement by Lamede, ventriloquized by Rees-Mogg, mark a turning point in discourse about Sweatshop within the Council and demonstrates the legibility of the project.

Following *Poppies*, Sweatshop had very distinct things it wanted to accomplish: these included fostering more women's work, carrying out a multicultural policy and establishing something like a permanent home. The company revised its constitution in 1984, adding a new policy strand about working with disabled people and clarifying the 'directorships', – the two people in the company designated by the Arts Council as having ultimate financial responsibility for it. The company became a dramaturgical force: its work during this period consisted of play readings (both staged and developmental), the commissioning of writers, offering writing workshops, staging festivals of new works such as on their tenth and twelfth anniversaries and touring full productions. The company began to wonder what it would mean to have a permanent relationship with a venue such as the Albany (GS, 1986, 1/2/4b). At that moment, Sweatshop might have been on its way to following the trajectory Paines Plough took in the 1990s under Anna Furse, Penny Ciniewicz and Vicky Featherstone, aiming to become a centre for developing and launching new writers, with an added emphasis on gay subjectivity. But, as the company approached its fifteenth anniversary, a new negotiation of its mission took form.

In summary, the members of Sweatshop always thought that they were on the way to creating an established theatre company. However, by the time Lois Weaver and James Neale-Kennerly accepted their appointments as joint Artistic Directors in 1992, the 'edifice' of Sweatshop felt like something they had to struggle with. Lois Weaver said that by then she felt that they were asked to work 'very much within a middle class idea of theatre and what a theatre was meant to be' (Weaver, 2000). Weaver and Neale-Kennerly presided over Sweatshop's final phase of work, which had contradictory aims: on the one hand, there was an artistic push to 'radicalize' the company into the realm of queer performance. On the other, there was a mandate to preserve what had been gained, and to focus on and consolidate the mission to tour new plays.

Sweatshop's working methods during its last five years varied widely because of these different aims: the company commissioned narrative-based plays, staged them and toured them, while some experimental pieces were devised, like *The Hand* (1995) or *In Your Face* (1994). Weaver ran vibrant 'Queer School' classes, development programmes, and networking opportunities; the company staged nights of solo performances (*One Night Stands* in 1992; *It's Not Unusual* in 1994) and performance art (*Club Deviance* at the Almeida in 1997) and hosted readings by Chloe Poems and Weaver with her Split Britches collaborator Peggy Shaw. As Sweatshop became less writer-centred, it experienced mixed reactions from its board of directors and the Sweatshop as it entered a new political conversation changed by queer theory. In 1994, the company admitted that these divergent policies were going to pull them apart. Between 1988 and 1994, Sweatshop's new-writing mission demonstrated the convergence of alternative and mainstream goals until the tension of what Roberts calls being 'between gay and queer' became too acute and Weaver in particular felt the company could no longer serve these two different policy strands (Roberts, 2000, 178; Case, 2000, 257–60). Sweatshop was neither fully radical nor fully established, or, to put it positively, the company was both radical and established and felt all the discomforts of both positions. Sweatshop was 'of' 1975, 1978 and 1984 much more than the '1968' described by Catherine Itzin. The company's notion of politics concerned representation far more than revolution and Osment's company history charts how its members believed in expressing themselves from the heart by means of passionate, reconciliatory public discourse.

Funding and Company Structure

Sweatshop never had an official artistic director prior to the appointments of Lois Weaver and James Neale-Kennerly in 1992. Volunteer management committees (sometimes called Administration) accompanied by paid part-time administrators ran the company and membership determined policy. Originally, the company was run as a collective during its first two years. Sweatshop also conducted its business by having regular company meetings with the people in its shows (Osment, 1989, lv). By 1980, this structure presented problems. Minutes from a 1980 meeting contain a proposal authored by Greig, Paul Hines, Philip Timmins and Gean Wilton, who argued that project being conceived and executed on an *ad hoc* basis did not create a true company.

Instead, they proposed 'the formation of a mixed Artistic Collective, comprising of 5 Men and 5 Women'. The proposal stipulates that the Artistic Collective needed a lifespan of at least one year for members to 'express and demonstrate long-term commitment to the company' (GS, n.d., 1/2/4). The proposal clarified that the Artistic Collective would only be paid directly for work on specific shows, since Sweatshop did not have funding for management salaries at any point prior to 1992. The goal was for the Artistic Collective to have responsibility for both artistic and administrative policy in order to guide a consistent 'programme', where initial directions would be set by them and carried out by the general membership. Final decisions about policy would also rest with the Artistic Collective. Year by year, the Artistic Collective would be reconstituted, retaining half its membership while bringing in a new cohort of five, for continuity. This proposal did not see implementation because of the closure in 1981, but it broadly set out the way in which Sweatshop was to organize itself after 1983, despite a struggle to achieve a 50:50 balance between the sexes.

Prior to 1981, Sweatshop had received annual support from the Arts Council of an amount that varied from modest up to a maximum of £31,000.[1] They also relied on in-kind support and small grants from other groups. When the *Poppies* project grant allowed Sweatshop to reconstitute itself, Greig and Timmins were listed as Directors of the company for Arts Council purposes. Across 1983–4, Sweatshop received £13,000 from the Arts Council. In the wake of *Poppies*, Sweatshop received project grants from the Arts Council for specific tours, and leveraged its new and belated understanding of funding opportunities from the Greater London Council and other local and regional arts organizations to support other projects (Osment, 1989, liv).

A management committee emerged, made up of Greig, Timmins, Kate Owen and administrator Martin Humphries, with Philip Osment joining later. The committee then agonized about its gender imbalance and as a result commissioned Sue Frumin to write an all-female play and asked Tierl Thompson (who had been working with the Women's Theatre Group) to join the management committee and administer the tour of Frumin's show, *Raising the Wreck* (Osment, 1989, lv–lvi). Next, the management committee conceived the idea of the company's x10 festival and appointed a Festival Committee of eight people (the management committee plus Bernardine Evaristo, co-founder of The Theatre of Black Women, and Diane Biondo, an American writer and founder of the theatre group No Boundaries). The x10 Festival programme received financial support in the form of a guarantee against loss from the Greater London Arts Association and funding from Shape, a charity funded by various sources that focus on access to the arts for disabled people, including lesbian and gay writers with disabilities (GS, 1985, 3/17/2/1/3).

Between Osment's narrative and archived company meeting minutes, key figures in each period of the company's history emerge. By the late 1970s, the men's company was controlled by Griffiths, Greig and Sweatshop's first paid administrator David Thompson, while the women's company coalesced around the leadership of Kate Crutchley, Julie Parker and Nancy Diuguid. When the separate men's and women's companies dissolved, Greig, Diuguid, Philip Timmins, Stephanie Pugsley, Sharon Nassauer, Angela Stewart-Park, Jill Posener and new administrator John Hoyland formed what Osment calls a 'new nucleus', starting in 1978 (Osment, 1989, xlii). Gean Wilton replaced Hoyland in 1980 and together he and Greig handled things when the company went into its hiatus. Martin Humphries was the administrator who oversaw Sweatshop from *Poppies* to the x12 Festival. Suad El-Amin followed and stayed through 1991. Later came Mark Ball, then Rose Sharp (GS, 1992, 1/2/7).

After 1985, Greig began to step back from the management committee and took work in Sheffield, moving to a position at the Theatre Centre in 1987. Owen and Osment were the backbone of the committee through the late 1980s. Timmins and Osment had a disagreement in 1986, which caused Timmins to post his resignation letter to company management on 11 April 1986 (GS, 1986, 1/2/4a.). By 1987, Osment and Owen were both ready to leave, and their resignations, along with Tieri Thompson's, became official in 1988. The company recruited leadership from the x10 and x12 participant pool, inducting Cordelia Ditton, David Benedict, Richard Sandells and Carole Woddis to the Management Committee (GS, 1988, 1/2/5; GS, 1989, 1/2/5c). The meeting minutes throughout 1988 show that terminology begins to shift as the Management Committee gave way to Artistic Directors. The playwright Bryony Lavery passed through the management structure between 1989 and 1991 as organizer of a never-to-be-realized 'women's project' for 1990; instead, she wrote *Kitchen Matters,* or *The Guinness Book of Lesbians* as it was known in its early stages, for the company (GS, 1989. 1/2/5g; Aston, 2003, 100).

At the end of 1989, Sweatshop faced a challenge that proved unique in its history of funding. The new patronage scheme Pals of Sweatshop

(POSH) had been running for a year and a half (Woddis, 1987, 10). The company also won a 1988 Charrington London Fringe Special Award for 'continuing excellence in an adverse social climate' (GS, 1989, 1/2/5d). Methuen agreed to publish the company history and collection of plays that Osment proposed (GS, 1989, 1/2/5a). Most importantly, the Arts Council reached out and indicated unprecedented approval, inviting Sweatshop to apply for a cycle of three-year funding for 1990–93. However, the company couldn't make the tight proposal deadline because things were imploding with the production of *Paradise Now and Then* Greig's script in celebration of the twentieth anniversary of the Stonewall riots, and Sweatshop's fifteenth anniversary.

In retrospect, Greig may well have been the most remarkable dramaturg and visionary of Sweatshop's history – the company's most productive years, from 1977–87, came during his tenure. He was able to mentor artists in the company at all levels, place the right directors with compelling pieces of work and create a strong group dynamic. His playwriting set the company's agenda on more than one occasion (*As Time Goes By, Dear Love of Comrades, Poppies*). But *Paradise Now and Then* laboured under crossed stars. The originally contracted director (Annie Castledine) hated the script, David Benedict vied to direct it, and the ambitious musical production did not have enough resources and was poorly reviewed (GS, 1989, 1/2/5/f). This was exactly the type of show that elicited jaded commentary about old-fashioned alternative theatre, with its 'right-on' politics that now looked tiresome on the cusp of the 1990s (Lavender, 1989 1356; Caplan, 1989, 1356; Hiley, 1989, 1506). Shortly thereafter Woddis resigned from the management committee and Sweatshop's funding from the Arts Council was put in doubt.

In fact, throughout 1989, Sweatshop faced huge external pressures because of paradoxes surrounding its funding and fears stemming from the passage of Section 28. How could a company in one moment be asked to apply for a guaranteed cycle of franchise funding and in the same moment be threatened with the complete elimination of its funds? The answer lies partly in the way Sweatshop found support in the 1980s by overlapping Arts Council support with grants from the GLC and Regional Arts Authorities (RAAs) when on tour. The abolition of the GLC in 1986 choked off this funding. Then in 1988 Section 28 was passed and this prohibited local authorities providing money for the promotion of homosexuality. This included teaching about the acceptance of homosexuality or any 'pretended' family relationship and chilled the climate for the local funding bodies that remained (Freshwater, 2009, 107–9). The rest of the answer comes from the changes in funding categories employed by the Arts Council. Because of its work as a new-writing company, Sweatshop had legitimated itself with the Arts Council and received an invitation to apply for revenue funding. But because of the bruising evaluation received by *Paradise Now and Then*, Sweatshop's status as a leading *gay* company took a hit. Bryony Lavery noted in an interview with Lizbeth Goodman and Jane DeGay that *Kitchen Matters* was written in the wake of the Art's Council's 'attempt to close down Gay Sweatshop' because 'there were other groups doing gay work' (Goodman, 1996, 40). The company became embroiled in a type of stature paradox: their achievements in fostering new writing by gay artists made them important, but their treatment of gay themes made them old hat.

In 'Funding a "Company of Identity"' Matthew Jones, administrator for Tara Arts, identifies a 'classic funding pattern' for groups he compares to Tara such as Sweatshop, Women's Theatre Group (WTG) and The Black Theatre Cooperative (Jones, 1997, 370). Jones calls the three-year franchise funding from the Arts Council the 'final phase' of a developmental process that turns on the receipt of revenue funding that demonstrated 'the funder's willingness to recognize the organization' not just the 'value of any individual project' (Jones, 1997, 370). Sweatshop's 'developmental moment' came very late in its history and skipped over revenue funding entirely. For Sweatshop, revenue funding was never secured, even after its identity as a gay organization had been recognized. Moreover, the company's vicissitudes meant it did not have a record of three continuous years of project funding that would automatically make it into a franchise client. In the space between Section 28 and the invitation to apply for a franchise, Sweatshop rallied even as it suffered from lack of funds: it called an open meeting about the company's future in March 1990. The meeting was meant to mobilize public support and help to make the case that a gay company was still needed: Ian McKellan's high-profile presence as a patron of the company and his attendance at the meeting carried weight (GS, 1990, 1/2/6/2).

Kitchen Matters opened at the Royal Court's Theatre Upstairs on 6 November 1990, with its run entirely sold out (Benedict, 1994). The reviews all declared that this would be Sweatshop's last production (Kingston, 1990, 1498). However, on the strength of *Kitchen Matters*, the Arts Council awarded project funds for a tour of x10 Festival alumnus Carl Miller's *The Last Enemy* in 1991 and Sweatshop was awarded a franchise for 1992–5 (Goodman, 1993, 80). Ian Brown,

Robert Brannen and Douglas Brown's analysis of the funding of touring franchises after 1986 notes that until 1988 there was not a separate 'touring franchise'. In 1988, the instatement of a new system meant that '22 middle- and small-scale touring companies then receiving revenue funding were placed on staggered three-year franchises' (Brown et al., 2000, 381). Along with Actors Cabal, Black Mime Theatre, Double Edge, Gloria and Kaboodle, Sweatshop became one of six new companies taken on in 1991–2, and received £116,000 for its operations. Tables in an article that showed categories of touring theatres supported by the Arts Council didn't contain a line for 'gay' companies, although it included black, disability, experimental and women's groups (Brown et al., 2000, 383–4). The Arts Council's invitation to apply for a touring franchise back in 1989 signalled a readiness to take Sweatshop on as a gay, new-writing company, but it took until 1991 for all the pieces to fall into place.

In June 1991, the company began creating a 'new and improved Gay Sweatshop': one with artistic directors, a board of directors, official job descriptions and new office space (GS, 1991, 1/2/7). The desire to affirm both a male and female presence in leadership brought about the structure of joint artistic directors. This also allowed the company to reach out to a prominent figure like Lois Weaver. Because each appointment was technically a job-share, she would be free for part of each year to work in America, teach and create her own work. The company moved into gear, thinking about sponsorship and different projects: Ewan Marshall of Graeae reached out to the company about a co-production and the group hoped to connect with Bette Bourne, a leading drag artist and activist who performed with Hot Peaches and founded the Bloolips performance troupe, to develop some crossover projects between the groups (GS, 1992, 1/2/7).

Sweatshop made every effort to look and function like a high-level established professional company, even to the point, in August 1994, of sending three board members on a training session to learn how to seek private funds, only to have them conclude, in typical institutional fashion, that an outside specialist would have to be hired (GS, 1994, 1/2/8a). However, by 1994, Weaver's work in particular was judged to be both of insufficient quality and out of keeping for the type of leading, new-writing company Sweatshop was supposed to be. Weaver countered that Sweatshop was really a small-scale, experimental touring company; she perceived that Sweatshop's Board and the Arts Council saw Sweatshop as a middle-scale 'mainstream, narrative based' touring company and she wanted to dispel that thought (Weaver, 2000; GS,

1995, 1/2/9). Overall, disparity between the small scope of Sweatshop's work and the size of their audiences – which were usually under 300 – and a larger sense of their reputation and influence produced confusion as to whether the company was small- or middle-scale, established or alternative.

The Brown/Brannen narrative about funding decisions affirms Sweatshop's position as a new-writing company in the Arts Council's mind and specifies the reason why the company lost franchise funding in 1995 as the result of 'failure to produce as a result of conflict in the company which arose between those who wished to maintain the company's long term focus on new writing' and those pushing towards performance art (Brown et al., 2000, 385). In 1996 James Neale-Kennerly announced his resignation as Artistic Director and Arts Council England sent a letter that gave Sweatshop a year's notice to heed its recommendations: integrate the Queer School and new-writing activities, market its programme coherently and focus on strategic development (GS, 1996, 1/2/9). After two years of revenue funding in 1996 and 1997 to allow Sweatshop, as Weaver put it, to 'get their act together', all funding was withdrawn: the company no longer fitted the category under which it had legitimated itself (Weaver, 2000). Mel Kenyon summarized the situation by declaring that it was 'clear that they are not happy with the company in its present incarnation', but wanted 'the idea of Sweatshop as a concept … to survive'. This was a concept about new writing from a gay perspective, with a strong institutional profile, and not one about experimental form and community politics (GS, 1996, 1/2/9). Sweatshop, which up to then had been able to address both those sets of concerns, closed when it had to choose between them.

Key Work and its Impact

Surveying the nature of political theatre in the early 1990s, Brannen and Brown proposed that a new kind of countercultural theatre emerged. Theatres were no longer 'beating a single drum of opposition' driven by 'intellectual debate from the broad left of the sixties and seventies' (Brown et al., 2000, 385). The authors contend that companies 'appeared to be freed from single-issue politics and were able to explore a diversity of issues important to them and their audiences' (Brown et al., 2000, 385). Here, they cite the examples of Black Mime Theatre as a black company presenting work about women's issues and Graeae as a disability company dealing with gay themes (Brown et al., 2000, 385). If alternative theatres were ever beating a unified political drum, which is doubtful, Sweatshop never fitted this mould. Sweatshop propelled the creation of *More* seven years before the Graeae piece Brown cites that identified the relationship between disability and homosexuality in terms of both style and content. Maro Green and Caroline Griffin's piece received scholarly attention precisely because of its profound sense of intersectionality around disability and homosexuality and its sophisticated interweaving of theatrical idioms of style and genre, in both its text and performance conventions (Goodman, 1993, 109–13). Indeed, intersectionality characterized Sweatshop's work all along, which is why its coming-out plays feel inadequate when over-empha-sized as signatures of the company. *Mr X* and *Any Woman Can* distill a complex understanding of the personal and the political into a confrontational style that Aleks Sierz recognizes as an early precursor of in-yer-face aesthetics (Sierz, 2001, 25). But Sweatshop's aesthetic goal was never to be visceral *per se* – the goal was dialogue. This is why *As Time Goes By*, *Care and Control* and *Dear Love of Comrades* are such critical touchstones. These plays opened dialogue that still define the terms of gay theatre histories.

Likewise, *Compromised Immunity* constitutes one of the first home-grown British AIDS plays. In 1985, Sweatshop caught a theatrical moment exactly. The tenth-anniversary festival provided the launching pad for *Compromised Immunity*, prior to the London opening of Larry Kramer's *The Normal Heart* (1985), the play that launched activism about the AIDS epidemic in the US. While *Compromised Immunity* received its readings at the x10 Festival, American import *Torch Song Trilogy* (1978–81), by Harvey Fierstein, and The Bush's production of Manuel Puig's *Kiss of the Spider Woman* (1985) were playing in the West End, showing the journey to mainstream visibility for gay plays about the costs of being publicly identified as homosexual. In distinction, Sweatshop's project insisted on dialogue about the newest, most pressing issue for the gay male community with a play that humanized the medical issues of AIDS and put caring relationships at its centre, especially those between medical personnel and patients. Less confron-tational than *The Normal Heart* and less a state-of-the-nation play than Tony Kushner's later *Angels in America: Millennium Approaches* and *Perestroika* (1991), *Compromised Immunity* followed the trajectory of British alternative and community theatre by providing a space for artists and audiences to connect while confronting massive social and personal changes taking place in the world.

Sweatshop fought hard to bring *Compromised Immunity* to full production and take it on tour around Britain. After a London run that received strong show reports from ACGB reviewers Jonathan Lamede and Nick Worral, Philip Osment submitted a proposal for an Arts Council-funded tour in January 1987, citing the 'huge demand to see it outside London' and the way the play 'confronts the prejudice and hysteria around the disease in an accessible way' (ACGB, 1987, 41/19/9). Drama Panel Chairman Tony Church wrote to Osment encouraging the tour, noting, 'It is the first play I have seen about AIDS that dared to be both tough and funny at the same time', opining that the 'central performance was fascinating: funny and dangerous, as good acting should be', and declaring that 'I think it is important that this play should be seen in as many areas and types of community as possible' (ACGB, 1986, 41d). Bob Crossman, the newly out gay mayor of Islington Borough Council, wrote a letter supporting the tour and expressing how as 'a governor of a large secondary school and someone who is involved in adult education, I would see this play as a very important experience for people in their late teens and early adulthood as this is the group at the greatest risk from further spreading the aids virus' (ACGB, 1986, 41e). Theatre scholar Paul Heritage also argued that the show 'must not remain confined to the fringes of the London Theatreworld. The anger, the humour, and the emotion of this production will work on audiences across the country, providing the essential theatrical counterpart to the present education campaign [that the government is now pursuing]' (ACGB, 1986, 41c). In fact, the play toured for almost two years and brought Sweatshop to a wider general audience in venues it had not visited before, sometimes for week-long runs. The audience was often populated by nursing professionals (Osment, 1989, lx).

Sweatshop periodically returned to this subject until its closure. Productions included Carl Miller's *The Last Enemy*, which situated AIDS as one of many deathly enemies a group of friends face as they age and Malcolm Sutherland's 1994 adaptation of Dale Peck's novel *Fucking Martin*, with its story of gay rites of passage, its presentation of a long demise due to AIDS and its aggressive title earning it a place in that year's debate about whether a 'plague of pink plays' (Shulman, 1994) were taking over British theatre. This was also the theme of Osment's *The Undertaking*, which unites a group of friends at a funeral on the Irish coast, yet none of these latter-day AIDS plays made a statement of immediacy like *Compromised Immunity*.

In addition to the coming-out plays, Sweatshop's long-term theatrical and political project was realized through its anniversary festivals in 1985 and 1987 and in the full productions of *Compromised Immunity*, *This Island's Mine* and *Twice Over* that came out of those celebrations. Osment and Jackie Kay initially wrote their plays for other venues, but Sweatshop nurtured the shows in the x12 festival at the Ovalhouse. Full productions reached the stage in 1988 as the effects of Section 28 became clear. Because of the intersectionality in these works, the way they replied to Section 28 became distinctively eloquent. Osment's play imagines Britain, 'this island', in the title's borrowed phrase from Shakespeare's *The Tempest*, as a nation of immigrants, refugees and others who have been internally exiled. These included Jewish women who came to England during the Second World War, black British artists and gay men of different generations who all formed a community as important as any heritage vision of the past. Kay's play, *Twice Over* (1987–8) eviscerated anxiety about 'pretended families' in a humanistic way by making Cora and Maeve's interracial lesbian romance exactly the family history that allowed a young woman to really understand herself and her world. With these beautifully written plays, Sweatshop strengthened when other companies weakened. Compare, for instance, Joint Stock's shows of 1987 and 1988. On a shoestring budget after losing revenue funding, Joint Stock also strove to present multiracial and politically motivated shows during this hard period in the late 1980s. *A Child in the Heart* and *Promised Land*, both by Karim Alrawi and both produced in 1988, made nowhere near the impact of *This Island's Mine* and *Twice Over* – in terms of reviews, scholarship and general commentary.

In many ways, Bryony Lavery's *Kitchen Matters* should be considered the paradigmatic Sweatshop piece. This play exemplifies Sweatshop's chaotic way of working in the moment and irrepressible desire to upend the mainstream (or what Lavery's main character calls 'upstream') on its end. In a *City Limits* review of *Kitchen Matters*, Antonia Denford describes the piece as both a 'swansong and a knees-up' (Denford, 1991, 1498). Its anarchic energy connects to the type of cabaret Sweatshop employed to close the 1985 x10 festival, when it gathered The Communards, Janice Perry, Simon Fanshawe, The Insinuendos and Hard Corps to party at the Drill Hall. Lavery's play ravages the greats of dramatic literature, forming them into a gleeful pastiche of Euripides, Noël Coward, Alan Ayckbourn, Pirandello and more. She also acutely skewers social types – gay and straight alike. This side of Sweatshop mattered as much as its 'serious' work. The success of Lavery's play caused Jeremy Kingston to look back to Sweatshop's history and reflect in *The Times* that 'strong doubts exist that a work as subtle as the anti-war *Poppies* could now be mounted by anyone else' (Kingston, 1990, 1498). *Kitchen Matters* also presages Sweatshop's queer turn in the 1990s: its mode makes space for *Stupid Cupid* (1993), *Threesome* (1993) and *In Your Face* (1994), plays that received quite positive reviews and, like *Kitchen Matters*, demonstrated a rapprochement between gay and lesbian camp sensibilities, solo performance, drag acts and the British push for new writing. Sweatshop's work with Lavery, Phil Wilmot (*Stupid Cupid*) and with Phyllis Nagy, Claire Dowie and David Greenspan (*Threesome*) suggest there was a sophisticated comic and socially critical path to be charted for Sweatshop 'between gay and queer' that used the postmodern dramaturgical techniques and fractured language that came to prominence in the 1990s. It is apposite that as Sierz's 'in-yer-face' wave of British playwriting emerged, Weaver was devising a piece about gay and lesbian 'superheroes of the post-punk queerzine scene' with the title *In Your Face*. In the hope of ripping open dilemmas about commodifying queer sexuality for a heterosexual audience in order to obtain greater visibility within wider culture, Weaver wanted to explode more formalized theatrical structures. *In Your Face* was created by a playwright, a choreographer and six artists who came from different modes of performance. These included a drag artist, a performance poet, a visual artist and a cartoonist (Cornwell, 1994).

Critical Reception

Critical reception of Sweatshop follows a pattern of opinions that improved in retrospect, so that often a successful play, like *Poppies*, would first receive a wide range of critiques and then several years later surface in a review as a key example of the company's achievement. A similar scenario occurred with Kingston's of *Kitchen Matters*. Sweatshop did not polarize critics as much as seep into their consciousness, winning them over time with the thrust of their artistic and social dialogues. Sweatshop collected several notable supporters among the regular newspaper reviewers during the 1980s and 1990s, including Jim Hiley, Lyn Gardner and Nicholas de Jongh. Writing for *City Limits* and other gay-focused publications, Hiley critiqued Sweatshop for its less-polished work, but his voice consistently affirmed the company's importance. Hiley organized a National Theatre platform event that accompanied the release of *Gay Sweatshop: Four Plays and a Company* in 1989. He tried to secure Richard Eyre's introduction for the proceedings, but at the event at the Lyttelton on 7 July, Ian McKellan did the honours (GS, 1989, 1/2/5e). Throughout the 1980s, Gardner placed Sweatshop's work in context with the history of the 1970s and ongoing developments in the alternative scene.

As an out-gay reviewer in the mainstream press, Nicholas de Jongh positioned himself in relation to Sweatshop in a more prickly way. He wrote consistently about the company, reviewing their shows and tracking them in his book about homosexuality on stage, *Not in Front of the Audience*. However, his reviews regularly found the company lacking in attention to dramatic structure and he seemed constantly on-guard against potentially simplistic political messages. His review of *Poppies* exhibits these characteristics most clearly (de Jongh, 1984, 103). Around *This Island's Mine*, however, de Jongh experienced a turning point. Overall, the reviews for this show consistently expressed preemptive concern about it being a prime site for an 'angry or didactic stance', only to be surprised by the complexity of the social world presented in the play. De Jongh, unlike many other reviewers for this show, even embraced Osment's deconstructive, story-telling drama-turgy in the piece – structures Osment developed via his time with Mike Alfreds and Shared Experience. For de Jongh to conclude that the 'kaleidoscopic' structure of the piece began to 'shimmer and attract' and that it allowed the 'political, social, and emotional points' to strike home marks an opening up of more restricted views about dramatic writing and political theatre (de Jongh, 1988, 236).

A younger reviewer, Lydia Conway, in *What's On*, tracked the same journey with *This Island's Mine*, but in more effusive tones: 'When I went to Gay Sweatshop's new play', she opened, 'I was all ready to defend my heterosexual stand, steel myself against right-on confessionals and laugh nervously at jokes I was not party to.' But then she is transformed: 'What a breath of inspiration this hilarious play proved to be. Tears of laughter ran streaming down my face from line one.' Conway asserts that Osment successfully fused *The Tempest* with a gay liberation theme, 'bringing the art of lyrical storytelling back to the stage'. Her final line emphasizes 'it is *so* funny' (Conway, 1988, 236). Conway's explicit narration of late 1980s expectations and prejudices about political theatre and gay politics demonstrates the forces at work in mainstream critical reception of Sweatshop and also explains why this company needed support from the gay press and from gay and feminist scholars. Management committee members Woddis and Benedict also did a fair amount of work as journalists, so they themselves assured that Sweatshop continued to receive attention.

Conclusion

In her assessment of Sweatshop, Lizbeth Goodman cites its most important achievement as being 'its continued viability across the 1980s and into the 1990s' (Goodman, 1993, 80). Viability relates to visibility and Sweatshop strove to stay visible, even taking on the politics of this with *In Your Face*, which questioned how much power derived from mainstream recognition. For example, is receiving attention from fashion magazines worth it? Following Peggy Phelan's argument in *Unmarked: The Politics of Performance* (1993), theatre scholars have become more sensitive to the idea that visibility is not the same thing as liberation. I argue instead that Sweatshop's greatest legacy is the path it opened for artists to be able to speak to audiences in a project of mutual liberation. This was Drew Griffith's fundamental intention for the company, and the ideal around which Greig, Osment, and Kate Owen built Sweatshop in their decade, from 1978 to 1988. Osment, the only company member to work with the group across a full 20 years, and who occupied the roles of actor, director, administrator, playwright, historian and conscience of the company, narrates that this was a project of love. His title for the company's history is *Finding Room on the Agenda for Love*. The effects of love create a legacy in a wide arena, nicely encapsulated by the trajectory of Carl Miller, author of *The Last Enemy*. Miller submitted a play to Sweatshop for the x10 Festival while he was still at university and it was given a reading. His festival programme biography paints a portrait of him at that moment: 'Carl Miller is twenty years old, and after coming out at school, began dividing his time there between studying for his 'A' levels and discovering politics, theatre, and sex; roughly – he says – in that order (GS, 1985, 3/17/2/1/3). After *The Last Enemy*, while developing his career as a playwright, Miller published a historical study of gay theatre, *Stages of Desire: Gay Theatre's Hidden History*, in 1996. Between 1997 and 1999, Miller, like early Sweatshop member Gerald Chapman before him, ran the Royal Court Young People's programme. After that, he became literary manager for the Unicorn Theatre, which has been his home-base since 2002 across numerous productions and commissions at theatres from Watford to the National. In Miller, Sweatshop fostered a theatre artist able to build a career, both inside and outside of gay companies, in a way that Sweatshop's founding members dreamt about.

Sweatshop as an institution never moved fully from the fringe into the mainstream, but its profile did. The company's artistry and work guaranteed that both fringe and mainstream theatre included a greater range of approaches to homosexuality, storytelling and social dialogue. The passing of the revolution-focused model of historiography and theatrical activism followed by Itzin allows us to see what Sweatshop really achieved: good shows, advocacy for new writing, formal experimentation, artistic homebuilding, dramaturgical development, support for social change, sustained organization, individual transformation and community building. Sweatshop pioneered and endured; it created both success and protest; it made insightful work in several different modes across three distinct decades, all the while achieving greater liberty for gay and lesbian artists and a fuller cultural consideration of the human dynamics of desire, identity, gender, community and love.

Chapter 5

THÉÂTRE DE COMPLICITÉ

Michael Fry

Introduction

Of all the companies discussed in this volume, Théâtre de Complicité (the name was officially abbreviated to Complicite in 2000, the French accents having waned early on) can legitimately lay claim to moving swiftly and conspicuously from fringe to well-acknowledged mainstream within just five years over a similar number of productions.

Neither expressly committed to touring nor new writing, the four-strong company's initial vision was an intuitive – later unashamedly articulated – reaction against the conformist, text-based theatre they perceived as preponderant in Britain at the time and a proselytizing of their own more European methods. From the outset Théâtre de Complicité's work was distinctive, idiosyncratic and less quantifiable than many of its peers and predecessors (one of the reasons why the über-categorizing Arts Council was initially tentative in its support). While not obsessively physical in approach, the work displayed impressive athleticism and clowning; while not overtly political or offering the polemics of many fringe companies during the 1970s, the early productions often reflected an inherent critique of the economic and social pressures of the early Thatcher years (particularly the 1985 Perrier Award-winning *More Bigger Snacks Now*); while not directly concerned with gender politics, the performers switched effortlessly between the sexes in their characterizations, and the generic challenges for both men and women formed a significant part of the subject matter for *Put It On Your Head* (1983), *Please, Please, Please* (1986) and *Anything for a Quiet Life* (1987); while their starting point was never the text, the dialogue that emerged was consistently droll, sharp and poignant. Most paradoxically, although many of the actors were European, the early plays were principally about the obsessions of the British.

The Complicite company of today is largely unrecognizable from the impulsive and madcap work of the 1980s. Recent large-scale productions have a more reflective tone with a focus on innovative technology to support the narrative. But innovation has always been a key to the company's *raison d'être*. Simon McBurney, the company's enduring Artistic Director, has consistently maintained that each production need have no relevance to a previous one, in terms of impetus and genesis, and that his guiding principle over the past 30 years has always been 'to create whatever he feels he is not seeing on Britain's stages' (Costa, 2010, n.p).

Early Background and Genesis

With a distinctive genesis in Paris, Théâtre de Complicité was founded in 1983 by four very different creative artists: Annabel Arden and Simon McBurney, both Cambridge educated, the Italian Marcello Magni, who had studied clowning (and mathematics) and Fiona Gordon, an Australian/Canadian actor.[1] McBurney, Magni and Gordon had taken the two-year training programme at Jacques Lecoq's eponymous school, and all four took evening classes with Monika Pagneux and Philippe Gaulier, both of whom had originally taught at Lecoq and who had similar (though not identical) views on training and performance.

Although Arden and McBurney seem to have articulated the conception of the company and Arden, in particular, propelled it organizationally in its first years, it was McBurney and Magni's paired work in Lecoq's *auto-cours* (weekly semi-prepared improvisations, based on a 'provocation' given by Lecoq) that seems to have been the spur for its foundation. Josef Houben, who joined Complicite for its second production and who was also a Lecoq contemporary, noted that their scenes were invariably the funniest. 'They weren't afraid. They weren't precious. There was some chemistry at work, a meeting of minds' (Lane, 2005, n.p).

Théâtre de Complicité's early marketing refers to slightly different derivations depending on who was writing it. The first programme notes (written by Arden) affirm that 'The Company consists of four very individual performers whose common points of reference include: the work of Philippe Gaulier and Monika Pagneux in Paris; an interest in movement-based theatre; creation of their own work and performing in various spaces and to different people' (ACGB, 1984a, 41/45 2). The brochure for the accompanying workshops (written by McBurney) asserts that:

> the work of Théâtre de Complicité has its roots in the shared training of its members at the Jacques Lecoq School in Paris. The Lecoq approach begins with the assumption that the individual performer is an author of the work, not a cipher through which the writer or director expresses his or her ideas. All the work is based on observation and the study of reality and the contributions the performers make are the source material of the subsequent work, not something outside or additional to it. (Complicite archives, 1984[2])

There is palpable validity, rather than contradiction, in both statements, but McBurney's description is a particularly lucid summary of Lecoq's fundamental influence on the company.

L'Ecole Jacques Lecoq is unique and influential. Founded in 1956, it has had a profound impact not only on many of Complicite's actors over the years, but also on such significant and eclectic theatre makers as Ariane Mnouchkine, Dario Fo, Steven Berkoff, Luc Bondy and Julie Taymor. Indeed, the incremental propensity in late-twentieth-century theatre to incorporate a more self-conscious use of movement to communicate story and character seems indirectly to owe much to the school. Lecoq placidly challenged the (Western) performer's reliance on psychological naturalism with its focus on text – and subtext – and with scant regard to physical embodiment.

Funding and Company Structure

Complicite's rise to prominence was comparatively fleet, but it was by no means straightforward. The company received very little financial support during its first few years, and the actors often worked unsalaried, deriving a minimal income from workshops in schools and community centres. 'We will be living on social security, and rehearsing out of London to save money on housing and rehearsal space as well as in many other ways', they wrote to the Arts Council in a largely fruitless 1984 grant application, for which they were awarded £1,500 (ACGB, 1984c, 34/155/1). Although early productions received mostly favourable and sometimes rapturous press reviews, funding continued to be negligible. For pragmatic rather than philosophical reasons, Complicite chose to ally itself with other emerging 'mime' companies, despite an early insistence that mime was precisely not what they were advocating – 'I have never done mime in my life', claims McBurney (Fry, 2013a). The Arts Council had a small mime sub-committee on the Dance Panel and the company calculated that it stood a better chance of funding by identifying itself as a dance/mime troupe than a theatre group. In interview, Arden acknowledged that 'we accepted mime because that's what there was, and because the wonderful Sue [Hoyle] at Dance Umbrella and Joe Seelig of the mime festival were really supportive of us' (Fry, 2013b). The two companies with whom Complicite particularly aligned were Trickster and Trestle, who were treading similar paths in what is now retrospectively referred to as physical theatre. Whereas Moving Picture Mime Show, the leading company of the 1980s 'mime' theatre groups – in terms of early repute and ACGB support – did indeed perform a rejuvenated rendering of the art form, Complicite, Trickster and Trestle were mime companies in only the very loose sense that they used little or no text. Trickster and Trestle tended to employ dancers or movement practitioners; Trestle worked entirely in masks and Trickster strutted a range of startling technical skills and comparatively complicated sets. Complicite, however, used actors who might have initially been cast for their nimbleness, but who had a more eclectic range of performance styles – including speech. 'Complicite trod more dangerous ground than its mime colleagues', wrote Kenneth Rae, 'because it had no visual gimmicks: the emphasis was wholly on the actors playing together as an ensemble with minimal scenery and props' (Rae, 1994, 37).

The combined cluster of Trestle, Trickster and Théâtre de Complicité was an assertive and rallying force. In one of many jointly signed letters to the Arts Council they quoted figures pointing out that the total budget for mime in 1984–5 was £80,362, of which £20,000 went to the International Mime Festival and £33,598 to Moving Picture Mime Show. Trestle received an annual grant of £2,500, Trickster £10,000 and Complicite £8,000. Piquant comparisons were made with equivalent companies funded by the Drama department, particularly Paines Plough (£65,000), Avon Touring (£73,000) and Shared Experience (£95,000), none of whom offered as many annual performances as Complicite (ACGB, 1985b, 41/45/4). By shrewdly forwarding copies of this letter to the directors of each of the Arts Council's Regional Arts Associations, they elicited strongly worded statements of support, suggesting to the Dance Panel that without Trestle, Trickster and Complicite, touring venues would be significantly disadvantaged in their programming and that the companies were in their view(s) critically underfunded, considering the calibre of their work and the flexibility of the venues they were prepared to play in. With the help of their new administrator, Catherine Reiser (an adroit bureaucrat who had also, perhaps not incidentally, trained with Philippe Gaulier) guiding them to more coherently drafted applications, Complicite steadily increased its project grants annually, although the Arts Council continued to generally ignore the counsel of some of its advisers. They recommended an annual grant of £70,000 for 1988–9, for instance, but the Arts Council offered only £35,000. Additional support came from GLA (Greater London Arts) in the form of £8,500 for London-related work, and Reiser negotiated long-term private support from Beck's beer, who provided £16,000 in 1988–9 and from the British Council, who contributed £3,769 for a tour to Zarazoga, Spain.

It was not until 1989 that responsibility for the company finally transferred from Dance to the Drama department and it received revenue (as opposed to project) funding of £70,000 for the first time. By 1994 this had increased to £135,653. With such an apparent declaration of faith from the Arts Council, the company grew progressively more ambitious about the status of its work and more belligerent in its funding applications, to the extent that in 1991 Ian Brown, the Arts Council Great Britain (ACGB) Drama Director, felt obliged to write to Roger Graef, the Chairman, complaining that a drama officer had been verbally attacked for suggesting that Complicite keep their three-year bid to a 'no-growth' estimate (ACGB, 1991, 34/155/3).

Company Development: Education, Internationalism and Politics

Complicite always stressed the educational side of its work in ACGB submissions, which indeed most companies were required to pledge (on paper at least) if they wished to receive any funding during the latter part of the 1980s. But to this day Complicite has always made training, workshops and outreach projects an integral part of its philosophy. Initial marketing to venues offered workshops in 'Maskwork, Clowning, Commedia dell'Arte and Movement', and both Arden and McBurney attest that some of their later performance techniques, particularly the sense of engagement and a tendency towards aggrandizement, emerged through their large-scale community ventures: a production of *Romeo and Juliet* (1984) rehearsed in just under a week for the Pegasus Youth Theatre in Oxford incorporated a cast of 60 and 100 masks; *Foodstuff* (1984), a community production at the Albany Empire, used a cast of 25 that intermingled Complicite actors with the Greenwich Youth Theatre. *Foodstuff*, like many later plays, had only a title at the beginning of its three-week rehearsal period, but finished up as a kind of sketch show celebrating the attitudes and manners of eating. The second half involved a large family gathering to celebrate the hundredth birthday of a great-uncle. There turned out to be problems in the offstage kitchen, resulting in increasing kindred tensions, a finale riot with food thrown about and a scene of complete desolation. Many of the actors were new to the company and included Gerry Flanagan (of Shifting Sands company), Hamish McColl (later to co-found the Right Stuff), and Mick Barnfather, Celia Gore-Booth and Linda Kerr Scott, who were each cast in Complicite's next production (*Please, Please, Please*, another family celebration with no less ensuing chaos), and who became established company members.

Théâtre de Complicité's early international work also affected the direction of the company and the working relationships of its members. Sponsored by the British Council to take *A Minute Too Late* to Chile in 1984, they found themselves performing not, in the end, the existing production, but quick, impromptu extracts as a kind of street theatre, in shanty towns and Santiago's soup kitchens. Playing to large crowds of mostly impoverished, subjugated (under the Pinochet regime), Spanish-speaking people was eye-opening, according to Marcello Magni:

> We performed on streets with cement, rubble and dust and it was scary and amazing. At first no one was around, but we carried on regardless, and then doors opened slightly and we had to work harder to win over whoever was behind them. More and more people gradually came out and suddenly we were playing to hundreds of people and we had to play more vigorously and make them understand and enjoy our routine. We, in turn, understood what they were experiencing when Pinochet's army passed by on one occasion, and a soldier suddenly saw what we were doing. But the crowd protected us, and absorbed us and made us disappear into their circle until the convoy disappeared. (Fry, 2013c)

Magni cites two outcomes, in particular, from the tour: 'We learned that there are two parallel levels of performance: what are you saying, and who are you engaging with. It was also a very bonding experience with Simon and Jos [Houben], not simply a cultural experience, but a human experience which impacted on our working relationships' (Fry, 2013c). Annabel Arden goes further: 'Teaching, community and international work was absolutely central to our experience and development – quite apart from being financially necessary – and we learned more about what we were doing and found new people who we would never have come across through standard auditions' (Fry, 2013b).

Simon McBurney now asserts that 'all our initial references and points of the work at the beginning were to do with the society we were living in and the situations we found ourselves in, in the middle of furious political firmament' (Fry, 2013a). Annabel Arden had joined from a radical feminist collective known as the 1983 Theatre Company, and McBurney was flat-sharing with Neil Bartlett (already heavily involved in gender and sexual politics) on a council estate in the Isle of Dogs – an area of particular social deprivation. Moreover, according to McBurney, 'our political commitment took the form of action and governed whatever and wherever we played. We worked in prisons, with young people in difficult circumstances, in depressed schools. Even our international touring was a conscious statement that you can do what you want on no money' (Fry, 2013a).

However, the medium seems to have quickly transcended the message. None of the company's early marketing and publicity refers to any sense of political action or social outrage, and all the emphasis is on the articulation of method: of Lecoq's theories, an evangelization of visual theatre and a display of its own particular performing strengths. One of the reasons for the name of the company, in any case, was that the founders had initially thought they were going to be based in France, where the political climate (under François Mitterand) was less radical and divisive than in Margaret Thatcher's Britain and the nature of theatre more connected to the art of performance than to conviction.

The politics and the art form are not, of course, mutually exclusive. McBurney cites Joan Littlewood, with her combination of political engagement and vibrant theatricality, as his heroine. An early aspiration, stated in an Arts Council application, to 'speak directly to the audience and implicate them in the characters and their actions on stage' (ACGB, 1984d, 34/155/1) is both assimilative and political and Arden has suggested that inclusivity was a key aim: 'A kind of theatre that could be performed anywhere and touch anyone' (Fry, 2013b). But in fact, she and McBurney in other interviews have talked much more about theatrical philosophies than agitprop: 'We wanted to make theatre which was more concerned with a totality of experience, visual, musical, than just writer-led' (Fry, 2013b).

Company Development: Early Productions

Marcello Magni's take on the budding origins of the company are, typically, more prosaic. He thinks that Complicite's initial achievements were less about self-conscious values and more to do with the specific personalities of the actors. 'You took four different types of performer and they *collided*. Who we were, and the dynamics between the characters was the essence of everything we did in the early productions' (Fry, 2013e). During their first collaboration, *Put It On Your Head* (1983), Fiona Gordon, a tall, thin actor from Canada, played a gawky Canadian. British-born, socially outlandish McBurney played a timid, well-heeled young Englishman. Magni, still struggling with his English, played a number of contrasting, ebullient Italians. Arden, less performance-trained, more interested in production and convinced that McBurney had invited her to join the company 'because I had experience of booking a tour' (Fry, 2013b), played a rotund schoolboy who observed most of the action and provided the accompanying sound effects and props when required.

Taking Lecoq's theory that if the actors just sit on stage and do nothing, something will happen, McBurney and Gordon sat on deckchairs 'and we didn't do anything for about an hour and yet we made people laugh'.

> The piece was deeply influenced by Jerome Deschamps, so it's all deliberately anti-narrative, in a Beckettian way, a kind of desire to make something about nothing and about how banal the majority of our lives were, and how nothing meant anything and yet how a *moment* of nothing, like drinking a cup of coffee, can mean everything, all the despair is behind that cup of coffee. (Fry, 2013a)

In other words, subtext without the text: McBurney is keen to point out that Chekhov much preferred Meyerhold's productions of his plays to Stanislavski's, where the focus on movement seemed to elaborate the underlying meaning more than the words.

Set on an English beach, *Put It On Your Head* deals with seaside etiquette and repressed (British) emotions. Complicite's marketing described it as: 'Four characters who fail to comprehend the changes which overtake them. A series of scenes presented with minimum set and maximum rhythm' (Complicite archives, 1983). What some critics found original about the production (although, it should be said, others found it juvenile and clichéd) was its unique blend of clowning and character. Despite its physical pyrotechnics (Gordon discreetly trying to remove her stockings and getting her feet stuck in a collapsing deckchair), uproarious revue (McBurney's prim Christian mangling of his biblical references and dropping his spectacles to avoid seeing Gordon's legs) and sight and sound effects (Magni's Italian spiv and clucking Latin mother, Arden's authentic marine and telephone impressions), there was clear narrative, an underlying despair and a visual poetry in the mostly decor-less action.

The singular boldness and risk-taking by the actors was particularly noted. 'They were really pushing barriers', says Mick Barnfather, who joined the company a year or so later. 'I didn't realise you could be quite so stupid on stage. It was very clownesque and instead of hiding their eccentricities, they all used them to daring effect' (Fry, 2013e). Only the Arts Council was underwhelmed. For example, dance and mime officer Ruth Glick commented, 'But what in total do these scenes amount to? ... The complaint is of hollowness and finally, near horror at the deeply pretentious ending ... Having said all this it <u>was</u> entertaining' (ACGB, 1984b, 41/45/2).

Complicite's second production, in 1984, offered less sketch show and more reflection. Performed by McBurney, Magni and (Belgian) Jos Houben, and with Arden credited as director, *A Minute Too Late* stayed in the repertoire for over 20 years – it was revived, after an extended gap, at the National Theatre in 2005. Whereas *Put It On Your Head* had been inspired by fragmentary readings of the Bible, *A Minute Too Late* was based, following the death of McBurney's father, on a DHSS pamphlet on how to deal with bereavement. 'It grew out of registering the death and everyone's reactions to me afterwards, where friends would cross the street rather than talk to me' (Lane, 2005). Billed as 'a civic comedy of municipal mourning', the production explored the aftermath of death rather than actual mortality, and the bureaucracy and ritual that the bereaved encounter. McBurney recounted, on *Desert Island Discs* in 2012, how even his father's funeral had moments of dark humour. 'We chose drop handles for the coffin and they, as it turns out, are like the ends of skipping ropes, and they swing, and as the undertakers carried the coffin, these handles kept on hitting their ears, and we all got the giggles' (BBC, 2012).

Although there were as many routines in *A Minute Too Late* as there were in *Put It On Your Head*, there was a more rounded sense of dramaturgy. McBurney's character went on a dramatically consistent journey, even if it was partly told backwards – the news about his wife's fatal diagnosis was imparted by a doctor in the second half – and elliptically. In a National Theatre programme note on the tone of the play (2005), McBurney refers to erratic impressions stored in the brain's unconscious. The production shifted effortlessly from detailed observation to surrealism. It also had the confidence and finesse to end on a moment of genuine poignancy as the narrative simply petered out at the graveside, with the mournful strings of an orchestra appropriating the emotions – the first sign of Arden and McBurney (in particular) revealing their eclectic musical sensibilities.

Complicite's third production, *More Bigger Snacks Now*, was directed by Neil Bartlett, while McBurney, Magni and Houben were joined by the much older (deaf) actor Tim Barlow. Opening at the Edinburgh Fringe Festival in August 1985, it was the company's most socially pertinent work, yet also – as the Perrier award for comedy denoted – its zaniest. A picaresque, increasingly phantasmagorical journey through 1980s Britain it reflected, as Complicite's grant application to the Arts Council suggested:

> those situations in which someone discovers that they don't actually have enough to live. At the same time they realise that they are inexplicably spending what little money they have on things which they don't really want. Into this life of greyness comes a man… who can conjure unlimited wealth and happiness. (ACGB, 1985d 34/155/1)

The production started off, teasingly interminably, in a dilapidated flat with strewn crisp and cigarette packets, and with the cast watching television (a deafening operatic aria), while dunking tea bags, spilling milk and smelling their feet. In due course the audience was conjoined into lending them cigarettes and cash, before being taken on a rapid journey out of destitution and into incongruously urbane scenes in expensive restaurants and exotic foreign locations. The company's technical agility was at its strongest. Fernau Hall in the *Daily Telegraph* compared their work to the *lazzi* (visual joke) in *commedia dell'arte*. 'They bring together long sequences of modern *lazzi* and often combine totally unrelated ones with skill and perfect timing so as to create extraordinary multiplication effects' (Hall, *Telegraph*, 1985).

The performer David Glass, in his show report for the Arts Council, found the mixture of social commentary and zany humour problematic: 'Whilst Simon was telling me that the piece was meant to be about waste and greed, a young lad came over and said to Simon it was the best show he'd ever seen. He then went back to his friends and proceeded to smash up 6 glasses' (ACGB, 1985e, 41/45/3). But McBurney was pleased with the production, and its widespread attention: 'Satirical and absurdist laughter was one of the few ways you could challenge the orthodoxy. To be able to tear up real money on [the popular BBC TV chat-show] *Wogan* mystified the viewers – and Terry Wogan' (Fry, 2013a).

Two further devised productions that helped to define Théâtre de Complicité's style and approach, before it branched off in a somewhat different direction, were *Please, Please, Please* and *Anything for a Quiet Life*. The company's press release encapsulated *Please, Please, Please*, directed by Arden, as 'snow falls outside, furniture flies within' (Complicite archives, 1986). More parochial than *More Bigger Snacks Now*, with domestic themes of sex, love and jealousy, it showed an unusual (perhaps) family Christmas, with aggression and self-interest and all the characters blaming each other for lack of the good time they should be having. Starting once again with audience address, and a bag lady emerging from the aisles with a diatribe about the want of Christmas spirit, the play climaxed 80 minutes later with three separate beds (and five occupants) joining to create one enormous, cavorting sheet. Particularly accomplished physical fare included Linda Kerr Scott as the mother, devouring a whole packet of biscuits, spraying crumbs across the stage, and snatching and swapping books in bed with Mick Barnfather as her indolent husband; Magni as the fat, sad, stay-at-home brother getting his finger trapped in the table flap; and McBurney as the lothario brother, who arrived through an invisible window to land on top of his sibling, subsequently having befuddled sex with his girlfriend ('I think I'm the wrong way up … ') and getting her chewing gum stuck in his teeth in an amorous clinch. More empathetically, it embodied a thoughtful subtext through the apparent inability of the characters to say what they really felt about each other.

Three projects that didn't in the end materialize, according to Arts Council archives, were referred to as the 'Fear Project', the 'Silent Project' and the 'Solo Project'. The 'Fear Project' was touted as 'fear of pain, disease, bankruptcy, lavatory seats and worst of all, <u>other people</u>. A show inspired by newspaper cuttings we have collected throughout the year, Webster's plays and Defoe's "Journal of the Plague Year"' (ACGB, 1986, 34/155/1). The 'Fear Project' was to have been jointly directed by Julia Bardsley and Phelim McDermott, while McBurney focused on the 'Silent Project', scripted by a writer but using only 'Grommelot' (gobbledygook), and the 'Solo Project' in which he would appear on his own, talking to the audience about growing up. All of these projects were shelved after discussions with the Arts Council (who offered only £30,000 out of the requested £81,913), in favour of *Anything for a Quiet Life* (ACGB, 1987, 34/155/1).

Anything for a Quiet Life was developed from a long rehearsal period, supported by the National Theatre Studio. Originally an exploratory project into 'The Chorus and the Nature of Fear' – 'just that one word, "fear", was the genesis for the production,' says Arden (Fry, 2013b) – although it was different from the previous 'Fear Project'. McBurney, as director, was inspired by an obscure Pushkin text and research by the company included revenge tragedy and Kafka's fiction. Set in a dreary but familiar office environment, the play, with its most considered narrative to date, dissected the lives and relationships of the employees, with ever more surreal meetings, drudgery and frantic indecision.

The set, designed by Jan Pienkowski (now better known as a children's illustrator, but who worked with Complicite on three productions), consisted of three very adaptive wardrobes, some office tables, chairs and numerous telephones. There seemed slightly less focus on physicality with a darker and more brutal element pervading the comedy. Marcello Magni believes that the production took the company's approach to character to a much more complex level. 'In a way the personification was still archetypal, like *commedia*, but the office context created more detail. It was an experiment about the tensions between the workers. In some ways', he adds, 'it was also a reflection of our company at that particular period ...' (Fry, 2013c). *Anything for a Quiet Life* was filmed and broadcast by Channel 4 in 1989. In the cast, performing with Complicite for the first time, was Kathryn Hunter, who was to have a significant influence on the company.

Significant Productions 1989–94

Théâtre de Complicité rapidly approached the mainstream when, at the end of 1988, they were invited by Pierre Audi, the artistic director of the Almeida Theatre, to be company-in-residence for 15 weeks, an astonishing accolade for a fringe group at the time, although by now Complicite was no small outfit – a report by Greater London Arts lists a full-time administrative team of five, with a further 46 actors and crew employed over the year, on a variety of British and international tours (Complicite archives, 1988).

Most of the previous productions were revived for the Almeida season and the company added two new music-theatre pieces – *The*

Food of Love (text by Nick Dear, music by David Sawer) and *Miss Donnithorne's Maggot* by Peter Maxwell Davies. Annabel Arden also directed an opera, *The Lamentations of Thel*, by Dmitri Smirnov, based on a William Blake poem. Tim Barlow performed his one-man autobiographical show *My Army*.

Complicite received the 1989 Laurence Olivier Award for Outstanding Achievement for the Almeida season. It was artistically successful and personally fulfilling for the founder members in particular. 'This itinerant company suddenly owned a theatre', says Magni. 'It was our home and I never felt as happy. It changed every week, it was full all the time and there was just this huge buzz' (Fry, 2013c). It also marked a culmination of the first phase of Complicite. 'It was the end of something, that season', says McBurney. 'I went off and started working in films and television and my relationship with the company changed' (Fry, 2013a).³ Magni regrets that the laurels generated by the Almeida ultimately changed the close relationships within the group. They also never devised (from scratch) again after *Anything for a Quiet Life*.

The principal new production at the Almeida was the company's first attempt at an existing text. Friedrich Dürrenmatt's *The Visit* had been suggested by Monika Pagneux and centred on the return to an indigent town of a wealthy divorcée, Clara Zachanassian, bent on revenge for a childhood injustice.

The production was an unexpectedly faithful interpretation of Dürrenmatt's text, in Maurice Valency's standard-English version (with a few unacknowledged updates). Although Valency's translation is fairly naturalistic in tone, the actors played up the potential for hyperbole and satire in their characterizations. While some critics thought that Complicite had unnecessarily imposed its own style on the production – Michael Billington, in particular, wrote that 'one comes out hymning the company rather than talking about the play' (Billington, 1991) – Dürrenmatt's widow called it the most revealing she had seen, in that each moment of tribulation was quietly complemented by the humour. This in turn echoes Dürrenmatt's own comments on the relationship between comedy and tragedy: 'Comedy alone is unsuitable for us, but the tragic is still possible even if pure tragedy is not. We can achieve the tragedy out of the comedy' (Dürrenmatt, 1976, 84). 'Our approach was the same', says Mick Barnfather about the rehearsal process. 'It still felt just as exploratory. Yes, there was a text, but we were experimenting and doing exercises in a similar way to find the style' (Fry, 2013e). In fact, Annabel Arden's production (with McBurney), while giving each cast member ample opportunities to show their particular legerdemain, had more sense of directorial rigour than previously, with an abundance of arresting tableaux. In the first five minutes the actors created one of Complicite's most memorable *coups de théâtre*, as an express train sped through the ramshackle town, simultaneously blowing the actors off course, clothes and hair miraculously flying in the same direction, and with airborne leaves and a deafening sound. A cast of 11 – the largest to date – played over 30 parts and were able to switch flawlessly from townsfolk to international hit squad in seconds. Where Dürrenmatt suggests that the actors should play trees in two scenes set in a park, this prompted the cast to additionally offer birdlife, gambolling deer – and branches that would helpfully light cigarettes for the protagonists.

The Visit also had what Marcello Magni describes as 'our first proper set' (Fry 2013d). Whereas the company had generally used designers on their productions to help create images with carefully chosen, flexible furniture and props, the aesthetic for *The Visit* was on a different scale. Rae Smith's judiciously conceived and colourful construction was an abstract collage, able to regularly change tone and hue (accompanied by Luke Sapsed's effectively moody lighting) and vaguely reminiscent of a fascist past. Kathryn Hunter's performance in the central role was extraordinary. Despite the frenetic athleticism of the rest of the cast, her casual, vengeful tranquillity was often the most riveting thing on stage – 'a bejewelled, sinister reptile on gilded crutches, corrupting her home town with a deathly grin', as John O'Mahoney put it in a *Guardian* feature (O'Mahoney, 2004) – she wore an ever-changing array of flush, festooned outfits, usually with dark glasses and an inscrutable demeanour. At the same time, her depiction laid bare both the cynical assurance of prosperity and the anguish of her destitute youth – exiled from the town after Simon McBurney's Schill (now an elderly, paunchy man whose self-assurance and physical demeanour both palpably diminished during the performance) refused to acknowledge the paternity of her unborn child and his false depiction of her as a well-known nymphet.

Hunter won an Olivier Award for her performance and McBurney and Arden acknowledge that the phenomenal success of the production (it toured for two years and was invited to play a season at the National Theatre in 1991) was principally down to Hunter. 'I saw her at a workshop I was organising for Philippe Gaulier', says Arden, 'and I had never seen eyes as bright as hers, she was always electric. I got myself cast in a season at the Traverse so I could be close to her and persuade her to join us' (Fry, 2013b). Hunter trained at RADA and was one of the first actors chosen by the company not to have worked principally from a physical perspective. However, what she brought to Complicite was an ability to combine corporeal imagination with a sharper focus on language and temperament. 'The company lifted when Kathryn came in,' says Magni: 'she wasn't scared of Complicite, she was confident of her own theatre language – character and text' (Fry, 2013c). 'I think I could say', says McBurney,

> that Complicite would not have done *Anything For A Quiet Life*, *The Visit* or *Help! I'm Alive* without Kathryn. She definitely changed the company. She forced us to think about attention to detail and would always challenge us if she didn't believe in our characters. We became less larger-than-life after that and perhaps this motivated the kinds of plays and subject matter we started to choose. (Fry, 2013a)

The Winter's Tale was Complicite's second established text. Co-directed by Annabel Arden and the veteran British theatre director Annie Castledine, it opened at the Lyric Hammersmith in 1992, but was not universally admired. While it cast some of the company's most gifted players, including Magni as Autolycus (with a lot of audience banter), McBurney as a wild, rather aggressive, Leontes and Kathryn Hunter in the striking trio of Maximilius, Paulina and the Old Shepherd, it was thought to be textually slack with a surfeit of contemporary revisions, and with little regard for psychological veracity. There was some particularly riotous sheep-shearing and a fiercely witty bear, but on the whole most critics felt that the romance and anguish had been dropped at the expense of the broad comedy. 'Our production of *The Winter's Tale* is a bit buried now', says Arden, 'but it sowed a seed of tackling the classics which Simon has pursued – *Measure for Measure*, *The Chairs*, *All My Sons* ...' (Fry, 2013b).

More extolled – and arguably Complicite's most acclaimed work to date – was the next production, an adaptation by Simon McBurney and Mark Wheatley of the collected short stories of the Polish writer and artist Bruno Schulz. This was the first production where a playwright had been brought into the rehearsals.

Schulz's singular imagination, both in his fiction and his painting, arose from the observations and experiences of his childhood. Born in 1892 in Drogobych, a small town in Poland[4] where he stayed for most of his life, he had an eccentric Jewish upbringing, with a mentally ill father to whom he was close but whose behaviour became increasingly bizarre, and a restless career as an art teacher at the local school. During the Nazi occupation he was confined to the district ghetto but given less onerous tasks because a particular Gestapo officer liked his drawings and gave him work sorting out appropriated Jewish books in the library. In 1942, however, he was shot dead in the street by a rival SS officer. His stories were reissued in Poland, France and Germany in 1957 and he has become increasingly internationally venerated as an author. Evidently a complex personality, his drawings are usually awash with images of naked women, erotica and sadomasochism, and his prose frequently references paedophilia and bestiality – 'only at a later stage did [Father's love of animals] take that uncanny, complicated, essentially sinful and unnatural turn, which it is better not to bring into the light of day' (Schulz 1998, 22).

For what was known originally as the Bruno Schulz Project, Complicite was invited to spend five weeks at the National Theatre Studio, exploring the stories using a mixture of National Theatre actors and Complicite regulars (many of whom were, rather controversially, not invited to participate in the subsequent production). In the BBC *Late Show* documentary on the rehearsals and preparation for *The Street of Crocodiles* (one of the only times that Complicite has let the media into the rehearsal room), McBurney describes it as an 'utterly ridiculous project … No narrative, no dialogue. Very peculiar. People don't know him. We have no relationship with a small village in Poland in the 1920s.' At the same time he admits that Schulz and Complicite are well suited. 'He's incredibly funny about the human condition. A complete interconnectedness of character, object, music, word, sound and image … which is what we've done since we started' (BBC, 1992).

The opening of Complicite's production immediately evoked the themes and world of the novel. McBurney has often iterated the need to grab the audience's attention from the start with unusual, startling images, and here, in semi-darkness, a man in a library sat reading a book, plucked deliberately from a large pile. There were plangent strings (Martynov's 'Come In!'), shadowy movements, the sound of German voices and marching. Then, astonishingly, a man walked vertically down a wall; hands and then a body emerged from an incredibly small dustbin; a woman materialized from under a pile of books. Another man began narrating, while somersaulting. 'There is a mythological dimension to the characterisation,' says McBurney, 'so I wanted the performance itself to have the feeling of a dream … At the beginning he should be calling them up, so the actors are called from all different parts of the theatre, like spectres' (BBC, 1992).

In most of his short stories, Schulz uses regular personification, whether for animals, furniture or even the town itself. This of course tallied entirely with Complicite's own dramatic approach and here books turned into flapping birds (Schulz's father hatched unusual eggs) and raised chairs became woods. The choreographed movements, particularly in the school classroom, with clattering chairs and desks and a lot of slapstick, were as finely manipulated as in *The Visit*. Every inch of the stage was used, including elevation – Father's room was halfway up the proscenium – and objects would rapidly drop from the flies.

McBurney has commented on how music was an important part of his childhood, and he started to use it increasingly in Complicite productions from *The Visit* onwards, nearly always in collaboration with his composer brother, Gerard McBurney, and generally from an unpredictably eclectic range of periods and styles. Some programmes list over 20 miscellaneous musical references. The emotional content of *The Street of Crocodiles* was particularly enhanced by authentic or arousing melodies. At one point the cast even played (live, with violin, oboe, clarinet, percussion) a kind of klezmer for a romantic dance, and many less conspicuous musical moments cued an affecting response.

After criticizing *The Visit* and many of the previous productions, Michael Billington finally admitted that Complicite had found 'the ideal synthesis of form and content. The triumph of the show is that Complicite's talent for visual effects is always put to the service of Schulz's vision' (Billington, 1992).

The final production discussed in this phase of the company's history, *The Three Lives of Lucie Cabrol*, was Complicite's fickle take on John Berger's short(ish) story, the last and longest in *Pig Earth*, his series of fictional and poetic reminiscences based on his experience of living in a remote and unsophisticated village in the French Alps. Berger, the British novelist and art critic known for his Marxist politics, moved to a rural community in the Haute Savoie region of France during the 1970s in an attempt to experience the traditions and ordeals of the inhabitants he refers to (objectively) as 'peasants'. *Pig Earth* is the first volume of a trilogy, *Into Their Labours* ('Others have laboured and ye are entered into their labours', from the biblical John 4:38). The novella charts the life (only partly in triplicate) of a woman of stunted growth, whose gracelessness, unconventional habits and incongruously masculine strength cause her, in her 'first life', to be misunderstood by her family and largely ostracized by the village. Cast out to a remote mountain hut to fend for herself in her 'second life', which she does with extraordinary enterprise and accomplishment, she is eventually murdered for her money. In a nod towards magic realism, she then returns, in a 'third life', as a spectral presence to Jean, the man she has always loved and to whom she once proposed marriage (and procreation). She enlists other dead villagers to help build them a marital home, but eventually dematerializes once Jean has acquiesced, carnally, to this uncanny arrangement.

Lilo Baur, a stalwart of the company since *The Visit* and who had already demonstrated her power and diminutive strength in *The Street of Crocodiles*, was perfectly cast as Lucie Cabrol. Only slightly taller than the Lucie described in the novella, and by no means impeded by her size, she was able to show both the 'tough-as-a-mountain goat' qualities and a restrained vulnerability. There was the subtle mixture of masculinity, androgyny ('she had neither hips nor bust' [Berger, 1979, 17]) and feminine needs that Berger describes, as well as an astonishingly consistent vitality.

As in all the stories in *Pig Earth*, Berger supplies a plethora of descriptions of peasant farming life with both tangible and metaphorical images. Complicite's production recreated many of these images. The stage was covered in (pig) earth. The actors, whose clothes were already stained and bloody at the start, became increasingly dirty as the performance progressed. Tim Hatley's set, using only buckets, chairs, tables and tools, offered a particular adaptability, the actors' efforts at creating their own environments serving as a shrewd metaphor for the active life of the farming folk.

Upturned tables were used for expeditions and mountain routes. Chairs were thrown and constantly rearranged to provide obstacles and challenges on a journey across a peak track. A series of wooden planks were hurled around to represent some surprisingly passionate lovemaking (less representational were the semi-naked bodies, licking milk off each other). For the third, more surreal life, the tiled black back wall disintegrated, replaced by a panoramic blue sky.

Focusing on Lucie and Jean (played by Simon McBurney) as the pivotal relationship in the narrative, the other five actors played all the remaining characters between them. Like a functioning chorus, they provided everything that was needed to enact and comment on Lucie's story. They not only portrayed cows, pigs and horses, but also a cart, a cattle shed and even the earth itself, rolling over as the blade passed by them. Perhaps some of the narrative in the adaptation is too stuck in the original Berger prose and insufficiently dramatic, but most of the time Mark Wheatley and Simon McBurney as co-writers subtly transformed the text from chronicle to animated dialogue, and it was one of the first of Complicite's plays to be published. The production did not have the flagrant theatricality of *The Visit* or *The Street of Crocodile*, but it had a majesty and poignancy that was to become more of the mark of the company over the succeeding years.

Critical Reception

As has been seen from earlier sections, the response to Complicite's early work, while generally approving, was by no means wholly positive and it was not until *The Street of Crocodiles* and *The Three Lives of Lucie Cabrol* that the company garlanded the hyperbole it has by and large received ever since. The newspaper critics were, perhaps unpredictably, generally more responsive to the company's innovative bravado than the Arts Council – the body supposedly set up to support the new and the provocative. Arts Council show reports were sometimes so subjective and dismissive that they merit inclusion here as a notable part of a critical overview.

One of the perennial problems of Arts Council assessments is that they were and are frequently written (anonymously) by someone from a company's peer group. This is presumably to ensure a greater degree of theatrical authority, but since that peer group may also be vying for the same pot of Arts Council subsidy, their authority (and objectivity) is evidently sometimes outweighed by their pragmatism. Perhaps the Arts Council assessment panels inevitably had to be more judgemental than the newspaper critics, with their own responsibility for funding and accountability in a wider context than just one particular production. Nevertheless, there is something distinctly begrudging about the tone of some of their assessments on Complicite's early work, compared to the journalists.

Nigel Jamieson, the artistic director of Trickster, wrote the first report for *Put It On Your Head*: 'I felt it needed to develop some sense of purpose, some ambition in terms of what it was trying to say or do, or at the very least a change of gear' (ACGB, 1983, 41/45/10). At the same time, Clare Colvin in *The Times* concluded that 'the evening is a beautifully constructed mixture of buffoonery and mime and, at one hour ten minutes in length, avoids any danger of spinning the joke out too far' (Colvin, 1983).

Even the Arts Council officers themselves frequently submitted carping and rather personal criticisms, safe in the knowledge that they would be unidentifiable (until now).[5] 'Simon is starting to milk his little man character', noted Ruth Glick about *A Minute too Late*: 'he turned theatre into cabaret and it would have been better if he hadn't. He needs a much stronger director' (ACGB, 1985a, 41/45/3). 'I would rather see them do something more structured', wrote Jane Nicholas in a particularly disparaging report on *More Bigger Snacks Now*, '… I found the deliberate dirtiness rather off-putting and when McBurney started eating a plant I wanted to throw up. I am confident that they are all clever mimes, but this message really puts me off' (ACGB, 1985c, 41/45/3). However, Lyn Gardner in *City Limits* found that *More Bigger Snacks Now* had 'a rare ability to combine side-splitting buffoonery with incisive social comment' (Gardner, 1985) and Charles Spencer wrote in *The Stage* that 'it offers 90 minutes of inspired lunacy and in Simon McBurney the group is blessed with a performer of delirious eccentricity' (Spencer, 1985). Using the tick-box format stipulated by the assessors, Jane Nicholas, the Arts Council's Director of Dance and Mime, awarded Complicite a majority of twos and threes out of a possible six for *Please, Please, Please*. Yet Michael Ratcliffe in the *Observer* referred to it as 'one of the funniest and most inventive shows around' (Ratcliffe, 1986).

There is a constant theme running through the Arts Council's show reports that criticizes the company's lack of discipline and proper organization (precisely, in a sense, what motivated its work) and how as a group, members seem highly likely to disband. This is given as a reason to offer the company only project and not revenue funding – ironic in view of Complicite's remarkable longevity and Simon McBurney's status as one the UK's longest-serving artistic directors. However, there are some tantalizing minutes of a Complicite board meeting from 1992, which started an hour late 'because Simon and Annabel's rehearsal over-ran: Chairman furious' and goes on to record that 'some angst was aired about where the company is going, how the core members relate to Simon and how they select their future projects' (ACGB, 1992, 34/155/4), which gives more credence to the Arts Council's vacillation.

The situation was slightly reversed with *The Visit*. This was the production that finally convinced the Arts Council to offer permanent annual funding to the company, yet the press was actually more divided. While Claire Amitstead in the *Financial Times* suggested that 'one emerges convinced that one has seen a great play, rather than a great production, which is just as it should be' (Armitstead, 1989), Jane Edwardes in *Time Out* found that 'the play's own rhythm is sacrificed to the temptation to revel in moments of typical Complicite fooling' (Edwardes, 1988), and Nicholas de Jongh thought that 'they render the play as if it were some dramatic cartoon. Characters are reduced to stereotypes' (de Jongh, 1988).

Similarly, while the Arts Council admired the imagination and energy of *The Winter's Tale*, the critics stymied its progress beyond one short season at the Lyric, Hammersmith, complaining about the quality of the verse-speaking and seeming insensitivity to Shakespeare's more romantic nuances. Paul Taylor in the *Independent* dismissed it as 'just a pretext for an exhibition of inventiveness' (Taylor, 1992) and Michael Arditti in the *Evening Standard* described McBurney's Leontes as 'completely over the top, with too little Othello and too much Master Ford ...' (Arditti, 1992).

From *The Street of Crocodiles* onwards, both the newspapers and the Arts Council itself (by now Arts Council England and with Complicite devolved to the Drama Department) have mostly lauded the company's achievements and changing artistry. Complicite's archives offer an increasingly impressive array of international reviews, and the company regularly receives one of the largest annual grants for non-building-based companies in the Arts Council's client list.

Conclusion

In many ways the words 'Complicite' and 'McBurney' are interchangeable when reflecting on the work, not simply because of the longevity of the latter's commitment to the company, nor that nearly all recent productions bear his name both as author and director, but because he seems to have continuously been the inspiration and visionary behind it. 'It was always Simon carving the shapes and thinking about the next project' says Magni (Fry, 2013d). 'He is the recurrent genius,' says Mick Barnfather. 'You could always feel his influence no matter who was directing the production. Although Annabel directed *Please, Please, Please* and *The Visit*, and her clarity and imagination are immense, she and Simon would talk most evenings and his perception of how a piece was going would manifest itself in rehearsals the following day' (Fry, 2013e).

McBurney's paradoxical blend of intellectualism, artistry and populism – as well as his indubitable acting and comedic skills (he still thinks of himself predominantly as a working actor) – have contributed to the company's transcendence. Although many existing theatre groups have demonstrably been influenced by Complicite's physical wit and intrepidity, none have matched the eclectic and unpredictable choice of source material, the poetry in the stage ambience and the astonishing visual metaphors, the narrative accessibility and the conviviality. Few companies have focused so much attention on *being* a company (including the involvement of the production and administrative teams) or on such protracted rehearsal periods. 'We have always invested hugely in research and development time', says Arden. 'It is a major difference between us and many groups. We spend a lot of money on it' (Fry, 2013b). Few other ensembles have as many staunch actor associates, some of whom have spent years with Complicite, either as performers or workshop leaders.

Complicite rehearsals are genuinely collaborative, although not inevitably democratic. 'Simon will listen to other people's views and use them, but he can also blank them out if he thinks they're wrong. He has total faith in himself', says Magni (Fry, 2013d). McBurney admits that his rehearsals are challenging. Nothing ever stays the same and productions are reworked and re-evaluated constantly during the run(s). The structure of each rehearsal period is quite similar – 'how are we going to tell the story and what preparatory props should we have in the room to advance it initially' (Fry, 2013e) – but the way the rehearsals evolve is unpredictable. McBurney acknowledged on *Desert Island Discs* that the beginning of each rehearsal is like a painful birth because he doesn't know what he's doing for much of the time. 'It's like going into the jungle with a mad explorer who doesn't know where he's going' (BBC, 2012).

'It's not for everyone', says Richard Katz, a regular performer since 1999. 'Lots of us don't want to be in the shit, to get lost in the labyrinth. For this is where you will spend your days. In a world of fumblings, blind alleys, lost causes' (Ainslie, 2010, 97). Barnfather, who has been a leading member of the company for many years, gives an especially evocative depiction of the rehearsal process:

> The first one is always the hardest. After that you know what to expect. Simon is like a demented rodent. He really doesn't know what the end product will be, and we are asked to continually invent new things, and then he offers even more propositions, or crazy solutions to problems. Design is left very much to the last minute. The last week is awful as Simon works faster and faster and there is

rarely a dress rehearsal. It can get very intense with lots of blow-ups, but these are always about the process, not the philosophy. Simon himself appears to go for days without sleeping or eating – and he's always thinking about the next project as well. The rest of us are dead on our feet. (Fry, 2013e)

As the company celebrates its thirtieth anniversary (39 productions, 52 international awards) it has been rather more mainstream than fringe for a preponderance of those years. From rehearsing in Boy Scout huts for three weeks, with negligible resources and the company sleeping on dingy floors, it now rehearses for as long as 19 weeks (*The Master and Margarita*), has draconian accommodation and *per diem* conditions for any theatre or international festival hoping for a booking, and sometimes finds even the largest rehearsal room in London – Three Mills Island – too small for its purposes. Nevertheless, it remains, at heart, a fringe company in its philosophy and approach, and in its ramshackle base offices. 'I still feel very much on the outside of things,' says McBurney, 'and I think we are still on the outside of things. But like limpets we've managed to stick in there' (Wagner, 2013).

Principal Complicite Productions Between 1983 and 1994

Put It On Your Head, devised by the company, Almeida, 1983

A Minute Too Late, devised by the company, directed by Annabel Arden, UK tour, 1984

More Bigger Snacks Now, devised by the company, directed by Neil Bartlett, Assembly, Edinburgh Fringe Festival, 1985

Foodstuff, devised by the company, directed by Simon McBurney, Albany Empire, 1985

Please, Please, Please, devised by the company, directed by Annabel Arden, ICA, 1986

Anything for a Quiet Life, devised by the company, directed by Simon McBurney, Almeida, 1987

The Visit, Friedrich Dürrenmatt, directed by Annabel Arden with Simon McBurney, Almeida, 1989

Help! I'm Alive, based on Ruzzante's *Il Bilora*, adapted and directed by Marcello Magni and Jos Houben, Almeida, 1989

The Winter's Tale, Shakespeare, directed by Annabel Arden, Seymour Centre Sydney, 1992

The Street of Crocodiles, adapted from Bruno Schulz by Simon McBurney and Mark Wheatley, directed by Simon McBurney, Cottesloe, 1992

The Three Lives of Lucy Cabrol, adapted from John Berger by Simon McBurney and Mark Wheatley, directed by Simon McBurney, Manchester City of Drama Festival, 1994

Chapter 6

FORCED ENTERTAINMENT'S EARLY TO MIDDLE YEARS: MONTAGE AND QUOTATION

Sarah Gorman

1995 – Bad year and hard winter
1996 – Nothing recorded
1997 – Two fights on a fire escape
1998 – Nothing written down
1999 – Bad year, plenty of heartache
2000 – Some twins born in Rotherham
2001 – Stanley Kubrick film
2002 – News blackout and several small explosions
2003 – Birth of St Barratt the Blessed in the border zone
2004 – Nothing written down
2005 – The wreck of the Amoco Cadiz
2006 – Nothing written down
2007 – First gay man on the moon
2008 – Nothing recorded
2009 – An energy crisis
2010 – The opening night of a nightclub called Paradise
2011 – No problems
2013 – Some problems but nothing written down
2014 – No more, my love, no more my love, no more …

… Thank you and goodnight …
(Forced Entertainment, *Hidden J*, 1994)

Introduction

As part of the opening and closing sequences of *Hidden J* (1994), Forced Entertainment's eleventh theatre piece, Robin Arthur and Cathy Naden read from what appears to be an almanac or town chronicle, with references to crop yields and remarkable trans-historical events listed against 20 chronologically listed years. Positioned downstage, Arthur wears a pair of joke-shop devil's horns and Naden a plastic halo. The listing of years and the agricultural entries in particular are evocative of cod-Domesday Book entries. Alongside attempts to fix chronology in *Hidden J*, the company also set out to 'map' events. Terry O'Connor develops metaphors of mapping as her colleagues strive to identify the year using the Judeo-Christian calendar. The company ground the events they describe in disparate years, holding up cardboard signs with years ranging from '1604' to '2014' scrawled on them in thick black marker-pen. At key points these placards are held aloft as a performer describes a quasi-historical event; however, rather than visually reinforcing the speaker's original attribution, for example, '1979', the signs contradict the given year, reading instead, for example, '1964'. Having witnessed Forced Entertainment's self-reflexive drive to simultaneously celebrate and deconstruct the practice of writing history in performances such as this, one might expect to find the experience of attempting to chart the company's history rather daunting. An enormous amount of labour has been dedicated to documenting, recording and analysing Forced Entertainment's work: so much so that any formal attempt to construct a history will be inevitably limited and partial.

At the time of writing, the company is best known for experimental theatre work, although it received a significant amount of critical attention both in the UK and abroad for realizing projects through a range of different art practices: installation art, site-specific performance, photographic projects, durational performance, online writing projects and digital performance. The work can be broadly characterized as being driven by questions about the viability of theatre as a representational medium in an age of simulation and postmodern anxiety.

Although several commentators have observed that the company enjoys greater appreciation in mainland Europe and abroad than in the UK, Forced Entertainment (originally Forced Entertainment Theatre Co-operative) has an appreciative following at home and is particularly celebrated by promoters, venues, artists and academics who champion what they see as the challenging and innovative nature of the company's work (Gardner, 2004). The company continue to tour extensively in the UK and its work is regularly put on the curriculum for students of A level Theatre Studies and BA and MA Drama and Theatre programmes (Lehmann, 2006, 7). Working at the interstices of theatre, performance and live art, Forced Entertainment has been celebrated as 'Britain's most brilliant experimental theatre company' (Etchells, 1999, p. 1). As an indication of the company's international profile, Eileen Evans, the current General Manager, is on record as reporting that:

> In 2006/2007 we visited 13 countries and made over 80 performances of our current repertoire to 17,500 people. This year we toured to Europe, Singapore, Rio de Janeiro and Vancouver. If there is a major UK tour taking place (once every two years currently) the split between UK and overseas touring is around 30/70. (Evans, 2007–8)

Furthermore, the company's large-scale 2013 theatre show *The Coming Storm* was co-commissioned by theatres in Essen, Avignon, Paris, Zurich, Vienna, London and Sheffield, demonstrating the extent of appreciation for the work in mainland Europe. Although this chapter deals with earlier sections of Forced Entertainment's career, it is important to note that, as it approach its thirtieth year, the company continues to produce new work and enjoy significant critical acclaim both in the UK and abroad.

This chapter will deal with what are known as the 'first' and 'second' phases of Forced Entertainment's work, charting the creation of the company in 1984 and its first show, *Jessica in the Room of Lights*, through to the end of 1994, when the company created *Ground Plans for Paradise, Dreams' Winter, Hidden J* and *Speak Bitterness* (Heathfield, 2004, 77). I will mention work from 1995 because several noteworthy events took place in that year. This period saw the company move from deconstructing recognizable film genres using a codified gestural language and mediated text to the exploration of romanticism and urban kitsch. During the early phase, the company moved from producing, on average, one theatre piece per year, to producing a range of different art forms (including seven different projects in 1993 and 1994). The years 1984 to 1995 marked a period of transition for the company as it grew in profile and gained first recognition then approbation in the UK and abroad. This chapter will chart the company's development, discuss key examples of work created during this time and provide an insight into significant aspects of the company's working process. It will provide an overview of the critical attention received, which, as I have indicated before, is considerable. Etchells has done much to make the company's artistic processes and rationale widely accessible, having written *Certain*

Fragments: Contemporary Performance and Forced Entertainment in 1999 and contributed to numerous publications as a writer and company spokesperson. In her preface to *Certain Fragments,* Peggy Phelan draws attention to Etchells' stated desire to 'produce witnesses rather than spectators', an idea that has been cited regularly in subsequent writing about the company. Members of Forced Entertainment regularly contribute to academic panels and after-show discussions and commissioned in 1999 a short documentary, lending insight into their devising process. In addition to work produced by the company, a large body of critical writing exists composed of responses by art critics, artists, promoters, performance academics and bloggers. In 2004 Judith Helmer and Florian Malzacher edited a collection of 13 chapters in English and German entitled *Not Even a Game Anymore: The Theatre of Forced Entertainment.*

Forced Entertainment's influence on the UK theatre scene has been such that some have observed that the company's work has become a pre-eminent mode of performance, copied and repeated by others. Simon Shepherd wrote in 2009 that the 'makeshift' aesthetic of *Emmanuelle Enchanted* (1992) 'became one of the regular tropes of contemporary work' and describes the 'theatre language' of Forced Entertainment becoming a 'dominant mode' (Shepherd, 2009, 177–8). However, in his contribution to writing about the 1990s theatre-scene, Etchells pointed out that when the company started working he could identify a *shared* set of concerns among artists working at that time:

> A prevalent idea is that both the character/performer and the stage are zones of possibility in which a number, or any number of contradictory things may lie, awaiting discovery. From this context conventions including verbal game playing, listing, obvious quotation of imagery or text, partial performance via video or PA systems, identical costuming, frantic costume-swapping or undressing, the construction of stage spaces with internal mirroring or echoing and the ceaseless re-arrangement of objects to produce fictions have passed into common performance language. (Etchells, 1994, 107–8)

Etchells described what he saw to be the 're-framing' of performance 'in light of postmodern identity theory' permeating the work of a number of different UK companies, including Impact Theatre Co-operative, Rational Theatre and Hesitate and Demonstrate. In the wake of these earlier companies, he reported a new wave of performance-makers emerging in the late 1980s and early 1990s. He noted that companies such as Dogs in Honey, Man Act and Appeal Products were working to deal with the 'implications of specific narrative trajectories ... [and] film' (Etchells, 1994, 110). He also cites Station House Opera, Gary Stevens, Fiona Templeton, Reckless Sleepers, Blast Theory and Stan's Cafe among his contemporaries (Etchells, 1994, 108–21). Founder member of Stan's Cafe Amanda Hadingue echoes Etchells' sense that a new urgency and vigour was emerging from the performance scene in those years: 'In the 1980s, theatre was definitely the coolest art form in Britain (visual art having disappeared up its own minimalist arse)' (Hadingue, 2007). Hadingue also provides an insight into the bias towards playwriting during that time, recalling that:

> David Edgar sent out a questionnaire in 1993 ... James [Yarker – director and writer] conscientiously replied, enthusiastically explaining how his writing worked in the context of Stan's Cafe – as a starting point or in response to improvisation, as poetry. We felt excited to have a chance to explain to the eminent David Edgar how our theatre worked. Weeks later, an article appeared ... 'British theatre is going down the drain because no one is writing plays'. (Hadingue, 2007)

Indeed, Etchells has also described this time as one of artistic conservatism. He has observed that 'we operated in a culture where definitions of form were sometimes keenly policed' (Etchells, 1999, 21).

In addition to a sense of artistic conservatism between 1984 and 1995, the company was also experiencing the downside of Thatcherism and particularly the embrace of free-market enterprise. Etchells recalls how 'walking around in 1984 and 1985 you'd never seen so many disused factories and fields of rubble' (Etchells, 1999, 32). Commentators repeatedly describe Sheffield, where Forced Entertainment was founded, as 'post-industrial', pointing to the effects of the Thatcher government's decision to privatize and sell off shares in Britain's manufacturing industries including, most notably for Sheffield, the UK steel industry. Writing for the *Observer* in 2013, shortly after Thatcher's death, Julian Coman pointed out that 'the north suffered the worst of the deep recession and high unemployment of the early years; and it benefited least from the eventual boom of the late 1980s' (Coman, 2013, 2).

History of the Company's Development

Forced Entertainment initially comprised seven graduates of Exeter University who had migrated to Sheffield by the summer of 1984. They were: Cathy Naden, Richard Lowdon, Robin Arthur, Huw Chadbourn, Deborah Chadbourn, Tim Etchells and Susie Williams. Although from different year groups, the members were united by a desire to resist a mode of teaching that Etchells felt was 'tremendously important' but a little 'stuck in the 60s, kind of white cube can be a bus or anything you like, sticks or staves and that kind of thing …' (Clarke, 2001, 330). The membership of the company has now shifted as a result of Huw Chadbourn leaving and Terry O'Connor joining in 1986, Susie Williams leaving in 1987, Deb Chadbourn stepping down as General Manager (but remaining on the Board of Directors) in 1999 and Claire Marshall joining in 1989. Although other performers and artists have collaborated with the company, its core membership has been stable since 1989 and comprises Tim Etchells, Terry O'Connor, Claire Marshall, Cathy Naden, Richard Lowdon and Robin Arthur. Key figures such as Nigel Edwards (lighting), John Avery (music) and Hugo Glendinning (photographer) have worked closely with the company over a long period of time.

At the very beginning of their careers the company founders were able to claim unemployment benefit and later 'Enterprise Allowance' (a Thatcherite scheme designed to encourage people to set up their own businesses, but widely considered as an attempt to massage unemployment statistics) while rehearsing and sharing work. Their first piece, *Jessica in the Room of Lights*, was performed at Yorkshire Arts Space in Sheffield on 14 December 1984. This is the only Forced Entertainment theatre piece not to have been captured on video, and Etchells describes it as follows:

> A love story … The cousin gets a job as an usherette. Falls in love with a bloke in mechanic overalls. The memory of the summer all mixed up with the movies the cousin has seen endlessly repetitiously in the cinema. Real life and the movies intertwined in bad memory. (Bailes, 2011, 79)

In 1985 the company produced two pieces, *The Set-Up* and *Nighthawks*. Etchells has described this work as 'single-genre based work', which saw them deconstruct 'particular filmic genres' (Kaye, 1996, 243). Over the next four years the company produced four shows and went on to create a trilogy of three of those pieces: (*Let the Water Run its Course*) *to the Sea that Made the Promise, 200% & Bloody Thirsty* and *Some Confusions in the Law about Love* in 1991. *(Let the Water Run its Course)* was the first project for which the company received Arts Council funding. For this piece Etchells took the decision to withdraw from performing and take up the role of director and writer on a more permanent basis. In addition to experimenting with a larger set, the company considered this piece a turning point because, as Naden explains, 'it was the first time we tackled urban experience and got into the whole industrial wasteland thing' (Benecke, 2004, 34). During this time, the company built up relationships with a number of small-scale regional venues and the ICA in London, playing *(Let the Water ...)* at 25 different venues between 1986 and 1988. Venues such as the Centre for Contemporary Art in Glasgow, Alsager Arts Centre in Crewe, The Nuffield Theatre in Lancaster, The Leadmill in Sheffield, Warwick Arts Centre in Coventry and The Arnolfini in Bristol played important roles at this time in supporting and promoting new and experimental work that often had difficulty securing a venue in London.

From 1986 the company was successful in securing project funding from the Arts Council of Great Britain and Yorkshire and Humberside Arts until 1994 when the Drama Panel, in response to a number of negative reviews of *Hidden J*, took the decision not to fund the next proposed project, *Speak Bitterness*. Etchells is clear that:

> It wasn't technically a cut and we never used the cut word ourselves ... although it was widely used by other people. Instead the year on year string of project funds we'd had since 1986 was broken ... throwing the stability (and viability) of the organisation very much into question. (Etchells, 2013)

As the company performed *A Decade of Forced Entertainment*, commissioned by the ICA to celebrate its first ten years, members experienced a sense of anxiety that the end of the company might be in sight. As Adrian Heathfield points out, 'the piece was written and performed by the company under the threat of closure' (Heathfield, 2000, 106). The company went out of its way to ascertain the grounds for the withdrawal of support, asking to read the reviewer's reports. It transpired that the decision was based on a total of five assessors' reports of *Hidden J*, two being positive and three negative. Etchells recalls company members visiting the Arts Council headquarters at Great Peter Street in London to copy out the reports by hand, as they were not allowed to photocopy them. He remembers that 'it was hard not to laugh ... writing out these negative assessments of our own work, like kids in detention' (Etchells, 2013). Deborah Chadbourn, the company's General Manager, organized a campaign to resist the withdrawal of funds and elicited a significant number of responses from artists, venues, promoters and academics who wrote to the Arts Council to articulate their misgivings about the decision. Etchells has declared that:

> The campaign was amazing ... drawing a lot of support from venues, academics, professionals and audiences – I think ACE were surprised by the depth and range of knowledge, support, feelings and passions for the company and its work. It was pretty humbling and amazing for us to see that. I don't think ACE had properly understood the work we were doing and I don't think they were very well placed to talk about its quality. (Etchells, 2013)

Etchells has spoken of his perception of the 'conservatism' in mainstream theatre in Britain during the 1980s and 1990s and it is highly likely that the public campaign against the Arts Council's decision invited policy-makers to review their perception of crossover art-form or multidisciplinary work. Given Arts Council England's current acceptance of site-specific and immersive theatre it is possible that this particular intervention forced a reappraisal of the disciplinary boundaries Etchells felt to be so keenly 'policed'. O'Connor has made explicit the company's intention to resist the model of theatre making that uses a preconceived and finished script as a blueprint for perfor-mance. She has written that 'as a company we have talked a lot over the years about destabilizing the hierarchical position of text on stage' (O'Connor, 2009, 89). Acknowledging this as a potential reason for the failure to recognize the value of the work, Hadingue has marked the moment when 'Forced Entertainment lost their funding' as significant in her treatise on the legacy of 1990s experimental theatre:

> One theory behind the cut was that Forced Entertainment, as a theatre co-operative, failed to appease the growing panic from the likes of David Edgar that British theatre was shrivelling up due to the lack of writers and directors. Insiders knew that Forced Entertainment actually had a very talented performance writer in Tim Etchells, and a team that were able to co-direct and act fantas-tically, but you couldn't point to any traditional theatrical role. (Hadingue, 2007)

Shepherd's survey of 1980s and 1990s theatre describes the emergence of a more 'aesthetic theatre' under the influence of companies such as Impact, and Lumiere & Son, and posits its emergence as a reaction 'against the realisms of the earlier period', which had presented themselves as 'rough-edged: committed to politics rather than aesthetics'. He described an 'aesthetic excitement around the forced interrelation of separated elements ... articulated in a favoured word of the 1990s – "hybrid"' (Shepherd, 2009, 176–7). Shepherd's appraisal of a reaction against the 'realisms of the earlier period' is significant in so far as it identifies the sticking point for many arguments about theatre that continue today. Britain has a long and respected tradition of playwriting and the new physical theatre languages reaching the UK via Impact, artists such as Pina Bausch and Jan Fabre, and the movement away from using the play script as a blueprint for performance-represented something of a threat to that tradition. In *Certain Fragments* Etchells points out that influences include, but extend beyond theatre:

> I've also been influenced by practitioners such as Pina Bausch, and the American company The Wooster Group. But what has influenced me most does not actually come from theatre; my references and inspirations are very broad: Mark Smith's work with punk band The Fall, Nicholas Roeg's cinema, especially *Performance*, Tarkovsky, fine art, films and performance art. (Etchells, 1999, 28)

It is perhaps the multidisciplinary nature of Forced Entertainment's influences that disturbed a received understanding of 'theatre' for mainstream critics and promoters. Socialist playwrights such as David Edgar, Edward Bond, Howard Brenton and Arnold Wesker had dominated the theatre scene in the 1960s and 1970s, with realism being the most recognizable form of 'political theatre'. It was also generally accepted that 'political theatre' meant socialist theatre – plays that were unequivocally *about* the plight of those oppressed under capitalism. Forced Entertainment has maintained that its work is political without feeling the need to explicitly cite or dramatize the socialist politics that informs its work through realism. The work of this period maintains a political stance in a more elliptical manner, insisting that the company writes from the perspective of not 'the people who made decisions but ... those people who were affected by decisions made in other times and other places' (Etchells, 1999, 32).

Key Work Produced and Impact

Etchells has revealed that during the early stages of their career company members were 'more interested in cinema or music culture' than theatre and borrowed references more readily from literature or fine art (Clarke, 2001, 299). Certainly, their work bore little resemblance to the realist theatre dominating the UK mainstream scene at this time. After *Jessica in the Room of Lights* came *The Set-Up* (1985), a piece selected to appear at the National Review of Live Art. Incorporating references to interrogation scenes in gangster films, this piece shifts in tone to include Bausch-like sequences of found movement in which the performers repeatedly dress and undress. Text is delivered via recorded voice-overs rather than delivered live from the stage. *Nighthawks*, also created in 1985, exists in two fictional spaces – a replica of a 1950s American bar and a windowed room with a high ceiling. Performers play out a pantomime of flirtation and machismo while a voice-over pastiches Chandleresque detective fiction. A range of relationships between the figures on stage is explored before a new space is revealed behind the back wall of the bar. The bespoke musical score moves from more meditative passages towards a heightened, frenetic crescendo. At times the soundtrack squeals as if capturing the sound of analogue tape being fast-forwarded. In the new space the performers repeat a more codified set of gestures as the music segues into piano and voices repeat that 'Coca Cola was seventy degrees in the shade' and 'It seems as if the rest of America is caught up in this nervous restlessness and no sleep' (Forced Entertainment, 1985). *Nighthawks* plays out the company's fascination with the experience of receiving American culture via media such as TV, film and literature and points to an early exploration of US cultural imperialism (Bailes, 2011, 67). *The Day that Serenity Returned to the Ground* (1986) ostensibly features a group of astronauts returned from a space mission who attempt to come to terms with the death of one of their party. Again, it features codified gesture and atmospheric soundtrack, but text is delivered from the stage for the first time in this piece. Performers are sealed off from the audience and work in a small, enclosed air-lock type space. At regular intervals, they approach microphones at the front of the air lock to deliver repeated sections of text.

(*Let the Water Run its Course*) *to the Sea that Made the Promise* was also created in 1986. In terms of its visual impact, this piece represented a move away from recognizable locations to a more ambiguous, atmospheric set. Funding from the Arts Council and Yorkshire and

Humberside Arts had allowed the company to spend money on a larger set, which was designed to resemble the damp, dark interiors of the abandoned Sheffield factories and warehouses in which they rehearsed. In this piece:

> The performers, there are four of them, play a kind of thing which is somewhere between a game and a ritual and a kind of exorcism. It's all done in this very brash, very big, physical, noisy style a bit like taking a cartoon and putting it on fast forward and distorting the dialogue and the sound of it. (Clarke, 2001, 305)

The performers compete in a game of emotional extremes. They play at crying, looking up from wretched sobs to check the effect their performance is having on their peers, then experimenting with performances of dying, squeezing tomato ketchup on to their bodies and repeatedly engineering creative acts of misadventure. Figures on stage deliver a nonsensical, garbled language that is suggestive but impossible to decipher. As mentioned above, this piece has been recognized as significant because it garnered a number of favourable reviews and marked the start of the company's engagement with Sheffield as a reference point in their work. It also represented the beginning of what Cathy Naden has described as an 'open, "see-what-comes"' attitude to generating material (Benecke, 2004, 35). A taped voice-over accompanied the verbalized sound effects of the on-stage characters. Featuring a male and female voice, it relayed an amalgamation of confession, child-like wonder and cynical obscenities seemingly quoted from popular culture. The text describes a series of cities, 'the City of Stones, the City of Wire, the City of Rain, the Stupid City, the Empty City':

> The sixth city was the City of the Variable stars. Someone put a note under the windscreen wiper of her car, 'I love you, but will never dare speak to you'. In another time, with another love in his heart, Mr Plastic choked and died in a hotel bathroom. (Etchells, 1999, 137)

Ben Slater has suggested that this piece represents the first in a series of 'survivors after a catastrophe' scenarios that continue in subsequent pieces. In response, Etchells revealed that:

> There's always a point when we're making our shows, even now, when you say "These are the only people left in the world, all they've

got are these ten bits of paper, and this great pile of crap and they've somehow got to sort it out'. (Slater, 1997, 11)

The interest in juxtaposing the naïve and urban continued in 1987 to 1990 with *200% & Bloody Thirsty* and *Some Confusions in the Law about Love*. *200%* saw the first use of TV monitors on stage, mounted to provide a medium for two 'real' angels to look down and comment upon the activities of the three drunken performers taking it in turns at pretending to be angels. Three figures repeatedly performed childlike re-enactments of the story of the Christian Nativity, stopping only to try to revive a friend out of his or her stupor. The set was constructed out of a series of steel frames, with a raised area towards the rear and an open space housing a bed and a sea of second-hand clothing. A neon sign reading '200% & Bloody Thirsty' was hung downstage and actual trees were erected at the sides of the main playing area. In terms of a factual review of the 'history' of the group's career, *200%* is notable because the 'open' rehearsal process of which Naden has spoken caused the company to 'hit such severe problems' that they took the decision to cancel the tour, opting instead to spend more time honing the piece so that it was ready for an audience (Benecke, 2004, 37). It was eventually very well received by venues and audiences, although, as Etchells records in *Certain Fragments*, one 'savage' review by the *Independent* stated that 'the whole performance is wholly out of control ... there is little to enjoy here and much to regret ...' This review provided the company with the final lines for the subsequent *Marina and Lee* (Etchells, 1999, 40).

Etchells has described key phases in the company's oeuvre, suggesting that for him the second phase ran from '*Marina and Lee* through *Emmanuelle Enchanted*, *Club of No Regrets* and *Hidden J*' (Heathfield, 2004, 77). Forced Entertainment produced *Marina and Lee* in 1991 and *Emmanuelle Enchanted: Or a Description of the World as if it were a Beautiful Place* in 1992, winning sponsorship from the Barclays 'New Stages' Award. *Marina and Lee* featured a neon sign stating 'Look No Further Here It Is', which illuminated a steel-framework set. These pieces have regularly been discussed in terms of 'narrative fragmentation' because they employ a montage of found texts and source materials and confound attempts to read for causal relation-ships or temporal progression. *Marina and Lee* drew allusions from Priscilla Johnson McMillan's book of the same title, without relying on it as an authoritative source (Kaye, 1996, 243). This stimulus was integrated alongside clumsy re-enactments of computer kung-fu games and science lectures with no single text being given priority. Claire Marshall, having joined the company for *Some Confusions*, took on the role of an awkward, childlike Marina, dressed as a hurriedly conceived cowboy complete with a scrawled-on beard and plastic penis. Richard Lowdon appeared on video as Lee Harvey Oswald, having broken his leg during the rehearsal process. This production prompted one of the first pieces of academic writing about the company's work from Andrew Quick, which was featured in a special 'Live Art' edition of *Contemporary Theatre Review* in 1994.

As in *Some Confusions* and *200% & Bloody Thirsty*, *Emmanuelle Enchanted* featured TV monitors in a number of scenes that were repeated and replayed over the course of the performance. The reassuring (yet withheld) potential of narrative is very much in evidence in *Emmanuelle*, as four seemingly disorientated figures repeatedly attempt to show and explain 'what happened the night the rain stopped' (Forced Entertainment 1992). For the first time the company used an obviously meta-theatrical 'stage-within-a-stage' configuration, with a gauze curtain hung over the front of a proscenium-like frame, enabling performers to do what Greg Giesekam has pointed out would be 'frontcloth scenes' in pantomime (Giesekam, 2007, 133). Giesekam cites the curtain as a self-reflexive device, pointing out that it illustrates 'the point that what is normally seen on the stage is always controlled and framed' (Giesekam, 2007, 139). The company play on the faux-naïvety introduced in previous productions with members performing a child-like sense of uncertainty as they gather to explain the premise of the show.

A much-admired section in this piece includes what Matthew Goulish, in a 'Compendium' of Forced Entertainment words, has called the 'fact people': 'personality aggregates appear as complete fragments in the form of Fact People', in other words, characters from popular culture, history, the company's imagination, scrawled on to pieces of cardboard. For example, designations such as 'BAD MOTHERFUCKER, A KING (USURPED), EX-LOVERS (NOT SPEAKING), ELVIS PRESLEY THE DEAD SINGER, AN ASSASSIN, THE HYPNOTISED GIRL, FANTASY FRED, A LOST MAN REMEMBERING THE ACCIDENT and A TILL GIRL WITH A GUN appear on individual pieces of corrugated card (Goulish, 2000, 142). During one of the opening scenes, underwear-clad performers dart between clothing racks, selecting placards and items of clothing before taking up a space in the playing area to adopt a crude gesture or stance to 'show' their 'character' to the audience. As four company members dress and undress, the remaining performer has the task of running on the spot upstage, as if running away from an explosion or site of disaster. This activity is set to a piece of frantic guitar music entitled *Emmanuelle Enchanted*.[1] The scene was adapted into the company's first durational performance, commissioned by the National Review of Live Art, in 1993.

Hand-held microphones, already used in *Some Confusions*, re-appeared in *Emmanuelle Enchanted*, providing an opportunity for the audience to experience both 'live' and 'mediated' voices simultaneously. The piece features what has been referred to as the 'Newsroom Hijack' scene in which performers take turns to sit at a small table and deliver lines into a table-top microphone. As they recite items from a list, they look into the lens of a video camera. The camera is linked by live relay to a television monitor at the side of the reconfigured playing area. In a manner similar to that of *Hidden J*, performers read from a long list of disconnected ideas, magazine article headlines, phrases, cultural artefacts and convoluted memories in what is a seemingly coherent list, as they state 'number one, number two, number three' (counting up to ten) before each item. For example:

> Number One: 'Her husband's death, loneliness, February 1953.'
> Number Two: A new game show called 'Long Faces.'
> Number Three: 'Builders on the roof at 7 am.'
> Number Four: 'Builders on the roof at 7pm.'
> Number Five: 'I Have a Horror Of The Truth But I Love The Truth.'
> Number Six: Crisis.
> Number Seven: The words 'Fuck face' and 'Seafood' are registered as trademarks by the manufacturer and they reserve the public right to be identified as such. (Etchells, 1999, 149)

A number of performances from this particular era (1992 to 1994) have attracted widespread attention from academics for a number of different reasons. Writing about the earlier work (*Some Confusions, 200% & Bloody Thirsty* and *Emmanuelle Enchanted*) was largely in response to the visibility of TV culture and the idea that the company was using digital technology onstage, 'to make theatre for those of us raised in a house with the TV permanently on' (Bayley, 1995; Gisekam, 2007, 120; Giannachi and Luckhurst, 1999, 29). Slightly later work (*Emmanuelle Enchanted, Club of No Regrets* and *Hidden J*) went on to be feted for the use of what was perceived to be a form of narrative deconstruction and a nostalgia for the reassurance of teleological narrative form. *Club of No Regrets* features a speech, which perhaps exemplifies the company's relationship to narrative:

Piecing together torn paper.

Simple as this work may appear yet it none the less presents numerous difficulties, and is often very awkwardly carried out. An investigator often receives numerous torn pieces of paper of small size, the content of which, once pieced together, is of the utmost importance ... (Etchells, 1999, 163)

Helen X, a character played by Terry O'Connor, reads this section of text out to the audience, stammering as if struggling to identify the words. The ordering of the scenes is determined by Helen X, who by her own admission is 'lost' and searching for meaning by attempting to order and make sense of the fragmented raw material she supposedly holds in her hands. For the first section of *Club of No Regrets* it is possible to build a quasi-realist rationale to 'explain' that Helen X is lost in a forest, that she comes to a clearing and two actors and two stage-hands (appearing to embody figments of her imagination) play out scenes from a random collection of popular cultural sources. The scenes include 'Scene 59: A Procedures Scene; Scene 93: A Questions Scene; Scene 6: A Troubled Scene; Scene 35: A Shoot-Out Scene and Scene 15: A Look How I'm Crying Scene' interspersed with a series of fictional telegrams (Etchells, 1999, 165–6). However, towards the end of the central section of the show, the crude 'room' constructed from four wooden flats is dismantled to clear the space, a chair is placed centre-stage and one of the stage-hands is gaffer-taped to the chair to re-play action from earlier in the show. Naden, as the restrained stagehand, desperately tries to escape as her colleague dances with cruel abandon beside her.

As indicated above, Etchells has acknowledged the company's interest in forensics as a potential metaphor for their attempt to construct meaning. He has revealed that the company came across Hans Gross's textbook *Criminal Investigation: A Practical Handbook for Magistrates, Police Officers and Lawyers* as it lay about in the rehearsal studio and it helped them recognize narrative reformation as the central activity for this particular show. Gross's text helped the company realize that 'the reconstruction of a narrative from clues, the reconstruction of an event from its objects, the reconstruction of a text from its fragmentary scenes were framed as the objects of our work' (Etchells, 1999, 73).

Something of a turning point occurred in 1993–4. In addition to touring two theatre pieces, *Club of No Regrets* and *Hidden J*, the company created its first durational performances, *12 am: Awake and*

Looking Down and *Speak Bitterness*, their first performance installations, *Red Room* and *Ground Plans for Paradise*, and its first large-scale site-specific performance, *Dreams' Winter*. In 1995 the company experimented with new forms in *A Decade of Forced Entertainment*, a performance-lecture, and *Nights in This City*, a site-specific piece located on a commercial coach. In response to the diversification of interests, the company dropped the 'Co-operative' part of its name and began to use simply 'Forced Entertainment' (Helmer, 2004, 62).

Written alongside *Hidden J*, *A Decade of Forced Entertainment* saw the company challenging conventional paradigms of history and attempting to make sense of its early years working as artists in Thatcher's Britain. The company shared material from past productions and generated new text, which was delivered from two facing tables. The performance–lecture was illustrated using images projected using a low-tech overhead projector. As in the quotation from *Hidden J* used at the start of this chapter, the company also playfully mismatched significant historical events with fictional years in *Decade*:

> They drew a map of the country and marked on it events from the rest of the world. On this map, the Challenger Space Shuttle had blown up in Manchester, 1985. The Union Carbide Bophal Chemical Works which exploded late in 1984 was located in Kent. The siege of the Russian Parliament Building in 1991 had taken place in Liverpool. (Etchells, 1999, 30)

Peggy Phelan has described this mapping as a 'complex process by which a public event arrives in the spectator's consciousness' and believes that it illustrates Forced Entertainment's 'primary interest ... in how individual readers suture this new information into ongoing narratives of their own affective and empirically specific histories' (Etchells, 1999, 12). These affective histories can be seen to grow out of an increasing interest in suffusing supposedly rational elements, which are traditionally considered to be fixed by objective and scientific means, with emotion. The resultant clash of discourses produces a productive tension that highlights the dominance of logical positivism in shaping and normalizing Enlightenment values of reason and order.

Ground Plans for Paradise (1994) and *Nights in This City* (1995) both represent a more explicit situating of the urban metropolis at the centre of the work. Forced Entertainment collaborated with photographer Hugo Glendinning on *Ground Plans for Paradise* creating 'an abandoned metropolis' out of multiple models of balsa-wood city blocks. The buildings were illuminated from inside and arranged along recognizable boulevards (Forced Entertainment, 1994). They were given names such as:

Heartbreak House
The Big MI5 Building
BUPA Hospital
The Last Chance Saloon
The Pentecostal Church of Elvis Alive
Retail World
Redemption House
The Leaning Tower of Derby
Carpet Wonderland
Horror House (Forced Entertainment and Hugo Glendinning, page 5)

Nights in This City took the form of a site-specific performance, using the city of Sheffield as its 'site'. Described as 'mischievous', this piece drew upon the Situationists' practice of 'drifting' and overlaying maps of different cities. Audiences were taken on a bus journey to see the 'real' people of Sheffield while being invited to imagine that they were part of a fictional narrative (Etchells, 1999, 61; Harvie, 2009, 49). A drunken tour guide created the illusion of the tour bus getting 'lost' and taking the participants, 'off route'. For Etchells, the role of the uncertain narrator or, in this instance, tour guide, exemplifies the destabilizing potential of performance: 'isn't that the definition of liveness? ... When the gatekeepers twitch nervously and the guides appear lost? Where safe passage back to the everyday is no longer assured?'(Etchells, 1999, 81).

Approaches to Devising

In terms of gaining an insight into the company's working methodology, Forced Entertainment has welcomed observers into the rehearsal room, so that in addition to company documentaries, *Certain Fragments* and company interviews, detailed reports exist from a number of scholars about the process of devising (Oddey, 1994, 85–104; Bailes, 2011; Clarke, 2001; Mermikides, 2002, 101–20).Working practices changed during the first phase of the company's process as roles became more fixed (early shows were directed and co-directed by Etchells, Naden, O'Connor, Arthur and Lowdon). The company moved away from the 'systematic repetitive choreographies' of the early work towards a 'rougher, more ragged physicality, and by structures built around the vital force of live, competitive, and playful performer interaction' (Benecke, 2004, 35). In brief, the company works by devising original material collaboratively as a group. Performers improvise around a set of concerns or ideas, often carried over from previous shows, and hone the material through a mix of extended play, reflection and detailed discussion. During the early to middle years the company continued to rework material during tours and between subsequent outings. However, the current commitment to touring abroad often means that Forced Entertainment has to 'fix' the activity in order for translations to be produced in the run-up to a foreign tour.

Forced Entertainment does not start from a pre-agreed premise or 'script': instead, the members engage with stimuli through associative play. A starting point will often be fragments of found text or images brought in by one or more company members. According to Paul Clarke:

> The composition can be described as textural and the company speak of combining texts in terms of their qualities and textures, as opposed to making decisions based on interpretations of meaning, or the significations of texts' contents. (Clarke, 2001, 323)

The company has a policy of not working in empty spaces, stating that 'we usually build some crude environment (to rehearse from Day One) in which to work, using materials from old sets or whatever else is to hand … We need a place to work. If you put us in an empty room we can't do anything (Giannachi and Luckhurst, 1999, 25). During the early and middle years, the company would work particularly closely with John Avery, a composer who wrote music in response to what he had witnessed in the rehearsal room. Funding has obvious implications for the length of available rehearsal time but during the middle-historical phase members would aim to work on a production 'on and off' for up to six months (Giannachi and Luckhurst, 1999, 25).

The company readily admits to 'getting stuck' during the devising process. Clarke's insight into rehearsals for *Dirty Work* (1998) and Alison Oddey's record of rehearsals for *Some Confusions in the Law about Love* (1989/90) demonstrate how each performance underwent significant (and often dramatic) changes as the company negotiated difficulties in making decisions about the length of various sections or how to realize an appropriately meaningful relationship with the audience. Etchells has admitted that the company anthropomorphizes the shows, and regularly asks 'What does it want? What does it need?' as if it 'had desires of its own' (Etchells, 1999, 62). The company alternates between improvisation and discussion, reviewing these on video, and admits that the discussions regularly take the form of 'arguments' that 'loop' endlessly and sometimes inconsequentially (Etchells, 1999, 63). One of Richard Lowdon's 'creative' decisions during the making of *Club of No Regrets* lends a fascinating insight into the process. The company had arranged four solid flats in the space so as to suggest a small domestic space, and Etchells recalls that:

> ... at a certain point in the process Richard got up and I think, without really asking, sawed a hole in one of the flats to make, effectively a very crude window, and when we talk about that we often talk about it as something between vandalism, set design and writing because, once you've got these windows, this whole piece of work totally changes. (Clarke, 2001, 303)

For Etchells, 'it's kind of obvious to say that if Richard hadn't done that that day this piece would be really different and that's for me, quite fundamental to the way that we're working with space ...' (Clarke, 2001, 299). Quick has written of the element of 'play' evident in Forced Entertainment performances, and it is clear that this becomes visible in performance because of its centrality to the devising process. The title of Malzacher and Helmer's book is taken from Etchells' admission that often, in rehearsal, the rules of 'play' are broken and superseded so that the performers find themselves going 'too far' so that its import can no longer be regarded merely as 'play' (Etchells, 1999, 70).

Critical Reception

Since its inception in 1984, Forced Entertainment has attracted both negative and positive press reviews, but has won an almost unanimously positive response from venue promoters and theatre academics. This support stood the company in good stead when it encountered opposition from a key funding body. Etchells' sense is that the Arts Council campaign in 1994 attracted such support from the wider artistic community because:

> ... all kinds of people – had the feeling that if we were vulnerable in this way then this was a very poor prospect for them. I mean

that people took our fate as something of a litmus test – a test for which way the wind was blowing, for what kind of practice ACE Drama were interested in supporting. So I think it was a community thinking about its own future as well as people supporting us and what we were doing. (Etchells, 2013)

As Caridad Svich has pointed out, members of Forced Entertainment have been widely discussed as 'postmodern provocateurs' (Svich, 2003, 31) contemplating Barthesian myths of popular culture, deconstructing modernism, drawing upon Lyotard's theory of the sublime and Foucault's heterotopias. In addition to the interrogation of form, academics and critics have tended to focus upon the company's exploitation of 'live-ness' and 'real-time' – features of contemporary performance that foreground the fact that theatre unfolds in the here-and-now and is prone to the risk of failure. In particular, the work can be seen to demystify the conventions of realist theatre, which works to promote the illusion of spontaneity and immediacy while suppressing signs of artifice. Etchells has described the work as being populated by 'real people in real time, really pretending (always acknowledging they are pretending)' but conversely with 'perhaps not enough fiction for theatre people to feel comfortable and not enough real time for performance purists' (Etchells, 2003).

Negative reviews have tended to dwell upon what critics see to be a lack of optimism or tendency towards the apolitical. In 1992 Deborah Levy observed that she saw 'a spiritual and aesthetic crisis … an avant-garde that has reduced itself to a flattened post-modern pastiche in which performers lament the death of everything in their thin fragmented shows' (Levy, 1992a, vii) and reviewing *Emmanuelle Enchanted* wrote 'thirty minutes into all this postmodern suffering and disaffection, we know exactly where we are' (Levy, 1992b, 9).

Simon Shepherd has also described the 1990s as 'the theory decade' for universities and in the field of theatre and performance studies this can perhaps be most usefully characterized in terms of a shift away from performances being analysed using cultural materialist frameworks and a move towards reading for signs of deconstruction or political 'resistance' (Shepherd, 2009, 176). The influence of Jacques Derrida and post-structuralism has been widely felt in many university drama and theatre departments and Philip Auslander's reworking of Hal Foster's influential essay 'Towards a Concept of the Political in Postmodern *Theatre*' (rather than postmodern *art*) has been influential in helping critics shape an argument for an active politics in the decon-structive theatre of companies such as The Wooster Group and Forced

Entertainment. Auslander points out that the 'didactic' theatre of Brecht is predicated on a politics of transgression and the assumption that the subject can stand apart from that which is critiqued. After Derrida, who held that there is no position outside of ideology (Derrida, 1967, 158–9, 163), or, in other words, that the subject is a product of, and implicated in, the very same political system he or she critiques, a politics of transgression no longer makes sense (Auslander, 1997, 58). In place of a politics of transgression, Foster and Auslander propose a politics of resistance and see the role of the artist in postmodern culture as being to offer 'strategies of counterhegemonic resistance by exposing processes of cultural control and emphasising the traces of nonhegemonic discourses within the dominant without claiming to transcend its terms' (Auslander, 1997, 61).

Sara Jane Bailes provides an insight into how Forced Entertainment has perhaps been caught between critics reading the work through postcolonial or cultural materialist and performative strategies. She demonstrates, on the one hand, how the company's work resists the limited horizons of 'success' proposed by Thatcher's Conservative government and argues that the self-referential nature of its work is anti-hegemonic. In particular, she argues that the use of a deliberate amateurism in *Club of No Regrets* 'becomes a radical method through which to perform cultural and political resistance' because it is a 'tactical wedge that prises apart theatre's apparatus' (Bailes, 2011, 94). The meta-theatrical nature of Forced Entertainment's work means that the company can be seen to be consistently undermining the apparatus of representation while testing its limits. Liz Tomlin has articulated the ethical concerns she had with the 1995 piece *Nights in This City* while celebrating the company's contribution to the experimental theatre scene elsewhere. In her essay, Tomlin constructed a critique suggesting that the company's decision to include a white, working-class estate on its tour represented a conservative act of cultural tourism. She wrote, 'we found ourselves participating in Forced Entertainment's creative process, changing the raw material from a working-class or underclass existence into art for a predominantly middle-class audience (Tomlin, 1999, 143). Tomlin underscored what she saw to be the lack of agency of the residents of the estate, reporting that 'some residents retaliated with aggressive gestures or verbal abuse; at this point, our touristic gaze was not perceived as humorously directed at 'nothing' but as offensively directed at them' (Tomlin, 1999, 144). Tomlin is at pains to point out that she feels these ethical problems to be associated with this particular project rather than relevant to the company's oeuvre as a whole (Tomlin 2013, 156). Bailes takes issue with Tomlin's reading of this piece, commenting that 'this argument seems predicated upon the assumption that the categories of the political and social on the one hand, and the aesthetic on the other, are antagonistic, mutually exclusive, or incompatible' (Bailes, 2011, 88). She suggests that Tomlin's stance suggests 'a fixed reality' and 'a homologous sense of experience' and that it ignores the ways that theatre encourages participants to 'experience' rather than 'observe' (Bailes, 2011, 89).

The difficult coexistence of cultural materialist politics and the supposed potential of performative resistance are cogently set out in Jen Harvie's *Theatre & the City*. Harvie writes:

> In contrast to cultural materialist analysis, performative analysis concentrates overwhelmingly on the ways people can and do act with freedom to self-author, exercising agency, control and power through everyday acts of self-articulation and self-creation. It does not generally see subjects as materially and socially trapped in restrictive, oppressive, self-denying social contexts already determined by the oppressions of inescapable material circumstances; it sees opportunities to challenge those conditions. (Harvie, 2009, 45)

Forced Entertainment's work, as I have already outlined, has been appraised through a number of different critical lenses. Reading the company's self-reflexive commentary in *A Decade of Forced Entertainment* it becomes evident that the company does wish to invest in the notion of change and self-authorship and sees performance as a way of staging small acts of resistance against the hegemonic ideal. An exchange towards the end of *Decade* highlights the company's ambivalent relationship to the idea of optimism:

> Richard: What was the question people asked most about the work?
> Terry: Er, whether it was optimistic or not.
> Richard: And what was the answer they got most often?
> Terry: They used to say the work was optimistic.
> Richard: In what way?
> Terry: We said there was an optimism in the struggle of it – an optimism in the way the on-stage protagonists used and re-used the material they'd been left with. (Etchells, 1999, 43)

When asked about his conception of the discourse that has arisen around the work of Forced Entertainment, Etchells acknowledges that 'people can say what they like, of course! Once it's out there it gets discussed and framed in ways you can't control – that's the reality you live by ...' but admits to slight frustration when critics or academics focus upon a limited set of emphases, for example, that 'people exaggerate certain things – how the pieces test people's patience/play with boredom etc', or the 'antagonistic audience-baiting' aspects of some shows or the 'deconstructing everything until nothing means anything anymore' (Etchells, 2013). For him, the work is more nuanced than these arguments suggest; it aims to 'pull people in' as much as test their patience and 'construct' as much as 'deconstruct' (Etchells, 2013). At the time of writing, critics remain divided about the political dimensions of the company's work, but what is clear is that the work is held in very high esteem by academics, critics, artists, programmers and international venues. Most critics are at pains to meet the company on its own terms, at least attempting to understand the rationale for the projects before passing judgement. Forced Entertainment represents one of the most prolific and celebrated theatre companies of the 1990s and remarkably has retained its core creative ensemble, which continues to produce challenging and provocative work into its third decade.

List of Shows

Jessica in the Room of Lights (first performance: December 1984, Yorkshire Arts Space)

The Set-Up (spring, The Leadmill, Sheffield); *Nighthawks* (October 1985, North Riding College, Scarborough)

The Day that Serenity Returned to the Ground (January 1986, The Zap Club, Brighton); *(Let the Water Run its Course) to the Sea that Made the Promise* (October 1986, Trent Polytechnic, Nottingham)

200% & Bloody Thirsty (October 1988, Trent Polytechnic, Nottingham)

Some Confusions in the Law about Love (February 1989/90, The Leadmill, Sheffield)

Welcome to Dreamland (trilogy of previous three shows, July 1991, The Leadmill, Sheffield); *Marina & Lee* (March 1991, Nuffield Theatre, Lancaster)

Emmanuelle Enchanted (Or a Description of the World as if it Were a Beautiful Place) (October 1992, Nuffield Theatre, Lancaster)

Club of No Regrets (October 1993, Nuffield Theatre, Lancaster); *12 am: Awake and Looking Down* (durational piece – October 1993, National Review of Live Art); *Red Room* (performance installation with Hugo Glendinning – November, ICA, London)

Ground Plans for Paradise (installation with Hugo Glendinning – March, Leeds Metropolitan University); *Dreams' Winter* (site-specific work – July 1994, Manchester Central Library, Manchester); *Hidden J* (October, Nuffield Theatre, Lancaster); *Speak Bitterness* (durational performance – October, NRLA, Glasgow)

A Decade of Forced Entertainment (performance, lecture – February, ICA, London); *Nights in This City* (site-specific work – May 1995, Sheffield); *Speak Bitterness* (theatre piece – September, Alsager Arts Centre, Manchester)

Chapter 7

WOMEN'S THEATRE GROUP

Kate Dorney

Introduction

The Women's Theatre Group (WTG), renamed Sphinx in 1991, is one of the few alternative touring companies to have survived from the 1970s to the present day. The group's history encompasses all the snakes and ladders that beset alternative theatre companies during this period. Formed in 1973, WTG's aim was to provide roles for women in the theatre as directors, stage managers and writers and to produce work that reflected their struggle for equal rights. The company began as a women-only collective, devising and performing their own issue-based shows, which set out to challenge and remedy the lack of good roles for women and role-models for teenage girls. Members made work that debated and reflected the modern feminist experience, including sex education (*My Mother Says I Never Should*, 1975), career opportunities (*Work to Role*, 1976) and the fight for equal pay (*Out! On the Costa del Trico*, 1977). They toured work aimed specifically at young people to youth clubs and schools, played at small-scale regional venues such as community centres and also took part in the London fringe. In the late 1970s the company began commissioning writers (for example, Bryony Lavery, Deborah Levy, Lou Wakefield and Timberlake Wertenbaker), as well as devising their own shows. Throughout the 1970s and 1980s the WTG struggled with cashflow, unreliable vans, unsuitable venues and the tensions and tribulations of working as a collective. At the end of the decade the company changed to a management structure and began working on a 'rebrand' after years of gentle, and not so gentle, hints from the Arts Council.

WTG began the 1990s with a new name (Sphinx), a new, hierarchical management structure, a new Artistic Director (Sue Parrish) and a new mission statement. The company now addressed women's experience from wider formal and cultural perspectives, encompassing adaptation and translation as well as new plays. To some, the repositioning may have seemed like selling out, but it ensured the company's survival: at the time of writing, Sphinx is still in existence (albeit in a diminished form), while the Women's Street Theatre Group, Monstrous Regiment and Gay Sweatshop are not.[1] The WTG's work looms large in feminist theatre histories because of its longevity, openness to discussion, and because of the practitioners associated with it (such as Wertenbaker, Bryony Lavery, Nancy Duguid, Anna Furse and Libby Mason). WTG's sustained commitment to exploring 'herstories' and 'revisioning' women's place and experiences across an increasingly international and historical span united with the project of feminist scholarship to recover and celebrate women's contribution to culture and society. As Gabrielle Griffin and Elaine Aston, who edited two collections of WTG plays, note in their introduction:

> As regards *Herstory* [the title of the collected volumes], this concept has been widened to include a mythological and literary heritage from which the women playwrights whose work is included here sought to 'revision'. (Griffin and Aston 1991a and b, 8)

From its beginnings in the 1970s when its work focused on the immediate experiences of teenagers and factory workers, the company gradually expanded its gaze to historical and mythical figures as well experiences of women in other countries (*My Mkinga*, *Hanjo* and *Black Sail White Sail*). Monstrous Regiment, the other contemporary feminist touring company to receive both sustained funding and academic attention, was also committed to international work. Founder member of Monstrous Regiment Gillian Hanna, who documented the company's work in *Monstrous Regiment: A Collective Celebration*, notes in her introduction: 'We have always thought that we should be in touch with what women were writing about in other countries – Sisterhood is Global – so we have produced plays from the USA and translations from Italian, French, Spanish ... and Finnish' (Hanna 1991, xiv). The global reach of sisterhood, however, was not quite as embracing as that of capitalism and now only Sphinx remains as an emblem of the flowering of women's theatre companies in the 1970s and 1980s.

When writing about any organization, there is a danger of ascribing motives on the basis of outcomes and of assuming that the direction taken by the company is based on policy and ideology, where it may really be a matter of serendipity or necessity. An additional degree of caution is necessary when dealing with an alternative company that, like WTG, operated as a collective for a long period of time (1973–89). Whatever the theory, the reality is that, far from speaking and acting with one voice, the company's practice is a result of agendas that are continually shifting and colliding, as indeed was the membership of the group. Susan Croft and Jessica Higgs' remarkable project of retrieving and documenting the history of the alternative theatre movement entitled 'Unfinished Histories' contains hours of interviews in which the veterans of the women's theatre movement recall the rigours of collective working and the porous boundaries of the groups whose actors, directors and writers moved back and forth between Mrs Worthington's Daughters, The Punching Judies, Monstrous Regiment and WTG. Unlike a number of other enduring fringe companies (Foco Novo, Monstrous Regiment, Talawa), no individual or individuals stayed with WTG throughout its collective period. Actor Hazel Maycock appeared in many of the company's shows during the period under discussion and a number of directors, designers and writers worked regularly with the group, but there was no one guiding vision until Parrish took over in the 1990s. Minutes of company meetings and meetings with the Arts Council reflect the difficulties that accompanied this mode of operation. Work was conceived of or commissioned for a number of ideological and practical reasons – to address a particular aspect of women's experience, to build on successful working relationships or critical approbation or to provide opportunities for new artists – but these did not always translate to the finished product. Commissions fell through or departed from the brief; work was rushed into production before it was ready in order to fulfil touring commitments and was poorly reviewed as a result. The company had no signature style or preferred mode, although it generally included music and song in its shows and employed imaginative designers. It made documentary work (*Out! On the Costa del Trico, Dear Girl*, 1983 and *Anywhere to Anywhere*, 1985), abstract work (*Pax*, 1984) and work in verse and mask (*Witchcraze*, 1985). This eclecticism introduced an element of risk for the Arts Council and for bookers, who could never be sure that the next show would be like the last one. By the mid-1980s, the Arts Council, adopting an ever-increasing business-like attitude and the vocabulary to go with it, preferred its clients to deliver products of a consistent level of quality and format, and WTG, like many other companies, struggled with this move to a more corporate, homogenous model.

The 1980s and early 1990s were a crucial time in the development of WTG/Sphinx. At the start of the 1980s the company was settling into a more 'professional' phrase. It had begun to employ directors and designers to work on the shows and to allocate specific administration and stage management duties. It gradually moved away from work directed solely at teenagers, learned to work with playwrights, to negotiate the Arts Council's ever-changing funding system and policy shifts, to win grants from the GLC and to attract sponsorship. It also developed a committed equal opportunities policy far in advance of peers and provided opportunities for black actors, writers and directors. By the 1990s the WTG (and funders) felt the need to move from the barricades to the mainstream in terms of the presentation of, and meditations on, the role of women in theatre and the world. Alongside the company's new artistic direction on stage, it pursued a series of initiatives aimed at highlighting the debate about women in theatre. The most notable of these was the annual *Glass Ceiling* conferences (1991–2002), which debated all aspects of women in theatre and culture. These events, pulling practitioners and academics together in dialogue, brought the WTG full circle to the circumstances that led to the company's inauguration.

WTG was born of the Women's Movement and was supported by the trade union, activist and education sectors as part of the broader project to challenge sex discrimination. As a result of these allegiances, the company worked closely with a number of academics, including founding member Mica Nava, a specialist in gender and cultural theory, and Julie Holledge, who was conducting her doctoral research into the role of women in Edwardian theatre while working as a director with the group. WTG operated in a dense network, and became the focus of a great deal of academic work based on women and theatre in the 1980s and 1990s, notably by Lizbeth Goodman, Geraldine Cousin and Elaine Aston. When WTG became Sphinx in the 1990s, it continued these networks through the *Glass Ceiling* events, which brought academics, policy-makers and practitioners together to debate the position of women in society and culture.[2] The group's openness towards researchers and writers has contributed to its continued presence in British theatre's historical consciousness, but studies tend to focus on the production of *Lear's Daughters*, restaged and filmed by the Open University thanks to Goodman. An upsurge in the drive to publish new work by women in the 1980s means that WTG's work from that period is preserved in print for study, restaging and inspiration, alongside a video recording of *My Mother Says I Never Should* (made by the Inner London Education Authority) and an audio recording of *Dear Girl*. Additionally, the company's archive is housed in the Theatre and Performance department of the Victoria and Albert Museum, where it is available to researchers alongside the archive of the Arts Council of Great Britain.

History of the Company's Development

In 1973, the Almost Free Theatre in Soho hosted a Women's Theatre Festival. Founded by producer/director Ed Berman, the Almost Free was a lunchtime venue with an eclectic programme. Berman was keen to follow up the success of Pam Gems' double bill exploring women's sexuality (*My Warren* and *After Birthday*) with a season of work by women. Gems and a group of women writers, directors, stage managers and performers accepted his invitation and set to work. Anxious to avoid the hierarchical process they regarded as typical of the male-dominated theatre industry, they chose to work via a series of open meetings to which any interested women could come to read and discuss scripts. The aim was to allow ideas and productions to develop organically but, inevitably, the pressure of having a show ready for the deadline meant that the group decided on scripted shows cast in the conventional way. As a result, the final Women's Festival programme mostly included the work of established writers, including Gems (*The Amiable Courtship of Miz Venus* and *Wild Bill*) and Michelene Wandor (*Mal de Mère*), and only one hitherto-unproduced writer, Jane Wibberley (*Parade of Cats*). Buzz Goodbody, Lily Susan Todd, Dinah Brooke and Liane Aukin were also involved in the festival as directors and performers. Buoyed by the success of the season, the group decided to continue to work through open meetings, but a schism soon developed between those theatre professionals frustrated with the opportunities and work available to them (including Gems and Todd) and the other women in the group who were committed to collective working (including Lynn Ashley and Anne Engel). One group, including Gems and Todd, began to work under the name of the Women's Theatre Company while Ashley, Engel and others carried on using the name Women's Theatre Group.[3] The new WTG was composed of a collection of theatre professionals with experience of Theatre in Education (TIE) and youth work, socialist theatre, the West End and feminists with no theatre experience at all. The founding members were Ashley, Clair Chapman, Engel, Jean Hart, Mica Nava and Julia Meadows. The group opted to devise work collectively, incorporating music and song, and to focus on producing work for the community (teenagers in particular). They modelled themselves on existing agitprop collectives and tapped into those networks for support and touring venues. The early work – agitprop and epic in form – had much in common with alternative theatre of the time in that it was big on ideas and intent but less focused on smooth execution. The first show, *Fantasia* (1974), explored the fantasies of two different women, and secured them Arts Council funding. The second show, *My Mother Says I Never Should* (1975), addressed teenage sexuality and contraception head on and was hugely influential, touring for two years and being filmed by the Inner London Education Authority. At this stage, the political impact of the shows was enough to guarantee the enthusiasm of audiences, regardless of ability. Anne Engel remembers that 'we carried people who really couldn't act but we hit the political nail with *My Mother Says*' (Engel, Unfinished Histories). The issue of mixed ability was to be a recurring problem for the company.

In 1978, WTG employed writers for the first time, commissioning *Hot Spot* (1978) from Eileen Fairweather and Melissa Murray and then *Soap Opera* (1979) from Donna Franceschild. Bryony Lavery was the third writer to receive a commission from them, resulting in *The Wild Bunch* (1979), a play about teenagers. Encouraging new work by women had always been part of the company's remit, and from this point on commissioning new writing became a cornerstone of policy, although this did not guarantee the writer freedom from interventions by the company. By the 1980s, the group's focus was shifting to the cultural history of women throughout the world, taking in female explorers (Timberlake Wertenbaker's *New Anatomies*, 1981), female pilots during the Second World War (Joyce Halliday's *Anywhere to Anywhere*) and women during the Crusades (Julie Wilkinson's *Pinchdice and Co*, 1989), as well as drug dumping in Africa (*My Mkinga*, 1980), drug addiction (Paulette Randall's *Fixed Deal*, 1986) and contemporary lesbian relationships (*Double Vision*, 1982).

Minutes from the company's meetings suggest that the WTG struggled with a collective model for the best part of a decade. The company's structure encompassed administrators, actors and a musician/composer, while designers, directors and other performers were hired as freelancers. This often created problems, as writers had to submit to their work being rewritten by the company to suit the performers, while directors had little or no influence on casting and had sometimes to work with actors who could not sing or play instruments, or musicians who could not act. It was also difficult for the group to devise work that played to the strengths of everyone in the company. In interviews Engel and Adele Saleem, a member of WTG from 1980–83, acknowledged the tensions this caused and the impact on the quality of the work, and show reports on WTG's work, found in the Arts Council of Great Britain archive, return time and again to this problem. Director Kate Crutchley, then working as Theatre Programmer at the Ovalhouse, a venue that often booked WTG work, noted that in *Soap Opera*:

> some performances were very good; but the tendency in collectives is to drag along the hard-working good company members who can't actually do the job on stage. And most companies have one or two. (ACGB 1979, 41/51/8c)

As a former member of Gay Sweatshop, Crutchley was speaking from a position of authority. Arts Council Drama Officer Nick Barter, a self-described veteran of fringe theatre work, also reporting on *Soap Opera*, identifies another problem that the company struggled with; that of ideology winning out over aesthetics: 'it's no longer sufficient that these statements are made and these companies exist. They must make them well and imaginatively cf *Dear Love of Comrades* which was excellent' (ACGB 1979a, 41/51/8).

Soap Opera did not bode well for WTG's new decision to commission writers, and Lavery's *The Wild Bunch*, about girls in a youth club, was not much more successful. Watching a performance at Battersea Arts Centre, Gerald Chapman, then running the Young Writers' Programme at the Royal Court, pitied the performers 'lumbered with an abstract, formulistic script' (ACGB 1979b). While Drama Officer Sian Ede noted that although 'Les Girls swing, hang, perch, lie or drape fairly aesthetically though not with enough acrobatic skill for real success ... [they] can't really act' (ACGB 1979d). Both shows were directed by Julie Holledge, who having co-founded Mrs Worthington's Daughters that same year, was simultaneously working with WTG on an Arts Council's director's bursary. She also directed their next show, *My Mkinga* (1980), an investigation into drug dumping in the Third World inspired by *The Political Economy of Health* by Lesley Doyal and Imogen Pennell. Holledge and Kate Phelps researched and devised the show with Phelps scripting. Having begun work, it dawned on the group that the plot, showing a family planning team visiting a village in Tanzania, required a more ethnically diverse group of performers. They brought a black actress, Dorrett Thompson, into the collective for the first time. When Thompson left, the show was dropped from the repertoire earlier than planned because of the difficulty of recruiting another black actress to replace her. Maintaining black members of the collective was an enduring problem for WTG (ACGB 1980a).

By the mid-1980s WTG had an explicit policy on equal opportunities, and was actively engaged in a positive discrimination programme to recruit black and lesbian women. As they rather despairingly note during a discussion of policy in 1986:

> Company has a respectable feminist image but does not fulfil its policy of challenging women ... nothing spectacular – worthy, plodding image ... over the years WTG has lost its London audience ... publicity stunt to recapture those audiences ... it's no longer enough to be a feminist company, audiences which challenge now seem to be predominantly black and gay ... these audiences aren't being tapped by WTG'. (Sphinx Archive, 1986a)

However, company minutes reveal that the two black performers in the company, Delmozene Morris and Lennie St Luce, expressed discomfort at having to be 'experts' on black issues, and it was proposed 'that they have the breathing space to assemble their ideas as black women ... to be able to discuss with each other' (Sphinx Archive 1986a). As part of its programme to address an ethnically and socially diverse audience, WTG commissioned plays from Winsome Pinnock and Paulette Randall (a founding member of Theatre of Black Women), shared an Arts Council Director's bursary scheme with Temba (awarded to Decima Francis), made strenuous efforts to increase the diversity of the group and produced plays reflecting the experiences of black women. Unlike its sister companies, however, WTG struggled to find bookings or an audience in 'black' venues (Sphinx Archive, 1986b). As well as creating roles for specifically black and Asian performers, the company was an early adopter of colour-blind casting. Morris and St Luce appeared in Deborah Levy's controversial *Our Lady* (1986) and *Fixed Deal* (1986), which was commissioned from Randall, who re-scripted it using devised work by Tasha Fairbanks.[4] *Lear's Daughters* (1987) featured Sandra Yaw and Adjoa Andoh. Yaw then appeared in Pinnock's *Picture Palace* (1988) and later wrote a play for the company, *Zerri's Choice* (1989). Morris and Andoh continued to appear in plays with the company into the 1990s, by which time WTG had moved to a radical policy of positive discrimination, proposing that every appointment made to a white person should be on a one-year basis, to enable positions to be reserved for black actors. Although admirable in intent, and in spite of the Arts Council's commitment to equal opportunities that had been in operation since 1985, the Drama Department believed the policy would only increase WTG's staff problems (the company were finding it hard to retain stage management and administrators) and counselled against it (ACGB, 1990, 34/164).

WTG's transformation into Sphinx was a slow process. The Arts Council were keen to move the company, along with a selection of other clients, from small- to middle-scale touring, but that was only possible if it produced work of a certain type and quality. In 1986 WTG examined itself anew after a number of established members left the company and an Arts Council Review Panel suggested that it extend voting right to the newly established Advisory Board because it was felt that there was insufficient experience within the company core. At a company meeting, Advisory Board member Jenny Harris, a veteran of The Combination and Executive Director of the Albany Empire, asked searching questions about who the group thought its audience was, and pointed out two of the long-standing problems of collective management continuity – high turnover of staff and quality of work (the Arts Council had been raising these points for several years). The minutes also record Harris's candid assessment of the company:

> JH raised the lack of high profile of the Group. It was suggested that the Group's profile suffered because the Group did not engage directors of established reputation and that the use of such women would allow the company to move into the middle-scale venues as well as more community-orientated work. (Sphinx 1986b)

WTG was no longer the brightest or biggest jewel in the feminist alternative theatre crown. In fact, from the Arts Council's point of view, alternative theatre was the past, and middle-scale touring was the future – it represented a slicker, more stylish product for a slicker decade.

Key Works

The Hits

In 1980 Timberlake Wertenbaker was commissioned by WTG to write a play about male impersonators, including Vesta Tilley. Instead, she ended up writing a play about the Swiss explorer Isabelle Eberhardt who lived in Morocco as a man (Vesta Tilley was transformed into a minor character, Verda Miles, a successful male impersonator avowedly feminine in her offstage life). The show was widely trailed even before it had been written, and attracted actor Adele Saleem to the company because she wanted to work on the project (Engel, Unfinished Histories). Director Julie Holledge was also keen to work on it but, along with Saleem, had first to endure a run of *Breaking Through*, also by Wertenbaker, an anti-nuclear teenage sci-fi musical. Saleem, Holledge and Wertenbaker all agreed that it didn't really work, but the press reviews and Arts Council show reports suggest otherwise, hailing it as a remarkable piece of youth theatre. By contrast, and a good example of how companies were expected to please a variety of masters, *New Anatomies* (1981), widely reported as a success by the press, the company and academics, was viewed largely with disapproval and/or boredom by the Arts Council reviewers, whose overall impression was that it was 'very disappointing' (ACGB 1981, 41/54/8b), 'dull' (ACGB 1981, 41/54/8a) and 'tame and predictable' (ACGB 1981,41/54/8c).

The first hit show of the decade for funders and punters was, rather improbably, the anthology piece *Better a Live Pompey than a Dead Cyril* (1980), an evening of words and music using and celebrating the work of Stevie Smith. The show had no through-narrative: rather, songs and readings were grouped thematically and performed against an elegant set of Art Deco stained glass flats. The contrast with the group's next success, *Double Vision* (1982), could hardly be more pronounced. Devised by the company and directed by Libby Mason, it was a funny and engaging account of lesbian life and love in London. The main characters Sparky and Chum meet in a gay pub when Chum, a committed activist and 'political' lesbian, tries to recruit Sparky to a Reclaim the Night march. They begin a relationship; Sparky, a northern, working-class, apparently uncomplicated ambulance driver gently but persistently mocks Chum for her earnest efforts at consciousness-raising and fighting for feminist causes. As their relationship develops, Sparky finds herself acting the role of 'wife', cooking and cleaning, while Chum works on her various campaigns. Bored and unfulfilled, Sparky goes to the Greenham Women's Peace Camp at Chum's suggestion and returns animated and invigorated: Chum is both jealous and proud. Their relationship staggers on through several more crunch points of opposing ideologies, including their views on parenthood. Chum wants children, Sparky unexpectedly reveals that she was married, had a child and didn't enjoy the experience. The issue that finally separates them is direct action – a confrontation that begins and ends the play (in one of three alternative endings). Their action and behaviour is commented on by the figure of the Narrator, who also sings the songs that counterpoint each scene.

City Limits described it 'a Woody Allen script for lesbians' while Libby Mason, the play's director and leader of the improvisation workshops which fed the scripts, stresses the fact that:

> the piece was never conceived of as a 'lesbian' play, in that it does not attempt to offer generalisations from specifically lesbian relationships. We wanted to present a piece in which the central relationship *happened* to be a lesbian one, just as most plays 'happen' to have heterosexual assumptions, but do not purport to be 'about' heterosexuality. (Davis, 1987, 53)

Double Vision was certainly never advertised by the company as a lesbian play and the publicity refers to it only as a play looking at the relationship between the personal and political. Reading the script that Mason assembled, it feels like an important contemporary document recording how WTG felt about the various issues it was dealing with personally and professionally. Chum works for a feminist collective ('we don't have a leader' [Davis, 1987, 53]). Arranging their next date, having spent their first night together, she tells Sparky: 'I'm going to take you to see a play on Friday ... It's about women and self-image. No, don't say anything'(Davis, 1987, 35). WTG had done a play, *Pretty Ugly* (1977), on precisely this subject, raising the delightful possibility that they were making a joke about their own good intentions. Similarly, the play acknowledges the struggle of the women's movement, and leftist movements in general, to deal with the un-politically correct reality of mixing with the working classes. Chum, real name Bryony, is from the same kind of background as WTG's founding members: confident and middle class. She enjoys meetings, discussion groups and issue-based theatre. Sparky is an ambulance driver who enjoys snooker and pubs. The Narrator comments: 'more than occasionally, Chum would make a mental note to talk to Sparky about her behaviour, but more often than not she dismissed her doubts as being puritanical and slightly small-minded' (Davis, 1987, 36). Nevertheless she is unable to stop herself from snapping 'do not objectify your sisters' when Sparky makes a joke about winning the glamorous assistant on a TV quiz show (Davis, 1987, 36).

Double Vision was one of three shows the company produced in an attempt to move from agitprop issue plays into an examination of the 'personal as political'. The other two, *Dear Girl* (1983) and *Love and Dissent* (1983), were also successful in broadening the company's audiences and attracting bookings. *Dear Girl* was a documentary piece based on a collection of letters and diaries between four working-class women made available to WTG's administrator, Tierl Thompson. WTG asked Mason to direct, and she and Thompson also scripted the show. The tour was 'very successful indeed', with the group playing to capacity audiences in most venues according to WTG's minutes (Sphinx Archive, 1983a).

Anywhere to Anywhere (1985) followed the success of *Dear Girl* in investigating and presenting women's history in the form of a 'musical documentary' about the Air Transport Auxiliary, a civilian organization that employed women pilots to transport planes during the Second World War. Directed by Kate Crutchley, the script was produced from research, interviews and workshops. Having stated its reservations about the project, essentially that the show focused on middle- and upper-class women, the company eventually decided to use the show 'to reach more women and men over forty five and a generally wider audience' (Sphinx Archive, 1984b). The success of the show not only earned the company a surplus – it also encouraged audiences to book for the next piece, Bryony Lavery's *Witchcraze* (which turned out to be something of a flop).

Lear's Daughters, a 'prequel' to *King Lear*, was the company's biggest success in the 1980s, both critically and commercially. In an interview in *City Limits*, novelist, poet and translator Elaine Feinstein described leaving a production of *King Lear* at the National Theatre wondering how the daughters had become the people they were. She had been reading Melanie Klein's work on the way mothers influenced the development of their daughters, and this led her to speculate about Lear's queen and her relationship with her children. WTG commissioned Feinstein to write a play exploring women and power through the prism of Shakespeare's play which they then workshopped for five weeks before producing the eventual published script (jointly credited to Feinstein and the WTG).[5] Director Gwenda Hughes explained to *City Limits*: 'the strength of Elaine's idea, for us, was that it was a metaphor for all women and their fathers and all women, not just those women that then go on to be in *King Lear*' (Feinstein 1986, n.p). The play shows Lear's daughters growing up increasingly isolated from but obsessed by their father. They spend their days shut up in a tower with only their pastimes and the Fool to divert them. Regan loves to carve wood, Goneril likes to paint and Cordelia has a passion for words. They are cared for by Nanny while their mother slowly fades away and dies, exhausted by Lear's continual attempts to father a son. Even before her death, the mother is portrayed as a remote figure, reluctant to see the girl children who remind her of her failure to produce a boy. Nanny is the surrogate mother and the teller of stories.

The *Times Educational Supplement* praised the play as 'unflinchingly original, sumptuously theatrical and quite beautifully performed' (McFerran, 1987). It drew on epic techniques to create a powerful and visually coherent production. The Fool acts as master of ceremonies, directly addressing the audience, moving in and out of the theatrical frame, telling jokes, singing songs, assuming the roles of Lear and his queen, and unsettling the 'poor little rich girl' aspect of the narrative. Lear's daughters may be unloved or unregarded but they grow up provided for, unlike the Fool, who previously kept body and soul together 'as a singer of filthy and wanton songs' and as a wise woman who 'heard voices. For money', and is now obsessed with earning and hoarding money (Fischlin and Fortier, 2000, 121). Like the Players in Stoppard's *Rosencrantz and Guildenstern are Dead* (1967), the comedy of the role is offset by occasional reminders that life in those days was nasty, brutish and short and that money offered a means of protection. As cuts to public spending started to bite in Thatcher's Britain, the Fool's willingness to do anything for money would have been a stark reminder of the lack of opportunities for young people. In the WTG version, the Fool's deliberate androgyny ('Are you a man or a woman? ... Depends who's asking' [Fischlin and Fortier, 2000, 121]) is highlighted by an extraordinary motley form: a costume that combines a man's suit and a woman's evening gown complete with false bared breasts. Hazel Maycock, who originated the role, played it with frizzy hair and clown make-up, which calls to mind Gethin Price's costume for his showcase in *Comedians* (1975).

The play takes the elements of fairytale and subverts them. The princesses in the tower are not rescued by handsome princes, but released to Albany and Cornwall in a calculated financial transaction. The fairytale element divided the critics. Establishment (male) critics found it infantile and reductive. In the *Independent*, Peter Kemp complained that 'the regulation anti-male animus here capers around in nursery trappings' (Kemp 1987), while *The Sunday Times* described it as a 'piece of aggressive triviality and mindbending tedium' (Anon, 1987). The majority of critics and audiences did not agree and the show was toured again and has subsequently been restaged and written about extensively by academics.

Her Aching Heart (1990) proved third time lucky for Bryony Lavery and WTG. Lavery drew inspiration from the breathless-prose style of romantic novelists like Georgette Heyer to create one of the company's most successful shows. This funny lesbian romance juxtaposes a historical relationship with a contemporary one: the latter are reading the story of the former, and both couples are played by the same pair of actors. Lavery revelled in parodying the conventions of the romance genre – the historical Molly is a lowly peasant girl, while Harriet is a fierce and haughty member of the gentry. Elaborate and overwrought stage directions describe the characters' emotions and actions: 'her tears flow, like the River Dart, fast and furious' (Lavery, 1991, 89). Stereotypical characters abound – pert serving wenches, apple-cheeked grandmothers and lusty fops. Lavery also draws attention to the requirements for doubling up characters in a series of comic stage directions:

> **Betsy** *enters. Although in these penurious times she may seem physically similar to* **Molly Penhallow** *... she is a completely different character. Born in Cheapside, she is a pert member of the serving classes.* (Lavery 1991, 99)

The play was very successful, playing to capacity audiences and creating enough demand for a second tour. It was directed by Claire Grove, a member of the company who inspired the Arts Council's confidence and who it was thought might lead the company forward in its redevelopment. Instead, she left to work for the BBC.

The Roaring Girl's Hamlet (1992) was the company's second appropriation/reimagining of Shakespeare's work after *Lear's Daughters*. This time the focus was on examining the dynamics of a company of women performing *Hamlet*, led by Moll Cutpurse, the Elizabethan cross-dresser immortalized in Middleton and Dekker's *The Roaring Girl* (1607–10). The prologue, written by Claire Luckham, was developed through a workshop with Royal Shakespeare Company actresses Harriet Walter, Suzanne Bertish and Dinah Stabb. The play had mixed reviews, partly as a result of its appearance soon after fellow touring company Cheek by Jowl had premiered its much-acclaimed all-male *As You Like It*. It was the first show produced under the name Sphinx and was also the company's first co-production (with Croydon Warehouse). A second attempt to look at the historical plight of women in the theatre, in April de Angelis's *Playhouse Creatures* (1993), fared much better. An imaginative reconstruction of the lives of Restoration actresses Nell Gwyn, Mary Betterton and Doll Common, the play received reviews in the mainstream national press (a rare occurrence for the company who more often featured in *Time Out, City Limits* and *Spare Rib*) and augured well for the company's new direction.

The Misses

The mid-1980s were a difficult time for the company and resulted in some of its least successful work. This was partially due to the pressure of producing two to three shows a year, touring them and running additional writers' workshops and rehearsed readings. The burden of all these activities meant that if a show was slow to get off the ground or had problems in rehearsal, the company was compelled to send out unfinished or barely salvaged work. An example of this is *Witchcraze* (1985), a historical survey of women and witchcraft written by Bryony Lavery, which was poorly received by ACGB assessors and critics. The company decided to work with masks, and Lavery struggled to create a script, telling *Time Out*: 'It was very frightening and very different writing for masks: so much is visual that there's hardly any script and where normally there'd be some idea of character development there was nothing' (Rose, 1985). The published script bears out Lavery's comment about characterization, as with a number of WTG's other historical-survey shows, notably *Time Pieces* (1982). It is hard to distinguish between the characters in *Witchcraze* and to have any investment in their fates. The seed of *Witchcraze* is first minuted in a 'Future Plans' meeting on 11 December 1984, the agenda for which suggests the company was seeking a new (to them) direction but running short of ideas:

Agenda
1. Pendle witches
2. Miners
3. Thriller/Gothic horror
4. Women on the edge of time
5. Women in Thatcher's Britain
6. Writers
7. A[nywhere]To A[nywhere]. (Sphinx 1984c)

Many of the topics on the list had been treated by other women's groups and writers: Angela Carter's *The Bloody Chamber* (1979) had dealt with item 3 and Caryl Churchill had covered items 4 and (5 with *Top Girls* (1982), and some of 2 with *Vinegar Tom* (1976). *Witchcraze* was partly inspired by a comment Churchill had made about researching

Vinegar Tom (1976) for Monstrous Regiment (one of the company's most successful shows), to the effect that she had left 'to one side' the fascinating suggestion that witchcraft had its origins in pre-Christian religion (Griffin and Aston 1991a, 16). Lavery's script took this as its starting point but with verse, masks and a troubled rehearsal period, it failed to reach the expectations of the company or audiences.

Fixed Deal (1986), a play about drug addicts commissioned from Paulette Randall, also had a number of problems. Randall submitted the script late and incomplete so the company was forced to devise a new show using this script as a basis. Their Arts Council-funded black director, Decima Francis, had been employed to direct a complete script, and demanded an additional fee for working with the company on devising. The company also employed another director to work with it on the play to redirect/re-rehearse the show. The result, unsurprisingly, was a confused melange, attempting to look at drug addiction from a stylized, lyrical viewpoint rather than a realistic one. ACGB assessors Ian Brown (later to be Arts Council Drama Director) and producer Peter Tod struggled to find positive aspects of the production to praise. Brown noted:

> if the writing had lifted off, the whole thing might have come over like a heroin-addicted *Under Milk Wood* or a version of *AC/DC*. But it wasn't, so it seemed like a student exercise, lacking in coherence or impact. (ACGB 1986, 41/54/8a)

Tod was a little kinder:

> It was an evening of the inner hell totally out of control, and it is perhaps the complexity of the drug/addiction scene being now so big that the piece in trying to cover everything, failed in achieving anything. (ACGB 1986, 41/54/8b)

The second show of 1986, Deborah Levy's *Our Lady* (1986), described as a 'blasphemous thriller' in the pre-publicity, also ran into problems. The play followed three women, all claiming to be the Virgin Mary, being tried for heresy by a fifteenth-century Grand Inquisitor. Levy's abstract stylings and controversial subject matter led to cancelled bookings and a deficit for the company. Had it not been for the success of *Lear's Daughters* in 1987, the company might well have foundered.

Funding and Company Structure

WTG first received funding from the Arts Council of Great Britain in 1975. It was revenue funded for small-scale touring work from the beginning, and supplemented this with grants from the GLC (later London Borough Grants Board), Regional Arts Associations and additional bursaries from Arts Council's schemes for directors, writers in residence and other initiatives. Their adherence to collectivist principles meant that all company members were paid a salary, and freelancers were hired at Equity/ITC rates. The company's financial stability was dependent on venues booking the shows and paying the fees stated in the budgets: any shifts in this, or any unforeseen circumstances, could propel the company into deficit. In the early 1980s WTG had a real problem with cashflow because of the uncertain nature of touring, and spent many of their board meetings discussing the situation with the Drama Officer. This is a typical extract from their deliberations at the time:

> Ways of dealing with the financial situation in the longer term were discussed. It was pointed out that though the companies were expected to be artistically lively and interested in new work they were penalised for it because new initiatives had to be paid for out of a grant adjusted to previous work. (Sphinx Archive, 1981)

The company was very disgruntled that Monstrous Regiment was in receipt of a more generous grant and there was much rejoicing when it was awarded a 20 per cent funding uplift in 1982, which put the two on level pegging. WTG work always had a strong design focus, which went above and beyond making sure the set was a) light (as they had to transport and install it themselves) and b) adaptable. The group collaborated with a number of designers and worked hard to try to incorporate actors and audience in the same space through careful design. In 1983, it was awarded a sizeable performers' bursary 'for a two week training period in singing, choral speaking and the physical creation of theatrical images without the use of properties and set' (Sphinx Archive, 1983b). It is tempting to draw a direct link from this workshop to the company's later, more physical work (for example, *Witchcraze*, *Pax*, *Lear's Daughters*), but, as discussed in the introduction to this chapter, we should be wary about directly attributing influences in this way. The company's repertoire is a good example of this. The members planned diligently, discussed passionately and decided the whole programme of work on a collective basis, but sometimes commissions fell through or projects collapsed, and when that happened, they were left with little alternative but to produce whatever was left, which is how *Anywhere to Anywhere* (1985) ended up in the programme. The minutes record that some members of the company had reservations about the match between the group's politics and the show's content. As stated, the women who worked in the Air Transport Auxiliary were middle- and upper-class, and they were concerned that the only 'angle' on the play available was 'nostalgia' (Sphinx Archive, 1984a). The company was also discussing a play about miners' wives at the same time, a topic generally considered more 'apt' and topical. But eventually *Anywhere to Anywhere* was the only show ready to go, and so it went into production and, despite the company's initial reservations, was very successful (Sphinx Archive, 1984a).

Throughout the 1980s, it was increasingly clear to the company and ACGB personnel that WTG was struggling with the collective form. In 1986 the company voted to establish an Advisory Board because it wished 'to have a body which could provide an overview of the work of the company, give advice and bring to the attention of the Group areas for development' (Sphinx Archive 1986b). In the same year, the company was reviewed by the Arts Council, which had begun to shift to a more business-focused mode of operation, yet was keen to help WTG regain its reputation and bookings and assist its move into middle-scale touring. In 1989 the collective structure was wound down and a small management team was formed, along with a Board of Directors, whose expertize could help move the company towards developing and showcasing new writing and away from devised work.[6] Claire Grove was the first Artistic Director, quickly followed by Sue Parrish when Grove joined the BBC. Parrish had impeccable credentials: she had worked at the 'Half Moon Theatre, London' workshops and co-founded the Standing Conference of Women Theatre Directors and Administrators in 1979 and the Women's Playhouse Trust in 1980.

The company launched a concerted research campaign to find out what its audiences and peers in the theatre industry thought about WTG and used that work to provide feedback to a consultant, who worked on rebranding and repositioning. Part of the research was a survey to canvass public awareness of the company. The majority of those surveyed could not/did not distinguish the WTG from other women's companies and couldn't successfully identify its work. The survey results bore out on a grand scale what the group had learned on a smaller one. Collective identity, like collective working, had become a weakness rather than a strength and the WTG needed a separate, distinctive identity (Sphinx Archive, n.d.). WTG had wanted to rename itself the National Women's Theatre Company, which both the Arts Council and the branding consultant were against (Sphinx Archive, n.d). WTG thought the problematic part of the name was 'group', but much of the evidence pointed to the fact that it was 'Women': thus Sphinx was born. The publicity explained:

Why The Sphinx?
As the original national touring women's theatre company, the Women's Theatre Group has been developing and commissioning new theatre writing by women since 1973. Following a summer of extensive research into audience perceptions of the field, in which a number of our mailing list members took part, the company marks a new phase in its life with a new name, The Sphinx, and with the artistic maturity to take its place in the mainstream of British theatre. The Sphinx reflects the work of the company in all her qualities:
She is:

FEMALE – placing women's experience centre-stage;
CLASSICAL – proud of her past, developing the canon of women's writing;
STORY-TELLING – producing original, spectacular, high-quality theatre;
MULTIFORM – reflecting women in all their diversity and
  subjectivity;
DANGEROUS – challenging and risk-taking theatre;
ORGANIC – nurturing the development of women's writing.
She has:
A WOMAN'S HEAD – to be a leading voice in addressing the
  cultural disenfranchisement of women;
A LION'S BODY – to fight for the creative freedom of women
  artists. (Sphinx Archive, n.d)

Without wishing to sound unduly cynical, it is hard to see how this elaborate reasoning could be apparent to the woman in the street. The company may have aspired to reflect women in all their 'diversity and subjectivity', but, in common with other alternative companies, members were mostly playing to constituencies like themselves – middle-class by education, if not by birth. The key point about the new name, however, is that by the 1990s it was unusual for companies to have names that overtly advertised their politics. But it was not unusual for the Arts Council to be encouraging companies to use consultants and corporate language. As Sue Beardon, Monstrous Regiment company member and Administrator from 1976–8, noted in 1991:

> In the 1980s the priorities of an arts administrator are shaped by considerations of funding, marketing and managerial efficiency. Arts funding bodies, guided by the prevailing monetarist philosophy of the present government, set stringent criteria for companies, based on their organisational effectiveness and ability to obtain a range of sponsorship. This is the age of the business plan, the consultant, the strategist, incentive funding and expensive fund-raising training. The only growth area in the arts it seems and the only place anyone can make a decent living. (Hanna, 1991, xxvi)

Beardon's comment sums up the large-scale shift made by the Arts Council, and perforce its successful 'clients' in the 1990s. Sphinx's re-launch went unremarked in Arts Council publications, but did get a mention in a full-page interview with Lynn Greenwood, the consultant who effected it, in a brochure advertising the Association for Business Sponsorship of the Arts (Greenwood, n.d.).

Key Productions by the Company 1980–94

Note that tour details are not exhaustive. They are based on information drawn from Arts Council show reports, promotional material and press reviews and reports. Venues vary but usually include colleges and university arts centres, community halls, studio theatres and established fringe venues.

The Wild Bunch by Bryony Lavery, directed by Julie Holledge. Topic: girls in a youth club. Toured to schools and Battersea Arts Centre, 1979/80.

My Mkinga devised by the company, directed by Julie Holledge. Topic: drug dumping in third world. Performed at the ICA, Africa Centre, Tottenham College and Leeds Trade Council Club, 1980.

Better a Live Pompey than a Dead Cyril by Clare McIntyre and Stephanie Nunn. Topic: 'A personal musical view of Stevie Smith's

NOTES

Chapter 1: Historical and Cultural Background

1   A clip of the performance can be viewed on http://vimeo.com/43188922, making up part of a local news feature on the company.

2   The name of the show is not mentioned in Davis's report, but it is likely that she is either referring to *In Or Out* or *Killers*. Both plays toured as a double bill during 1980–1.

3   *The Gentle Touch* (1980–4) 'Private Views', Series 4. Network, 2010.

4   A recording of the song can be heard on the Women's Liberation Music Archive, http://womensliberationmusicarchive.wordpress.com/t/.

Chapter 2: British Theatre Companies 1980–1994

1   The article is undated and I have not been able to locate the original publication. When I wrote to Naseem Khan she replied, 'My guess would be 1978 since MAAS was set up in '76' (email to the author, 5 October 2013), but references in the article place it approximately in 1983.

2   Despite contacting Jude Kelly by email, the author received no reply to this query.

3   The proposal was rejected by NAPS and the show remained unproduced.

4   Despite extensive enquiries made to former Arts Council staff, I have been unable to identify the individual concerned.

5   See note above.

6   Guy Slater in his show report for *Meet Me* (1984) mentions the English/Urdu mix and reports an audience of around 60 'largely Asian, and very attentive'(ACGB, 1984, 41/30/4b).

7   Looking at the webpage of the festival's organizer, Madhav Sharma, there were a great deal more Asian performers than Tara gave credit for. See http://www.madhavsharma.com. I have also been unable to find or locate the Nigel Hawthorne production of Chekhov that Tara referred to.

8   David Sulkin from the Royal Court's Young People's Theatre also directed Tara's 1982 *Scenes in the Life*.

9   *Mind Your Language* was a long-running British television situation comedy that ran from late 1977 to 1986. Set in a language evening class, the series enjoyed huge popularity, and later notoriety. In both cases, this arose from humour generated by the crude racial stereotypes that made up the adult learners in the class.

10   Jenny Topper, then working as a director at the Bush Theatre, comments

that, on the night she saw the play at Theatro Technis, out of an audience of 13 or 14, none were Asian (ACGB, 1982, 41/30/4f), while Arts Council Drama Officer Paul Barnard, reporting from the Croydon Warehouse, observes that out of an audience of 40, eight were Asian (ACGB, 1982 41/30/4g). Similarly, Michael Quine in his report notes that out of an audience of 23, seven were Arts Council assessors (ACGB, 1982, 41/30/4e).

11   David Edgar is referring to two 1981 Shakespearian productions that he clearly saw as unsuccessful in their depictions of race. Michael Rudman's *Measure for Measure* at the Lyttleton Theatre used a cast of 31 black actors and set the play in the West Indies, while at the RSC Ron Daniels' *A Midsummer Night's Dream* cast the black actor Joseph Marcello as Puck.

12   Waldman also makes the same point for Graeae being the only professional disabled company.

13   During the meeting it was agreed that Rational Theatre's recent shows at the ICA were not deemed to be of sufficient quality and should not be considered further for revenue funding.

Chapter 3: Joint Stock Theatre Company: 1980–1989

1   I would like to express my thanks for the assistance and expertise offered by the staff of Blythe House at the Victoria & Albert Museum and Special Collections at University of California, Davis. In particular, I would like to extend special thanks to Patricia (Patsy) Inouye, State and Local Government Information Librarian at UC Davis, for exceptional research support.

2   Exceptions were Howard Barker's *Victory* and *Power of the Dog*, which did not follow the workshop process.

3   The term 'black' as used here also includes individuals of Asian descent.

4   Curiously, *Borderline* was presented at the Asian Festival, held 5–12 October 1981, of which Madhav Sharma was Artistic Director. As the festival's schedule would have been planned months in advance, and because *Borderline* did not receive its premiere until 1 October 1981 (at Jackson Lane's Community Centre, London), it is conceivable that Sharma was not familiar with the direction in which the play had developed. That he would publicly condemn a play presented at his Festival perhaps indicates the strength of his feelings.

Chapter 4: Gay Sweatshop

1   Lamede's internal memo summarizes total support by year: £1,950 in 1975–6; £14,557 in 1976–7; £17,000 in 1977–8; £23,400 in 1978–9; £26,375 in 1979–80; £31,025 in 1980–1 (Lamede, 1984, ACGB 41/19/9b).

Chapter 5: Théâtre de Complicité

1   Gordon only appeared in the first production and is no longer referred to as a founder in later marketing material.
2   The Complicite archives, at the company offices in 14 Anglers Lane, are copious, but unsorted, unreferenced and often undated.
3   Annabel Arden only directed one further production (the 30th-anniversary production of *Lion Boy* in 2013).
4   Actually in Austro-Hungary in 1892; Poland regained independent statehood in 1918.
5   Although originally anonymous, with the author removed from the heading, names have been restored in the Arts Council archives, held at the Victoria and Albert Museum's theatre and performance archive.

Chapter 6: Montage and Quotation: Forced Entertainment's Early to Middle Years (1984–94)

1   John Avery, *Emmanuelle Enchanted* from *Welcome to Dreamland*, 1991, remastered version available on itunes.com: www.//itunes.apple.com/gb/album/welcome-to-dreamland-remastered/id336852102

Chapter 7: Women's Theatre Group 1980–94

1   Sphinx lost it Arts Council Funding in 2007 and has subsequently reduced its artistic output, focusing instead on conferences and workshops.
2   For a list of events and participants see Cousin, 2000, pp. 103–4.
3   There are varying accounts of the schism recounted by those involved including Michelene Wandor's version in her book *Carry on Understudies*, pp. 47–53; Pam Gems in *Fringe First*, pp. 196–8, and Goodman, *Feminist Stages*, pp. 26–7. See also interviews with Anne Engel and Lily Susan Todd undertaken by Unfinished Histories. Excerpts from the interviews are on the Unfinished Histories. Website, http://www.unfinishedhistories.com/interviews/viewing-interviews/.

Complete interviews are available for consultation at the British Library, Bristol Theatre Collection and Victoria & Albert Museum Theatre and Performance department.

4   St Luce also appeared in *Holding the Reins*.

5   See Goodman, *Contemporary Feminist Theatres* for more details on this fraught process.

6   Monstrous Regiment also moved from a collective to 'management' structure in the same year. See Hanna, 1991, xiv.

BIBLIOGRAPHY

Chapters 1 and 2

Appleyard, Brian, *The Times*, 26 October 1981.

Argument Room (2013), 'Women's Theatre of the 1960s, 1970s and 1980s', 30 January, www.livestream.com/theargumentroom. Accessed 11 October 2014.

Arts Council of Great Britain (1984), *Glory of the Garden: The Development of the Arts in England – A Strategy for a Decade* (London: Arts Council).

Arts Council of Great Britain Archive, Victoria and Albert Museum (n.d.), Sadista Sisters, programme for *Red Bolt Without a Door*, ACGB 42/28/11.

—(1979a), letter to the Drama Panel, 'Mrs Worthington's Daughters', 2 January, ACGB 41/25/1.

—(1979b), John Faulkner, 'Drama Allocation 1980/1: Paper for Discussion', 6 June, ACGB 38/9/23.

—(1979c), Gerald Chapman, show report on Black Theatre Co-Operative, *Welcome Home Jacko*, 13 June, ACGB 41/45/1.

—(1979d), Memo from Chairman to the Drama Director, 'Letter from Dr Brian Mawhinney MP', 27 June, ACGB, 38/26/4.

—(1979e), Jonathan Lamede, show report on Sadista Sisters, *Duchess*, 27 September, ACGB 42/28/11.

—(1979f), Jonathan Lamede, show report on Spare Tyre, *Bearing the Weight*, 18 October, ACGB 41/30/1.

—(1979g), Jill Davis, show report on Sadista Sisters, *Duchess*, 16 November, ACGB 42/28/11.

—(1979h), Howard Gibbins, show report on 7.84 England, *Trees in the Wind*, 4 December, ACGB 41/51/6.

—(1980a), Jill Davis, show report (unnamed title) for *Clean Break*, 26 January 1980, ACGB 41/49/1.

—(1980b), Memo from Sian Eade to Dennis Andrews, '"My Companies" – Random Observations', 18 February, ACGB 38/9/23.

—(1980c), Anonymous show report on Temba, *Teresa (The Modern Black Woman)*, 25 February, ACGB 42/57/7.

—(1980d), Clair Chapman, project grant submission for *How do I Look?*, 22 May, ACGB 41/30/1.

—(1980e), Jill Davis, show report on Beryl and the Perils' *Wot's Cooking*, 27 May, ACGB 41/13/6.

—(1980f), Sian Ede, notes on WTG Board Meeting, 8 October, ACGB/34/164.

—(1980g), Anonymous show report on 7:84 England, *One Big Blow*, 10 October, ACGB 41/51/6.

—(1980h), Jill Davis, show report on Spare Tyre, *How Do I Look?* 19 October, ACGB 41/30/1.

—(1980i), Robert Aldous, show report on 7:84, *One Big Blow*, 20 October, ACGB 41/53/8.

—(1980j), Jill Davis, show report on Counteract, *Never Mind the Ballots*, 23 October, ACGB 41/6/6.

—(1980k), John Faulkner, memo to Secretary General, 'Spare Tyre Theatre Company', 10 November, ACGB 41/30/1.

—(1980l), Anonymous, show report on 7:84, *One Big Blow*, 11 November, ACGB 41/53/9.

—(1980m), Jonathan Lamede, memo to John Faulkner, 'Spare Tyre', 14 November, ACGB 41/30/1.

—(1980n), Cunning Stunts, Application for Programme Subsidy 1981–82, 1 December, ACGB 41/17/5.

—(1980o), Jonathan Lamede, show report on Monstrous Regiment, *Dialogue Between a Prostitute and One of Her Clients*, 4 December, ACGB, 41/51/3.

—(1980p), Marghanita Laksi, show report on Cunning Stunts' *Christmas Show*, 27 December, ACGB 41/17/5.

—(1981a), British Council Dance and Drama Advisory Committee: Reports on Tours, 'Hesitate and Demonstrate: Poland', October, ACGB 41/20/7.

—(1981b), Nicholas Barter, show report on 7:84 England, *One Big Blow*, 13 January, ACGB 41/51/6.

—(1981c), Rod Fisher, memo to John Faulkner, 'Graeae Theatre Company', 22 January, ACGB 41/42/2.

—(1981d), Jonathan Lamede, memo to Georgina Barrowcliffe, 'The Graeae Theatre', 22 January, ACGB 41/42/2.

—(1981e), Georgiana Barrowcliff, memo to Jonathan Lamede, 'Graeae Theatre Company', 29 January, ACGB 41/42/2.

—(1981f), Anthony Field, memo to Drama Director, 'Criticism of Performance', 18 February, ACGB 41/20/7.

—(1981g), Jonathan Lamede, show report on Clean Break, *Killers*, 18 February, ACGB, 41/49/1.

—(1981h), Dennis Andrews and Jonathan Lamede, 'Counteract – Secretary General's Memo of 13 March 1981', 17 March, ACGB 41/6/6.

—(1981i), Gerald Chapman, letter to Jonathan Lamede, 16 April, ACGB 41/30/4.

—(1981j), Jonathan Lamede, letter to Gerald Chapman, 22 April, ACGB 41/30/4.

—(1981k), Tara Arts, 'Asian Festival '81?? An Open Letter', 17 June, ACGB 41/30/4.

—(1981l), Projects Committee Meeting, Drama Officer's Report: Cunning Stunts, 26 June, ACGB 41/15/5.

—(1981m), Peter Mair, memo to Jonathan Lamede, 'Cunning Stunts', 30 June, ACGB 41/17/5.

—(1981n), Ruth Marks, 'Some Points to Consider in the Discussion of Small-Scale Touring', June, ACGB 99/46/2.

—(1981o), The National Theatre of Brent, 'Application for Project Funding, *Ben Hur*', 24 July, ACGB 41/25/2.

—(1981p), Jonathan Lamede, show report on Sadista Sisters, *Red Door Without a Bolt*, 30 July, ACGB 42/28/11.

—(1981q), Jonathan Lamede, show report on Cunning Stunts, *The Opera*, 30 July. ACGB 41/17/5.

—(1981r), Jonathan Lamede, show report, Black Theatre Co-operative, *One Rule*, 5 August, ACGB 41/54/2.

—(1981s), Jonathan Lamede, show report on Tara Arts, *Vilayat*, 25 August, ACGB 41/30/4.

—(1981t), Olwen Wymark, show report on *New Anatomies*, October, ACGB/41/54/8.

—(1981u), Guy Slater, show report on *New Anatomies*, 13 October, ACGB/41/54/8.

—(1981v), Clive Tempest, show report on *New Anatomies*, 15 October, ACGB/41/54/8.

—(1981w), John Russell Brown and John Faulkner, 'Proposal to Council from the Chairman of the Drama Advisory Panel', 29 October, ACGB 38/32/13.

—(1981x), Olwen Wymark, show report on Mrs Worthington's Daughters, *Angels of War*, 29 October, ACGB 45/25/1.

—(1981y), Norman Beaton, 'Prospectus', 10 November, ACGB 41/9/13.

—(1981z), Guy Slater, show report on Sadista Sisters, *Red Door Without a Bolt*, 28 July, ACGB 42/28/11.

—(1981aa), Clive Tempest, show report on Mrs Worthington's Daughters, *Angels of War*, 7 November, ACGB 45/25/1.

—(1981bb), John Bowen, show report on Staunch Poets and Players, *In Transit*, 19 November, ACGB 41/30/2.

—(1981cc), Clive Tempest, show report on Cunning Stunts, *Winter Warmer*, 18 December 1981, ACGB 41/17/5.

—(1982a), Jonathan Lamede, show report on Spare Tyre, *Woman's Complaint*, 15 January, ACGB 41/30/1.

—(1982b), Mrs Worthington's Daughters, 'Application for Project Funding: *Wyre's Cross - the Soap Opera You Can Really Relate To*', 25 January, ACGB 41/25/1.

—(1982c), Clair Chapman, 'Submission for Project Grant on *The Pattern of my Life*', 27 January, ACGB 41/30/1.

—(1982d), Ian Brown, show report on National Theatre of Brent, *Black Hole of Calcutta*, 23 February, ACGB 41/25/2.

—(1982e), Projects Committee Meeting, 26 February, ACGB 41/17/5.

—(1982f), Jatinder Verma, 'Application for Project Funding, *The Lion's Raj*', 25 March, ACGB 41/30/4.

—(1982g), Mike Alfreds, show report on Hesitate and Demonstrate, *Goodnight Ladies*, 7 April, ACGB 41/20/7.

—(1982h), Bradford Watson, show report on Hesitate and Demonstrate, *Goodnight Ladies*, 7 April, ACGB 41/20/7.

—(1982i), Jonathan Lamede, show report on Clean Break, *Avenues*, 23 April, ACGB 41/49/1.

—(1982j), John Buston, internal memo to Jonathan Lamede, 29 April, ACGB 41/30/4.

—(1982k), letter from John Faulkner to Anne Louise Wirgman, 4 May, ACGB 34/43/6.

—(1982l), letter from Jude Kelly to John Faulkner, 24 May, ACGB 38/9/23.

—(1982m), Chris Gordon, letter to Jonathan Lamede, 'Graeae Theatre Company', 27 May, ACGB 42/20/3.

—(1982n), letter from John Faulkner to Jude Kelly, 7 June, ACGB 38/9/23.

—(1982o), Jonathan Lamede, show report on Tara Arts Group, *Scenes in the Life*, 18 August, ACGB 41/30/4.

—(1982p), Jonathan Lamede, show report on Tara Arts Group, *The Lion's Raj*, 1 September, ACGB 41/30/4.

—(1982q), Guy Slater, show report on The National Theatre of Brent, *Gotterammerung*, 16 September, ACGB, 41/25/2.

—(1982r), David Edgar, letter to John Faulkner, 10 October, ACGB 41/13/14.

—(1982s), John Faulkner, letter to David Edgar, 'Actors Unlimited', 20 October, ACGB 41/13/12.

—(1982t), Yvonne Brewster, show report on Staunch Poets and Players, *Downside Up*, 11 November, ACGB 41/30/2.

—(c. 1983), Madhav Sharma, application for project funding, *British Asians and Theatre in English*, n.d, ACGB 41/13/1.

—(1983a), Robert Petty, show report on Tara Arts, *The Lion's Raj*, 26 January, ACGB 41/30/4.

—(1983b), Tish Francis, letter to Jonathan Lamede, 27 January, ACGB 41/42/2.

—(1983c), Madhav Sharma, application for project funding, *Hum Sub Chor Hain (We Are All Crooks)*, 28 January, ACGB 41/13/12.

—(1983d), Guy Slater, show report on Graeae, *M3 Junction*, 24 February, ACGB 41/42/2.

—(1983e), Letter from Michael Coveney to Dennis Andrews, 10 March, ACGB 38/32/2.

—(1983f), Sadista Sisters, application for project funding, *Rachel and the Roarettes*, 23 March, ACGB 42/28/11.

—(1983g), Ian Kellgren, show report on Tara Arts, *Ancestral Voices*, 19 April, ACGB 41/30/4.

—(1983h), Yvonne Brewster, show report on 7:84 Scotland, *Men Should Weep*, 24 June, ACGB 41/53/9.

—(1983i), Philip Hedley, show report on Tara Arts, *The Passage*, 18 July, ACGB/41/30/4.

—(1983j), Norman Beaton, 'Origins, Aims and Objectives of Company', 19 August, ACGB, 41/9/13.

—(1983k), Jonathan Lamede, show report on Red Shift, *The Duchess of Malfi*, 20 October, ACGB 41/28/3.

—(1983l), Philip Hedley, show report on Foco Novo, *Sleeping Policeman*, 5 November, ACGB, 41/53/4.

—(1983m), Madhav Sharma, Letter to Parminder Vir, 9 November, ACGB 41/13/12.

—(1983n), Jude Kelly, show report on Spare Tyre, *Just Deserts*, 10 November, ACGB 41/30/1.

—(1983o), 'New Projects – Subsidies Committed 1983/4', 22 December, ACGB 38/32/1.

—(1984a), Jonathan Lamede, show report on Spare Tyre, *Just Deserts*, 24 January, ACGB 41/30/1.

—(1984b), Arts Development Strategy: Paper by the Drama Director, 1 February, ACGB 38/32/1.

—(1984c), Alastair Black, show report on Tara Arts, *Meet Me*, 10 February, ACGB 41/30/4.

—(1984d), Letter from Jatinder Verma to Pippa Smith, 27 February, ACGB 41/30/4.

—(1984e), Guy Slater, show report on Tara Arts, *Meet Me*, 29 February, ACGB 41/30/4.

—(1984f), Clive Perry, show report on 7:84, *School for Emigrants*, 18 March, ACGB 41/53/9.

—(1984g), Red Shift Theatre Company, 'Submission for Project Grant: *Broken English – A Collage of Images – Britain in 1994*', 28 March, ACGB 41/28/3.

—(1984h), Penny Mays, letter to William Rees-Mogg, 4 April, ACGB 41/45/7.

—(1984i), Nicholas Kent, show report on Black Theatre Co-operative, *No Place to be Nice*, 28 April. ACGB, 41/56/1.

—(1984j), Cliffhanger, Programme of Work 1984/5, April, ACGB 44/92/2.

—(1984k), 'The Glory of the Garden: Study of Appeals by Companies Facing Withdrawal of Revenue Subsidy', 12 July, ACGB 28/32/5.

—(1984l), Yvonne Brewster, 'Paper for Inclusion in Council Paper: *One Step Forward – Developing Support by the Arts Council and RAAs of Ethnic Minority Arts*', 28 September, ACGB 38/32/4.

—(1984m), Ian Kellgren, show report on Monstrous Regiment, *Calamity*, 10 November, ACGB/ 41/53/18.

—(1985a), 'Ethnic Arts – Proposals for Development: Paper for Council by the Deputy Secretary-General', ACGB 99/46/2.

—(1985b), Letter from Carolyn Graham to Anna Waters, 11 April, ACGB 99/46/2.

—(1985c), Memo from David Pratley to Jodi Myers, 19 August, ACGB 44/91/2.

—(1985d), Fiona Ellis, show report on Black Theatre Co-operative, *Ritual*, 3 September, ACGB 41/54/2.

—(1985e), Minutes of the New Project's Committee, 21 September, ACGB 99/36/2.

—(1985f), Memo from David Pratley to Dickon Reed, 'Abolition', 20 November, ACGB 38/32/16.

—(1985g), Letter from Trestle, Trickster and Complicite to Luke Rittner, 10 December, ACGB, 1985, 41/45/7.

—(1985h), Council Meeting Minutes, 18 December, ACGB 99/46/1.

—(1985i), Letter from Peter Stark and Susanne Burns to Ruth Glick, 20 December, ACGB, 41/45/6.

—(c. 1986), Wendy Jordan, '1987/88 Drama Budget Working Group: Briefing Notes on Temba', ACGB, n.d., 38/32/18.

—(1986a), John Ashford, show report on Trickster, *Charavari*, 1 January, ACGB 41/45/6a.

—(1986b), Memo from Jonathan Pope to Jodi Myers, 10 January, ACGB 44/96/2.

—(1986c), Memo from David Pratley to Graham Devlin, '2% Shift Towards Funds for Ethnic Arts', 11 February, ACGB 99/36/4.

—(1986d), Trickster Theatre Company – Theatre Enquiry Response, 15 February, ACGB 41/45/6.

—(1986e), Ian Brown, show report on WTG's *Fixed Deal*, 10 March, ACGB/41/54/8.

—(1986f), Peter Tod, show report on WTG's *Fixed Deal*, 13 March, ACGB/41/54/8.

—(1986g), memo from Graham Long to Jodi Myers, 'Ethnic Arts and Touring', 3 April, ACGB 99/36/4.

—(1986h), Michael Haynes, 'Drama Department's Progress Report on Ethnic Minority Arts', 15 April, ACGB 99/36/4.

—(1986i), Letter from Trickster Theatre Company to the Arts Council's Dance and Mime Committee, 6 June, ACGB 41/45/6.

—(1986j), Letter from Nick Owen to Jodi Myers, 'National Tour of The Black Jacobins by Talawa Theatre Co', 25 June, ACGB 92/1/1.

—(1986k), Memo from Hugh Shaw to Pippa Smith, 'Ethnic Minority Arts Action Plan', 25 June, ACGB 99/36/4.

—(1986l), Trestle: Meeting with Penny Mays, 22 September, ACGB 41/45/7.

—(1986m), Penny Mays, letter to Ian Brown, 27 October, ACGB 41/45/7.

—(1986n), Meeting with Annabel Arden, Complicite, 31 October, ACGB 41/45/2.

—(1987a), 'Foco Novo Appraisal: Financial Appraisal', 3 March, ACGB 34/43/9.

—(1987b), Memo from Jenny Waldman to Ian Brown, 'Drama Projects – Thumbnail Sketch', 9 October, ACGB 38/32/2b.

—(1988), Jean Bullwinkle, 'Briefing Notes for Drama Budget Working Party', 11 October, ACGB 38/32/13.

—(1989a), Fiona Ellis, Show Report on Temba, *Mother Poem*, 28 February, ACGB 41/56/6.

—(1989b), Memo from Jenny Waldman to Elizabeth Jones, 'Revenue Company Briefing Notes', 2 March, ACGB 38/32/13.

—(1989c), Jack Blackburn, show report on WTG's *Pinchdice and Co.*, 10 March, ACGB 41/15/8.

—(1989d), Tim Harris, show report on Temba, *Mother Poem*, 19 May, ACGB 41/56/6.

—(1989e), Nicola Thorold, show report on Talawa, *The Gods are not to Blame*, 4 November, ACGB 41/56/6.

—(1989f), South West Arts Theatre Panel, Regional Arts Show Report, Temba, *It's All in the Game*, 12 November, ACGB 41/51/7.

—(1989g), Alastair Niven, show report on Talawa, *The Gods are not to Blame*, 23 November, ACGB 41/56/6.

—(1989h), Anthony Kearey, show report on Major Road, *Daybreak*, 15 December, ACGB, 41/52/7.

—(c.1990), Interim Paper on Funding Black Theatre, Monitoring Committee: 'Ethnic Minority Arts Action Plan', n.d., ACGB, 38/32/2.

—(1990a), Paul Ranger, show report on Temba, *Glory*, 30 March, ACGB 41/56/6.

—(1990b), Barbara Pemberton, show report on Tara Arts, *The Government Inspector*, 8 May, ACGB 41/56/6.

—(1990c), Paul Ranger, show report on *The Government Inspector*, Tara Arts, 31 May, ACGB 41/56/6.

—(1990d) Tony Lidington, report to Sheila Connolly on Tara Arts, *The Government Inspector*, 7 June, ACGB 41/56/6.

—(1990e), Anonymous, East Midlands show report, Tara Arts, 12 June, ACGB 41/56/6.

—(1990f), Stephanie Edmonds, touring report on WTG's *Her Aching Heart*, 14 June, ACGB 41/15/8.

—(1990g), Philip Bernays, letter to Claire Grove, 28 June, ACGB/34/164.

—(1990h), Philip Bernays, show report for W.T.G's, *Her Aching Heart*, 21 July, ACGB 41/15/8.

—(1990i), Robert Adams, show report on Tara Arts, *The Emperor* and *The Beggar* by Bertolt Brecht and *The Proposal* by Anton Chekhov, 30 October, ACGB 41/56/6.

—(1990j), Claire Grove, show report on Temba, *Mama Decemba* and *Streetwise*, 11 December, ACGB 41/51/7.

—(1990k), Katerina Duncan, show report on Temba, *Mama Decemba* and *Streetwise*, 12 December, ACGB 41/51/7.

Aston, Elaine (1995), *An Introduction to Feminism and Theatre* (London: Routledge).

—(2003), *Feminist Views on the English Stage: Women Playwrights, 1990–2000* (Cambridge: Cambridge University Press).

Baker, Kenneth (1993), *The Turbulent Years* (London: Faber).

Best, Katy (1982), 'Creating a Theatre Tradition for Asians', *The Stage*, 19 August.

Billington, Michael et al. (1982), reviews of Foco Novo's *Edward II: London Theatre Record*, 11–24 February, pp. 98–101.

—(1993), *One Night Stands: A Critic's View of Modern British Theatre* (London: Nick Hern).

—(2007), *State of the Nation: British Theatre Since 1945* (London: Faber).

Boon, Richard (1991), *Brenton the Playwright* (London: Methuen).

—(1993), 'Retreating to the Future: Brenton in the Eighties', in Hersh Zeifman and Cynthia Zimmerman (eds), *Contemporary British Drama 1970–1990* (Basingstoke: Palgrave), pp. 323–37.

Bosche, Susanne (1983), *Jenny Lives with Eric and Martin* (London: Gay Men's Press).

Brenton, Howard (1975), 'Petrol Bombs through the Proscenium Arch', *Theatre Quarterly* 5:17, pp. 4–20.

Brewster, Yvonne (ed.) (1987), *Black Plays* (London: Methuen).

—(1991), 'Drawing the Black and White Line: Defining Black Women's Theatre', *New Theatre Quarterly* 7:28, pp. 361–8.

—(2006), 'A Short Autobiographical Essay Focusing on my Work in the Theatre', in Dimple Godiwala (ed.), *Alternatives Within the Mainstream: British Black and Asian Theatres* (Cambridge: Cambridge Scholars Press).

—(2011), 'Home Thoughts from Abroad', conference paper delivered at *English Theatre and The Cork Report*, Kingston University, 10 September.

Brooker, Joseph (2010), *Literature of 1980s: After the Watershed* (Edinburgh: University of Edinburgh Press).

Brown, Colin (1997), *Fighting Talk: The Biography of John Prescott* (London: Simon and Schuster).

Brown, Ian and Rob Brannen (1996), 'When Theatre was For All: The Cork Report, After Ten Years', *New Theatre Quarterly* 12:48, pp. 367–83.

Brown, Ian, Rob Brannen and Douglas Brown (2000), 'The Arts Council Touring Franchise and English Political Theatre After 1986', *New Theatre Quarterly* 16:2, pp. 379–87.

Caine, Barbara (1997), *English Feminism 1780–1980* (Oxford: Blackwell).

Campbell, Beatrix (1987), *The Iron Ladies: Why do Women Vote Tory?* (London: Virago).

Campbell, John (2003), *Margaret Thatcher – Volume Two: The Iron Lady* (London: Jonathan Cape).

Carpenter, Humphrey (2000), *That Was Satire That Was: Beyond the Fringe, the Establishment Club, Private Eye and That Was the Week That Was* (London: Victor Gollancz).

Churchill, Caryl (1990), *Plays: 2* (London: Methuen).

Cochrane, Clare (2006), 'A Local Habitation and a Name: The Development of Black and Asian Theatre in Birmingham Since the 1970s', in Dimple Godiwala (ed.), *Alternatives Within the Mainstream: British Black and Asian Theatres* (Cambridge: Cambridge Scholars Press).

Cole, John (1987), *The Thatcher Years: A Decade of Revolution in British Politics* (London: BBC).

Cook, Matt, Robert Mills, Randolph Trumback and Harry Cocks (2007), *A Gay History of Britain: Love and Sex between Men since the Middle Ages* (Oxford: Greenwood).

Croft, Susan and April de Angelis (1993), 'An Alphabet of Apocrypha: Collaborations and Explorations in Women's Theatre', in Trevor Griffiths and Margaret Llewellyn Jones (eds), *British and Irish Women Dramatists Since 1958: A Critical Handbook* (Buckingham: Open University Press, 1993), pp. 135–51.

Cross, Felix, ' "We Have to Set our Stall out Artistically": An Interview with Felix Cross', in Godiwala, Dimple (ed), *Alternatives Within the Mainstream: British Black and Asian Theatres*, Cambridge: Cambridge Scholars Press, 2006, pp. 218–38.

David, Hugh (1997), *On Queer Street: A Social History of British Homosexuality 1895–1995* (London: Harper Collins).

Davies, Andrew (1987), *Other Theatres: The Development of Alternative and Experimental Theatre in Britain* (London: Macmillan Education).

The Economist, 9 November 1985.

Edgar, David (1988), *The Second Time as Farce: Reflections on the Drama of Mean Times* (London: Lawrence and Wishart).

—(ed.) (1999) *State of Play: Playwrights on Playwriting* (London: Faber).

Eldridge, David (2006), *Market Boy*, (London: Methuen).

—(2012), *Plays 2* (London: Methuen).

Evans, Eric, J. (2004), *Thatcher and Thatcherism*, 3rd edn (London: Routledge).

Faludi, Susan (1992), *Backlash: The Undeclared War Against Women* (London: Vintage).

Feinstein, Elaine (1986), 'Lear's Daughters', *City Limits*, 24 September–1 October.

Feist, Andrew and Robert Hutchinson (1990), *Cultural Trends in the Eighties* (London: Policy Studies Institute).

Field, Anthony (1984), 'The Art of Being Non-Political', *Guardian*, 5 October.

Godiwala, Dimple (2003), *Breaking the Bounds: British Feminist Dramatists Writing in the Mainstream Since 1980* (New York: Peter Lang).

—(ed.) (2006a), *Alternatives Within the Mainstream: British Black and Asian Theatres* (Cambridge: Cambridge Scholars Press).

—(2006b), 'Genealogies, Archaeologies, Histories: The Revolutionary "Intercultural" of Asian Theatre in Britain', in Dimple Godiwala (ed.),

Alternatives Within the Mainstream: British Black and Asian Theatres
(Cambridge: Cambridge Scholars Press), pp. 101–19.

Goodman, Lizbeth, *Contemporary Feminist Theatres: To Each Their Own*,
London: Routledge, 1993.

Gottleib, Vera (2004), '1979 and After: A View 2002', in Baz Kershaw
(ed.), *The Cambridge History of British Theatre, Volume 3 Since 1895*
(Cambridge: Cambridge University Press), pp. 412–25.

Greater London Council (1984), Mike Philips, 'Black Theatre Policy: A
Discussion Paper', 9 September, ACGB archive, 99/32/1.

Hall, Peter (1983), *Peter Hall's Diaries*, John Goodwin (ed.) (London: Hamish
Hamilton).

Hall, Stuart (1988), *The Hard Road to Renewal: Thatcherism and the Crisis of
the Left* (London: Verso).

Hamer, Emily (1995), *Britannia's Glory: History of Twentieth-Century Lesbians*
(London: Continuum).

Hanna, Gillian (1988), 'Quote Feminist Unquote Poetry', in Gillian Allnut et
al. (eds), *The New British Poetry* (London: Palladin).

—(ed.) (1991), *Monstrous Regiment: Four Plays and a Collective Celebration*
(London: Nick Hern).

Hart, Lynda and Peggy Phelan (eds) (1993), *Acting Out: Feminist
Performances* (Ann Arbor: University of Michigan Press).

Head, Dominic (2002), *Modern British Fiction 1950–2000* (Cambridge:
Cambridge University Press).

Hemmings, Sarah (1993), 'Sisters Doing it for Themselves', *Independent*, 13
January.

Hewison, Robert (1994), 'The Arts', in Dennis Kavanagh and Anthony Seldon
(eds), *The Major Effect* (London: Macmillan).

—(1995), *Culture and Consensus: England, Art and Politics Since 1940*
(London: Methuen).

Hingorani, Dominic (2010), *British Asian Theatre: Dramaturgy, Process and
Performance* (Basingstoke: Palgrave).

Hoggart, Richard (1994), *A Measured Life: The Times and Places of an
Orphaned Intellectual* (London: Hogarth Press).

Holdsworth, Nadine (1997), 'Good Nights Out: Finding and Activating
the Audience with 7:84 (England)', *New Theatre Quarterly* 13:49, pp. 29–40.

Hollingshurst, Alan (1988), *The Swimming Pool Library* (London: Chatto &
Windus).

Isaacs, Jeremy (1989), *Storm Over 4: A Personal Account* (London:
Weidenfield and Nicholson).

Itzin, Catherine (1980), *Stages in the Revolution: Political Theatre in Britain
Since 1968* (London: Methuen).

Jackson, Paul (1980), 'Play with New Art Form', *Western Mail*, 11 November.

Janaczewska, Noelle (1989), ' "Do We want a Piece of the Cake or a Whole
One"? Feminist Theatre in Britain', *Hecate*, 81.

Jenkins, Peter (1987), *Mrs Thatcher's Revolution: The Ending of the Socialist Era* (London: Jonathan Cape).

Jones, Simon (2004), 'New Theatre for new Times: Decentralisation, Innovation and Pluralism, 1975–2000', in Baz Kershaw (ed.), *The Cambridge History of British Theatre, Volume 3, Since 1895* (Cambridge: Cambridge University Press, 2004), pp. 448–69.

Kavanagh, Dennis (1987), *Thatcherism and British Politics: The End of Consensus?* (Oxford: Oxford University Press).

Kershaw, Baz (1992), *The Politics of Performance: Radical Theatre as Cultural Intervention* (London, Routledge).

—(2004), 'British Theatre, 1940–2002', in Baz Kershaw (ed.), *The Cambridge History of British Theatre, Volume 3, Since 1895*, Cambridge: Cambridge University Press), pp. 291–325.

Keynes, John Maynard (1982), *The Collected Writings of John Maynard Keynes: Volume 28*, Donald Moggridge (ed.) (London: Macmillan Press).

Khan, Naseem (c. 1983), 'Inside Out, ACGB 99/46/2b.

—(2013), email to Graham Saunders, 5 October 2013.

Kruger, Lauren (1990), 'The Dis-Plays the Thing: Gender and Public Sphere in Contemporary British Theater', *Theatre Journal* 42:1, pp. 27–47.

Lacey, Stephen, 'British Theatre and Commerce 1979–2000', in Baz Kershaw, (ed), *The Cambridge History of British Theatre, Volume 3 Since 1895*, Cambridge: CUP, pp. 426–47.

Lamede, Jonathan (2013), interview with Graham Saunders and Tony Coult, 25 March, Victoria and Albert Museum, Theatre and Performance Archive, Blythe House, London.

Lizbeth, Goodman and De Gay, Jane (eds) (1996) *Feminist Stages: Interviews with Women in Contemporary Theatre*, Amsterdam: Harwood Academic Press, 1996.

MacLennan, Elizabeth (1990), *The Moon Belongs to Everyone: Making Theatre with 7:84* (London: Methuen).

McFerran, Ann (1987), 'Where's Mrs Lear?' *The Times Educational Supplement*, 2 October.

McGrath, John (1984), 'No Politics Please, We're British', *Guardian*, 5 October.

—(1990), *The Bone Won't Break: On Theatre and Hope in Hard Times* (London: Methuen).

Maguire, Tom (2011), 'Women Playwrights from the 1970s and 1980s', in Ian Brown (ed.), *The Edinburgh Companion to Scottish Drama* (Edinburgh: University of Edinburgh Press), pp. 154–64.

McSmith, Andy (2011), *No Such Thing as Society: A History of Britain in the 1980s* (London: Constable).

Milling, Jane (2012), *Modern British Playwriting: The 1980s, Voices, Documents, New Interpretations* (London: Methuen).

Morgan, Kenneth O. (2001), *The People's Peace*, 3rd edn (Oxford: Oxford University Press).

Mulgan, Geoff and Ken Worpole (1986), *Saturday Night or Sunday Morning? From Arts to Industry – New Forms of Cultural Policy* (London: Comedia).

Neustatter, Angela (1989), *Hyenas in Petticoats: A Look at Twenty Years of Feminism* (London: Penguin).

Onlywomen Press Collective (eds) (1981), *Love Your Enemy? The Debate Between Heterosexual Feminism and Political Feminism* (London: Onlywomen's Press).

Osment, Philip (ed.) (1989), *Gay Sweatshop: Four plays and a Company* (London: Methuen).

Owusu, Kwesi (1986), *The Struggle for Black Arts in Britain: What Can We Consider Better Than Freedom?* (London: Commedia Publishing Group).

Pattie, David (2006), 'Theatre Since 1968', in Mary Luckhurst (ed.), *A Companion to Modern British and Irish Drama 1880–2005* (Oxford: Blackwell), pp. 385–97.

Peacock, D. Keith (1999), *Thatcher's Theatre: British Theatre and Drama in the Eighties* (London: Greenwood Press).

Peter, John (1988), 'How to Make a Play a Failure', *The Sunday Times*, 15 May.

Phillips, Caryl (2006), 'I Could Have Been a Playwright', in Geoffrey V. Davis and Anne Fuchs (eds), *Staging New Britain: Aspects of Black and South Asian British Theatre Practice* (Brussels: Peter Lang), pp. 37–46.

Pick, John (1987), 'The Arts Industry', *The Journal of Arts Policy and Management* 3:1, pp. 2–3.

Private Eye (1979) 12 October, unpaginated.

Quant, Leonard (1993), 'The Religion of the Market' in Lester Friedman (ed.), *British Cinema and Thatcherism: Fires Were Started* (UCL Press: London), pp. 15–29.

Ravenhill, Mark (2004), 'A Tear in the Fabric: The James Bulger Murder and New Theatre Writing in the "Nineties"', *New Theatre Quarterly* 20:4, pp. 305–24.

Red Shift Theatre Company, http://www.redshifttheatreco.co.uk

Rees, Roland (1992), *Fringe First: The Pioneers of Fringe Theatre on Record* (London: Oberon).

Reinelt, Janelle (1993), 'Resisting Thatcherism: The Monstrous Regiment and the School of Hard Knox', in Lynda Hart and Peggy Phelan (eds), *Acting Out: Feminist Performances* (Anne Arbor: University of Michigan Press).

Remnant, Mary (1986), *Plays by Women, Volume 5* (London: Methuen).

—(1987), *Plays by Women: Volume 6* (London: Methuen).

Rittner, Luke (1984), 'How the Garden Must Grow Now', *Sunday Times*, 8 April.

Saunders, Graham (2012), '"The Freak's Roll Call": The Arts Council of Great Britain's Experimental Drama Committee, 1969–1973', *Contemporary Theatre Review* 22:1, pp. 32–45.

Sharma, Madhav (n.d.), 'Actors Unlimited', ACGB 41/13/12.

—(2011), http://www.madhavsharma.com

Sierz, Aleks (2012), *Modern British Playwriting: The 1990s. Voices, Documents, New Interpretations* (London: Methuen).

Sinclair, Andrew (1995), *Arts and Cultures: The History of the 50 years of the Arts Council of Great Britain* (London: Sinclair-Stevenson).

Smith, Joan (1989), *Misogynies: Reflections on Myths and Menace* (London: Faber).

Southwell, Tim (1998), *Getting Away With It: The Inside Story of Loaded* (London: Edbury).

Spencer, Charles (1981), 'What a Beast', *Evening Standard*, 14 April.

Spencer, Kenneth (1986), *Crisis in the Industrial Heartland: A Study in the West Midlands* (Oxford: Oxford University Press).

Sunday Times Magazine (1980), 'Cunning Stunts', 27 July.

The Sun (1980) 12 November.

Taylor, D. J. (1989), *A Vain Conceit: British Fiction in the 1980s* (London: Bloomsbury).

Thomas, David (1993), *Not Guilty: The Case in Defense of Men* (New York: William Morrow).

The Times (1981) 16 October.

Timothy, Sue (2014), email to Graham Saunders, 10 January.

Trussler, Simon (ed.) (1981), *New Theatre Voices of the Seventies: Sixteen Interviews from Theatre Quarterly* (London: Eyre Methuen).

Turner, Alwyn W. (2010), *Rejoice! Rejoice! Britain in the 1980s* (London: Aurum).

Verma, Jatinder (1996), 'Punjabi Theatre in Britain: Context', Tara Arts, http://tara-arts.com. [accessed 4 May]. Unfinished Histories Website, www.unfinishedhistories.com [accessed 28 September, 2014].

Viner, Richard (2009), *Thatcher's Britain: The Politics and Social Upheaval of the 1980s* (London: Simon and Schuster).

Whelehan, Imelda (2000), *Overloaded: Popular Culture and the Future of Feminism* (London: The Women's Press).

Whybrow, Nicholas (1994), 'Young People's Theatre and the New Ideology of State Education', *New Theatre Quarterly*, 10:39, pp. 267–80.

Wolf, Naomi (1993), *Fire with Fire: The New Female Power and how it will change the 21st Century* (London: Vintage).

Women's Liberation Music Archive (2013), http://womensliberationmusic archive.wordpress.com [accessed 28 August].

Young, Hugo (1989), *One of Us: A Biography of Margaret Thatcher* (London: Macmillan).

Chapter 3

Arts Council of Great Britain Archive (1973), Nicholas Barter, internal memo to Sue Timothy, 9 July, ACGB 40/32.

—(1981a), Hanif Kureishi, insert for the *Borderline* Royal Court programme, undated, ACGB 96/90.

—(1981b), John Bowen, show report for *Borderline*, 10 November, ACGB 34/54/7.

—(1985a), Jonathan Lamede, internal memo to Drama Panel, 3 May, ACGB 34/54/6.

—(1985b), Jonathan Lamede, internal memo to Drama Panel with ACGB minutes of Joint Stock AGM, held 4 August, 9 August, ACGB 34/54/5.

—(1986), Ruth McKenzie, internal memo to Drama Panel, 14 November, ACGB, 34/54/3.

—(1988a), Ian Brown, letter to Rita Wolf, 8 January, ACGB 34/54/3.

—(1988b), Karim Alrawi, Nicholas Broadhurst and Souad Faress, 'A Proposal for Three Year Funding, 1989–1991', June, ACGB 34/54/3.

—(1988c), Jonathan Pope, internal memo to Ian Brown and Moss Cooper, 6 July, ACGB 34/54/3.

—(1988d), Jonathan Pope, internal memo to Ian Brown and Moss Cooper, 20 July, ACGB 34/54/3.

Bardsley, Barney (1984), 'Gems and Blunders', *Tribune*, 13 April.

Billington, Michael (1977), 'Savouring Joint Stock', *Guardian*, 19 February.

Bradby, David, Louis James and Bernard Sharratt (1980), 'After *Fanshen*: A Discussion With the Joint Stock Theatre Company, David Hare, Trevor Griffiths and Steve Gooch', in David Bradby, Louis James and Bernard Sharratt (eds), *Performance and Politics in Popular Drama* (Cambridge: Cambridge University Press), pp. 297–314.

Callow, Simon (1984), *Being an Actor* (London: Methuen).

Chambers, Colin (1980), 'Product into Process: Actor-Based Workshops', in Sandy Craig (ed.), *Dreams and Deconstructions: Alternative Theatre in Britain* (Derbyshire: Amber Lane Press), pp. 105–15.

Dawson, Jane (1987), letter in *TV Times*, 21 March.

Devlin, Joyce (1992), 'Joint Stock: From Colourless Company to Company of Colour', *Theatre Topics* 2:1, pp. 63–76.

Dewhurst, Keith (1974), 'Joint Stock', *Guardian*, 24 January.

Dunn, Tony (1985), 'Joint Stock: The First Ten Years', *Plays and Players*, pp. 15–17.

Freeman, Sara (2006), 'Writing the History of an Alternative-Theatre Company: Mythology and the Last Years of Joint Stock', *Theatre Survey* 47:1, pp. 51–72.

Hare, David (1975), 'From Portable Theatre to Joint Stock … Via Shaftsbury Avenue', *Theatre Quarterly* 5:20, pp. 108–15.

Itzin, Catherine (1980), *Stages in the Revolution: Political Theatre in Britain Since 1968* (London: Methuen).

Joint Stock Theatre Group Archive (1980a), JSA/26/89.

—(1980b), Minutes of Joint Stock Policy Committee Meeting, 18 January, JSA/26/89.

—(1980c), 7 September, JSA/26/89.

—(1980d), 8 October, JSA/26/89.

—(1981a), 13 May, JSA/26/90.

—(1981b), Minutes of Joint Stock AGM, 14 June, JSA/26/90.

—(1981c), Minutes of Joint Stock Policy Committee Meeting, 16 September, JSA/26/90.

—(1981d), 9 November, JSA/26/90.

—(1982), Minutes of Joint Stock Policy Committee, 1 February, JSA/26/91.

—(1983a), 10 April, JSA/26/92.

—(1983b), letter from Max Stafford-Clark to Lynda Farran and Anne-Louise Wirgman, 11 May, JSA/26/92.

—(1983c), Minutes of Joint Stock AGM, 31 July, JSA/26/92.

—(1983d), letter from Anne-Louise Wirgman to Max Stafford-Clark, 1 August, JSA, 26/92.

—(1983e), Minutes of Joint Stock Policy Committee Meeting, 16 August, JSA/26/92.

—(c.1984a), Document showing clause to be inserted into Joint Stock's Standard Writer's Contract (requested by Sue Townsend on *The Great Celestial Cow*), undated, JSA/26/91.

—(c.1984b), publicity leaflet for *The Great Celestial Cow*, undated, JSA/27/1.

—(1984a), 'Joint Stock and its *Great Celestial Cow*', anonymous pamphlet, 8 March, JSA/26/93.

—(1984b), Minutes of Joint Stock Policy Committee Meeting, 28 March, JSA/26/93.

—(1984c), Minutes of Joint Stock AGM, 24 June, JSA/26/93.

—(1984d), Minutes of Joint Stock Extraordinary Meeting, 28 June, JSA/26/93.

—(1984e), Minutes of Joint Stock Policy Committee Meeting, 11 July, JSA/26/93.

—(1984f), 12 July, JSA/26/93.

—(1984g), 'Report from Writers' Meeting' included with Minutes of Joint Stock Policy Committee Meeting, 16 October, JSA/26/93.

—(1985a), 'Finance Committee Statement', 15 June, JSA/27/3.

—(1985b), Anne-Louise Wirgman, 'A Response to the Finance Committee's Statement of 15.6.85', 16 June, JSA/27/3.

—(1985c), Minutes of Joint Stock Policy Committee Meeting, 20 June, JSA/27/3.

—(1985d), Minutes of Joint Stock AGM, 4 August, JSA/27/3.

—(1985e), Letter from Karim Alrawi to Joint Stock's Policy Committee, 25 August, JSA/20/7.

—(1985f), Minutes of Joint Stock Policy Committee Meeting, 10 October, JSA/27/3.

—(1986a), letter from Luke Rittner to Jane Dawson, 1 February, JSA/27/4.

—(1986b), Minutes of Joint Stock Policy Committee Meeting, 20 March, JSA/27/4.

—(1986c), 13 April, JSA/27/4.

—(1986d), letter from Jane Dawson to Luke Rittner, 1 May, JSA/27/4.

—(1986e), Jane Dawson, 'Administrator's Report (draft) for Joint Stock AGM', 23 June, JSA/27/4.

—(1986f), Souad Faress, 'Report from *Fire in the Lake* for Joint Stock 1986 AGM: Conclusions', 1 July, JSA/27/10.

—(1986g), Minutes of Joint Stock AGM, 13 July, JSA/27/4.

—(1986h), Minutes of Joint Stock Policy Committee Meeting, 9 September, JSA/27/4.

—(1986i), 2 December, JSA/27/4.

—(1986j), Minutes of Joint Stock Extraordinary Meeting, 11 December, JSA/27/4.

—(c.1987), Rita Wolf, *Sanctuary* Tour Report, undated, JSA/27/7.

—(1987a), Minutes of Joint Stock Policy Committee Meeting, 4 July, JSA/27/5.

—(1987b), Minutes of Joint Stock Extraordinary Meeting, 9 November, JSA/27/5.

—(1987c), Minutes of Joint Stock Policy Committee Meeting, 22 November, JSA/27/5.

—(1988), Minutes of Joint Stock Extraordinary Meeting, 14 November, JSA/27/6.

—(1989a), Minutes of Joint Stock Board Meeting, 5 June, JSA/27/7.

—(1989b), Minutes of Joint Stock AGM, 24 September, JSA/27/7.

Kelly, Tricia (2013), unpublished interview with Jacqueline Bolton, London, 17 May.

Ritchie, Rob (ed.) (1987), *The Joint Stock Book: The Making of A Theatre Collective* (London: Methuen).

Roberts, Philip and Stafford-Clark, Max (2007), *Taking Stock: The Theatre of Max Stafford-Clark* (London: Nick Hern).

Sharma, Madhav (1982), 'Unmasking the Pale Faces', *Guardian*, 6 February.

Tinker, Jack (1977), 'Hope Beyond the Fringe', *Daily Mail*, 1 March.

Woddis, Carole (1983), '"Joint Stock" Drama', *Quarterly Theatre Review* 149, pp. 17–18.

Chapter 4

Arts Council of Great Britain (1979), Jonathan Lamede, show report on Gay Sweatshop, *I Like Me Like This*, 6 September, ACGB 41/19/9.

—(1980), Gerald Chapman, show report on Gay Sweatshop, *Blood Green*, 14 September, ACGB 41/19/9.

—(1981), Noël Greig and Glean Wilton, letter to Drama Director, 21 January, ACGB 41/19/9.

—(1984a), Jerry Wiggan, letter to William Rees-Mogg, 1 February, ACGB 41/19/9.

—(1984b), Jonathan Lamede, internal memo: 'Gay Sweatshop Background Note', 7 February, ACGB 41/19/9.

—(1984c), William Rees-Mogg, letter to Jerry Wiggan, 29 February, ACGB 41/19/9c.

—(1986a), Nick Worral, show report on Gay Sweatshop, *Compromised Immunity*, 25 August, ACGB 41/19/9.

—(1986b), Jonathan Lamede, show report on Gay Sweatshop, *Compromised Immunity*, 26 October, ACGB 32/13/1.

—(1986c), Paul Heritage, letter to the Drama Department, 10 December, ACGB 41/19/9.

—(1986d), Tony Church, letter to Philip Osment, 13 December, ACGB 41/19/9.

—(1986e), Bob Crossman, letter to Jodi Myers, 5 December, ACGB 41/19/9.

—(1987), Philip Osment, letter to Jodi Myers, 9 January, ACGB 41/19/9.

Benedict, David (1994), 'On Theatre', *Independent*, 20 May, Arts and Entertainment. http://www.independent.co.uk/life-style/on-theatre-1437126.html

Caplan, Betty (1989), review of *Paradise Now and Then*, *Guardian*, 11 October.

Case, Sue-Ellen (2000), 'Lesbian Performance', in Elaine Aston and Janelle Reinelt (eds), *The Cambridge Companion to Modern British Women Playwrights* (Cambridge: Cambridge University Press), pp. 253–65.

Clum, John M. (1994), *Acting Gay: Male Homosexuality in Modern Drama*, rev. edn. (New York: Columbia University Press).

Conway, Lydia (1988), review of *This Island's Mine*, *What's On* (2 March).

Cornwell, Jane (1994), 'Leaping Pages', *The Pink Paper*, 6 May.

Craig, Sandy (ed.) (1980), *Dreams and Deconstructions: Alternative Theatre in Britain* (Derbyshire: Amber Lane Press).

Deeny, John (2006), 'Lesbian and Gay Theatre: All Queer on the West End Front', in Mary Luckhurst (ed.), *A Companion to Modern British and Irish Drama 1880–2005* (Oxford: Blackwell), pp. 398–408.

de Jongh, Nicholas (1984), review of *Poppies*, *Guardian*, 15 February.

—(1988), review of *This Island's Mine*, *Guardian*, 27 February.

—(1992), *Not in Front of the Audience: Homosexuality on Stage* (London: Routledge).

Denford, Antonia (1990), review of *Kitchen Matters*, *City Limits*, 15 November.

Freeman, Sandra (1997), *Putting Your Daughters on the Stage: Lesbian Theatre from the 1970s to the 1990s* (London: Cassell).

Freshwater, Helen (2009), *Theatre Censorship in Britain: Silencing, Censure, and Suppression* (London: Palgrave Macmillan).

Gay Sweatshop Archive (c. 1975–9), Royal Holloway Special Collections, 'Why a Gay Theatre Group', draft statement, n.d., GS 1/2/1.

—(c.1980), Noël Greig, Paul Hines, Philip Timmins and Gean Wilton, 'Proposal by Four Members of the Gay Sweatshop Collective Concerning the Future of the Company', n.d., GS 1/2/4.

—(1983), Noël Greig, application for Project Grant Funding for Gay Sweatshop, June–October. 1983, 28 January, GS 3/14/3.

—(1985a), 'Minutes of a Meeting of the Gay Sweatshop Management Committee,' 6 January, GS/1/2/4.

—(1985b), Gay Sweatshop x10 Programme Supplement, Week One: Tues 15 Oct–Sat 19 Oct 1985, GS 3/17/2/1/3.

—(c.1986), Paula Crimmens, 'Looking at Gay Sweatshop and its x10 Festival: As 10 Years Go By', *The Plot: Volume 1*, n.d., clippng, GS 3/17/4.

—(1986a), Timmins, Philip, letter to the Management Committee, 11 April, GS 1/2/4a.

—(1986b), 'Minutes of the Gay Sweatshop Management Committee', 21 December, GS/1/2/4b.

—(1988), 31 October 1988, GS/1/2/5.

—(1989a), 2 January 1989, GS 1/2/5.

—(1989b), 10 February, GS 1/2/5.

—(1989c), 13 March, GS 1/2/5.

—(1989d), 4 April, GS 1/2/5.

—(1989e), 18 April, GS/1/2/5.

—(1989f), 15 May, GS 1/2/5.

—(1989g), 23 October, GS 1/2/5.

—(1990), 'Minutes of an Open Meeting about the Future of Gay Sweatshop Theatre Company', 19 March, GS 1/2/6/2.

—(1991), 'Minutes of a Meeting of the Gay Sweatshop Management Committee', 3 June, GS 1/2/7.

—(1992) 'Minutes of a Meeting of the Gay Sweatshop Board of Directors', 2 February, GS 1/2/7.

—(1994a), Memo 'Meeting of Gay Sweatshop's Board of Directors', 29 September, GS 1/2/8.

—(1994b), 15 November, GS 1/2/8.

—(1995), 17 October, GS 1/2/9.

—(1996), 2 April, GS 1/2/9.

Goodman, Lizbeth (1993), *Contemporary Feminist Theatres: To Each Her Own* (London: Routledge).

—and Jane de Gay (eds) (1996), *Feminist Stages: Interviews with Women in Contemporary British Theatre* (Amsterdam: Harwood Academic; London: Routledge).

Greer, Stephen (2012), *Contemporary British Queer Performance* (London: Palgrave).

Hiley, Jim (1989), review of *Paradise Now and Then*, *The Listener*, 19 October.

Itzin, Catherine (1980), *Stages in the Revolution: Political Theatre in Britain Since 1968* (London: Methuen).

Jones, Matthew (1997), 'Funding a Company of Identity', *New Theatre Quarterly* 13:52, p. 370.

Kershaw, Baz (2004a), 'Alternative Theatres 1946–2000', in Baz Kershaw (ed.), *The Cambridge History of British Theatre Volume Three, Since 1895* (Cambridge: Cambridge University Press), pp. 349–76.

Kingston, Jeremy (1990), review of *Kitchen Matters, The Times*, 8 November.

Lavender, Andy (1989), review of *Paradise Now and Then, City Limits*, 12 October.

Miller, Carl (1996), *Stages of Desire: Gay Theatre's Hidden History* (New York: Cassell).

Osment, Philip (ed.) (1989), *Gay Sweatshop: Four plays and a Company* (London: Methuen).

Pattie, David (2006), 'Theatre Since 1968', in Mary Luckhurst (ed.), *A Companion to Modern British and Irish Drama 1880–2005* (Oxford: Blackwell), pp. 385–97.

Phelan, Peggy (1993), *Unmarked: The Politics of Performance* (New York: Routledge).

Roberts, Brian (2000), 'Whatever Happened to Gay Theatre?' *New Theatre Quarterly* 16:22, pp. 175–85.

Shulman, Milton (1994), 'Stop the Plague of Pink Plays', *Evening Standard*, 30 September.

Sierz, Aleks (2001), *In-Yer-Face Theatre: British Drama Today* (London: Faber).

Sinfield, Alan (1999), *Out on Stage: Lesbian and Gay Theatre in the Twentieth Century.* New Haven Yale University Press.

Weaver, Lois (2000), interview with Sara Freeman, Rose Buford College, 21 September.

Woddis, Carole (1987), 'Why Gay Sweatshop's Gone POSH', *The Stage*, 14 May, p. 10.

Chapter 5

Ainslie, Sarah (2010), *Complicite: Rehearsal Notes – A Visual Essay of the Unique Working Methods of the Company* (London: Complicite).

Arditti, Michael (1992), *Evening Standard*, 8 April.

Armitstead, Claire (1989), *Financial Times*, 11 December.

Arts Council of Great Britain (1983), Nigel Jamieson, show report on *Put It On Your Head*, September (undated), ACGB 41/45/10.

—(1984a), programme notes, 18 January, ACGB 41/45/2.

—(1984b) Ruth Glick, show report, *Put It On Your Head*, 19 January, ACGB 41/45/2.

—(1984c), grant application, 6 March, ACGB 34/155/1.

—(1984d), grant application to the Arts Council (undated), ACGB, 34/155/1.

—(1985a), Ruth Glick, show report, *A Minute too Late*, 2 April, ACGB, 41/45/3.

—(1985b), letter to the Dance Panel, 10 December, ACGB 41/45/4b.

—(1985c), Jane Nicholas, show report on *More Bigger Snacks Now*, 13 December, ACGB 41/45/3c.

—(1985d), application for *More Bigger Snacks Now* (undated), ACGB 34/155/1.

—(1985e), David Glass, show report on *More Bigger Snacks Now* (undated), ACGB 41/45/3.

—(1986), grant application for *The Fear Project*, 12 December, ACGB 34/155/1.

—(1987), grant award for *The Fear Project*, 27 January, ACGB 34/155/1.

—(1991), letter from Ian Brown, 3 December, ACGB 34/155/3.

—(1992), Minutes of Board Meeting, 27 August, ACGB 34/155/4.

BBC2 (1992), *The Late Show*, 21 September.

BBC Radio 4 (2012), *Desert Island Discs*, 15 July.

Berger, John (1979), *Pig Earth* (London: Writers and Readers Publishing Cooperative).

Billington, Michael (1991), *Guardian*, 15 February.

—(1992a), *Guardian*, 15 August.

Colvin, Clare (1983), *Times*, 27 September.

Complicite Archives (1983), press release for *Put It On Your Head* (undated).

—(1984) (uncategorised), accompanying workshop notes for *Put It On Your Head*.

—(1986), press release for *Please, Please, Please* (undated).

—(1988), Greater London Arts application (undated).

Costa, Maddy (2010), 'A Life in Theatre: Simon McBurney', *Guardian*, 11 September.

de Jongh, Nicholas (1988), *Guardian*, 25 November.

Dürrenmatt, Friedrich (1976), *Writings on Theatre and Drama* (London: Cape).

Edgar, David (1988), *The Second Time as Farce: Reflections on the Drama of Mean Times* (London: Lawrence and Wishart).

Edwards, Jane (1988), *Time Out*, 23 November.

Fry, Michael (2013a), interview with Marcello Magni, 22 January.

—(2013b), interview with Marcello Magni, 21 March.

—(2013c), interview with Mick Barnfather, 31 May.

—(2013d), correspondence with Annabel Arden, 13 June.

—(2013e), interview with Simon McBurney, 19 June.

Gardner, Lyn (1985), *Guardian*, 6 September.

Hall, Fernau (1985), *Daily Telegraph*, 2 September.

Lane, Harriet (2005), 'Send in the Clowns', *Observer*, 2 January.

Murray, Simon (2010), 'Jacques Lecoq, Monika Pagneux and Philippe Gaulier: Training for Play, Lightness and Disobedience', in Alison Hodge (ed.), *Actor Training* (London: Routledge).

O'Mahoney, John (2004), 'Simon McBurney: Anarchy in the UK', *Guardian*, 1 January.

Rae, Kenneth (1994), 'Ten Years of Mime Action Group', *Total Theatre* 6:3.

Ratcliffe, Michael (1986), *Observer*, 21 December.

Schulz, Bruno (1998), *The Collected Works of Bruno Schulz*, Jerzy Ficowski (ed.) (London: Picador).

Spencer, Charles (1985), *The Stage*, 19 September.

Taylor, Paul (1992), *Independent*, 9 April.

Tushingham, David (1994), *Live 1: Food for the Soul – A New Generation of Theatremakers* (London: Methuen).

Wagner, Erica (2013), 'The Pioneers', *Times*, 18 May.

Chapter 6

Auslander, Philip (1997), *From Acting to Performance: Essays in Modernism and Postmodernism* (London: Routledge).

Bailes, Sara Jane (2011), *Performance Theatre and the Poetics of Failure: Forced Entertainment, Goat Island, Elevator Repair Service* (London: Routledge).

Bayley, Claire (1995), 'Playwrights Unplugged', *Independent*, 24 February.

Benecke, Patricia (2004), 'The Making of … From the Beginnings to *Hidden J*', in Judith Helmer and Florian Malzacher (eds), *Not Even a Game Anymore* (Berlin: Alexander Verlag), pp. 27–47.

Clarke, Paul (2001), 'Collaborative Performance Systems', PhD thesis, University of Bristol.

Coman, Julian (2013), 'Margaret Thatcher 1925–2013: 20 Ways That She Changed Britain', *The Observer*, 14 April.

Derrida, Jacques (1967), *Of Grammatology* (Baltimore: Johns Hopkins University Press).

Etchells, Tim (1994), 'Diverse Assembly: Some Trends in Recent Performance', in Theodore Shank (ed.), *Contemporary British Theatre* (London: Macmillan, 1994), pp. 107–22.

—(1998), 'Valuable Spaces: New Performance in the 1990s', in Nicky Childs and Jeni Walwin (eds), *A Split Second of Paradise* (London: Rivers Oram Press), pp. 31–40.

—(1999), *Certain Fragments: Contemporary Performance and Forced Entertainment* (London: Routledge).

—(2003), 'Manifesto on Liveness', presented at Live Culture Event, London, 29 March.

—(2013), email to Sarah Gorman, 22 April.

Evans, Eileen (2007–8), *ISTA Scene* 1, September, www.ista.co.uk/downloads/ Forcedentertainment.pdf

Forced Entertainment and Hugo Glendinning (1994), *Ground Plans for Paradise*, transcript of text and building names produced by company, p. 1. Author's copy purchased from company in 2003.

Gardner, Lyn (2004), 'The Rest of the World Thinks Forced Entertainment is one of Britain's Greatest Theatre Companies: Why Don't We?',

Guardian, 25 October, www.guardian.co.uk/stage/2004/oct/25/
   theatre?INTCMP=SRCH

Giannachi, Gabriella and Mary Luckhurst (eds) (1999) *On Directing:
   Interviews with Directors* (London: Faber), pp. 24–9.

Giesekam, Greg (2007), *Staging the Screen: The Use of Film and Video in
   Theatre* (Basingstoke: Palgrave Macmillan).

Gorman, Sarah (2005), 'Chronicles of the Indeterminate: Ordering Chaos in
   the Retrospectives of Forced Entertainment', *Performance Research* 10:2,
   pp. 92–4.

—(2008), 'Theatre for a Media-Saturated Age', in Nadine Holdsworth and
   Mary Luckhurst (eds), *A Concise Companion to Contemporary British and
   Irish Drama* (Oxford: Blackwell), pp. 263–83.

Goulish, Matthew (2000), 'Compendium: A Forced Entertainment Glossary',
   Performance Research 5:3, pp. 140–8.

Gross, Hans (1967), *Criminal Investigation: A Practical Handbook for
   Magistrates, Police Officers and Lawyers* (London: Sweet and Maxwell).

Hadingue, Amanda (2007), 'Experimental Theatre and the Legacy of
   the 1990s: A Personal Account', February, www.stanscafe.co.uk/
   helpfulthings/experimantaltheatreessay.html [accessed 23 October
   2013].

Harvie, Jen (2009), *Theatre and the City* (Basingstoke: Palgrave Macmillan).

Heathfield, Adrian (2000), 'End Time Now', in Adrian Heathfield (ed.), *Small
   Acts: Performance, the Millennium and the Marking of Time* (London:
   Black Dog Publishing), pp. 104–11.

—(2004a), 'As if Things Got More Real: A Conversation with Tim Etchells',
   in Judith Helmer and Florian Malzacher (eds), *Not Even a Game
   Anymore: The Theatre of Forced Entertainment* (Berlin: Alexander Verlag),
   pp. 77–102.

—(2004b), *Live: Art and Performance* (London: Tate Publishing).

Helmer, Judith (2004), 'Always Under Investigation', in Judith Helmer and
   Florian Malzacher (eds), *Not Even a Game Anymore: The Theatre of Forced
   Entertainment* (Berlin: Alexander Verlag), pp. 517–6.

—and Florian Malzacher (eds) (2004), *Not Even a Game Anymore: The
   Theatre of Forced Entertainment* (Berlin: Alexander Verlag).

Kaye, Nick (1996), *Art into Theatre: Performance Interviews and Documents*
   (Amsterdam: Overseas Publishers Association), pp. 235–52.

Lehmann, Hans Thies (2006), *Postdramatic Theatre*, trans. Karen Jürs-Munby
   (London: Routledge).

Levy, Deborah (1992a), 'Introduction', *Walks on Water* (London: Methuen).

—(1992b), review of *Emmanuelle Enchanted*, *Hybrid Magazine* 1, p. 9.

Mermikides, Alex (2010), 'Forced Entertainment: The Travels (2002) – The
   Anti-Theatrical Director', in Jen Harvie and Andy Lavender (eds), *Making
   Contemporary Theatre: International Rehearsal Processes* (Manchester:
   Manchester University Press), pp. 101–20.

O'Connor, Terry (2009), 'Virtuous Errors and the Fortune of Mistakes: A Personal Account of Making and Performing Text with Forced Entertainment', *Performance Research* 14:1, pp. 88–94.

Oddey, Alison (1994), *Devising Theatre: A Practical and Theoretical Handbook* (London: Routledge).

Quick, Andrew (1994), 'Searching for Redemption with Cardboard Wings: Forced Entertainment and the Sublime', *Contemporary Theatre Review* 2:2, pp. 25–35.

Shepherd, Simon (2009), *The Cambridge Introduction to Modern British Theatre* (Cambridge: Cambridge University Press), 2009.

Slater, Ben (1997), 'Addicted to Real Time: An Interview with Tim Etchells', *Entropy* 3, pp. 10–13.

Svich, Caridad (2003), 'Tim Etchells in Conversation with Caridad Svich', in Caridad Svich (ed.), *Trans-Global Readings: Crossing Theatrical Boundaries* (Manchester: Manchester University Press), pp. 31–5.

Tomlin, Liz (1999), 'Transgressing Boundaries: Postmodern Performance and the Tourist Trap', *The Drama Review* 43:2, pp. 136–49.

—(2004), 'English Theatre in the 1990s and Beyond', in Baz Kershaw (ed.), *The Cambridge History of British Theatre Vol. 3* (Cambridge: Cambridge University Press), pp. 498–512.

—(2008), 'Beyond Cynicism: The Sceptical Imperative and (Future) Contemporary Performance', *Contemporary Theatre Review* 18:3, pp. 355–69.

—(2013), *Acts and Apparitions: Discourses on the Real in Performance Practice and Theory, 1990–2010* (Manchester: Manchester University Press).

Tushingham, David (2004), 'We Go In and See What Happens', *Financial Times*, 18 October, http://www.ft.com/cms/s/0/d60d8684-20a2-11d9-af19-00000e2511c8.html#axzz2lIhVmRZK [accessed 17 May 2014].

Chapter 7

Anon. (1987), Review of *Lear's Daughters, The Sunday Times*, 27 September.

de Angelis, April (1999), *Playhouse Creatures* in *April de Angelis Plays One*. (London: Faber).

Arts Council of Great Britain Archive (1979a), Sian Ede, Show Report on WTG's *The Wild Bunch*, 1979, ACGB/41/51/9d.

—(1979b), Nick Barter, Show Report on WTG's *Soap Opera*, 5 May, ACGB/41/51/8.

—(1979c), Kate Crutchley, Show Report on WTG's *Soap Opera*, 21 May, ACGB/41/51/8.

—(1979d), Gerald Chapman, Show Report on WTG's *The Wild Bunch*, 26 November, ACGB/41/51/9.

—(1980), Sian Ede, Notes on WTG Board Meeting, 8 October, ACGB/34/164.

—(1981a), Olwen Wymark, Show Report on *New Anatomies*, n.d October, ACGB/41/54/8.

—(1981b) Guy Slater, Show Report on *New Anatomies*, 13 October 1981, ACGB/41/54/8.

—(1981c), Clive Tempest, Show Report on *New Anatomies*, 15 October 1981, ACGB/41/54/8.

—(1986a), Ian Brown, Show Report on WTG's *Fixed Deal*, 10 March, ACGB/41/54/8.

—(1986b) Peter Tod, Show Report on WTG's *Fixed Deal*, 13 March, ACGB/41/54/8.

—(1990), Philip Bernays, Letter to Claire Grove, 28 June, ACGB/34/164.

Aston, Elaine (2003), *Feminist Views on the English Stage: Women Playwrights 1900–2000* (Cambridge: Cambridge University Press).

Cousin, Geraldine (1996), *Women in Dramatic Space and Time* (London: Routledge).

—(2000), *Recording Women: A Documentation of Six Theatre Productions* (Amsterdam: Harwood Academic Press).

Davis, Jill (ed.) (1987), *Lesbian Plays: Any Woman Can and Double Vision* (London: Methuen).

De Gay, Jane and Lizbeth Goodman (eds) (2003), *Languages of Theatre Shaped by Women* (Bristol: Intellect).

Engel, Anne, interview, Unfinished Histories, V&A.

Feinstein, Elaine (1986), 'Lear's Daughters', *City Limits*, 24 September–1 October.

Fischlin, Daniel and Mark Fortier (eds) (2000), *Adaptations of Shakespeare. An Anthology of Plays from the Seventeenth Century to the Present* (London: Routledge).

Goodman, Lizbeth (1993), *Contemporary Feminist Theatres: To Each Her Own* (London: Routledge).

—and Jane de Gay (1996), *Feminist Stages: Interviews with Women in Contemporary British Drama* (London: Routledge).

Greenwood, Lynn (n.d.), 'An Adviser's Story', Sphinx Archive, Relaunch Notes, THM/322/2/2.

Griffin, Gabriel and Aston, Elaine (eds) (1991a), *Herstory Vol.1: Lear's Daughters, Pinchdice & Co and Witchcraze* (Sheffield: Sheffield Academic Press).

—(1991b), *Herstory Vol.2: Love & Dissent, Dear Girl and Anywhere to Anywhere* (Sheffield: Sheffield Academic Press)

Hanna, Gillian (1991), *Monstrous Regiment. A Collective Celebration* (London: Nick Hern Books).

Holledge, Julie, interview, Unfinished Histories, V&A.

Itzin, Catherine (1980), *Stages in the Revolution: Political Theatre in Britain Since 1968* (London: Eyre Methuen).

Kemp, Peter (1987), 'Unnatural hags', *Independent*, 26 September.

Lavery Bryony (1991), *Her Aching Heart, Two Marias, Wicked* (London: Methuen).

McFerran, Ann (1987), 'Where's Mrs Lear?' *The Times Educational Supplement*, 2 October.

Rees, Roland (1992), *Fringe First: Pioneers of Fringe Theatre on Record* (London: Oberon).

Remnant, Mary (1987), *Plays by Women: Volume Six* (London: Methuen).

Rose, Helen (1985), 'Mystery Play', *Time Out*, 18 September.

Saleem, Adele, interview, Unfinished Histories, V&A.

Schiach, Don (ed.) (1990), *The Wild Bunch and Other Plays* (Walton-on-Thames: Nelson).

Sphinx Archive (n.d.a), Relaunch Notes, THM/322/2/2.

—(n.d.b), flyer for *Better a Live Pompey than a Dead Cyril*, THM/322/8/2.

—(n.d.c), flyer for *New Anatomies* in Minutes Folder, THM/322/8/2.

—(n.d.d), flyer for *Our Lady, Our Lady* Production File, THM/322/5/17.

—(1981), Minutes of Board Meeting, 23 September, THM/322/1/2.

—(1983a), Minutes of WTG Meeting, 15 September, THM/322/1/2.

—(1983b), 14 December, THM/322/1/2.

—(1984a), 10 May, THM/322/1/3.

—(1984b), 6 December, THM/322/1/3.

—(1984c), Notes from Future Plans Meeting, 11 December, THM/322/1/3.

—(1986a), Notes from Policy Discussion, 3 January, THM/322/1/3.

—(1986b), Notes from Meeting, 22 October, THM/ 322/1/4.

Times Educational Supplement, Review of *Lear's Daughters*, 2 October 1987.

Todd, Lily Susan, interview, Unfinished Histories, V&A.

V&A WTG/Sphinx Company File. Cuttings and Flyers collected by the museum as part of its core collecting policy (separate to the Sphinx Archive)

Wandor, Michelene (1984), *Plays by Women Volume 3* (London: Methuen).

—(1986), *Carry on Understudies: Theatre and Sexual Politics* (London, Routledge).

Chapter 8

Allfree, Claire (2011), 'The Big Interview: Talawa Theatre Company, from Feisty to Philosophical', *Metro*, 13 October.

Bassett, Kate (1994), 'Reviving a Happy Tradition', *The Times*, 14 December.

Billington, Michael (1992), 'The Love Space Demands', *Guardian*, 7 October.

Binns, Jillian (1989), 'Talawa Scores with "The Gods"', *Weekly Gleaner*, 21 November.

Brewster, Yvonne (2006), 'Talawa Theatre Company 1985–2002', in Geoffrey V. Davis and Anne Fuchs (eds), *Staging New Britain: Aspects of Black and South Asian British Theatre Practice* (Brussels: Peter Lang), pp. 87–105.

—(2008), 'Ritual', in *Trading Faces: Recollecting Slavery* [pdf], available online: http://www.tradingfacesonline.com/docs/aesthetic-legacy/pdf/Ritual_Essay.pdf [accessed 21 January 2014, pp. 1–2].

Coveney, Michael (1986), 'The Black Jacobins/Riverside Studios', *Financial Times*, 27 February.

Cumper, Pat, Personal Interview by Kene Igweonu. Talawa HQ, London, 20 October 2011.

Curtis, Nick (1992), 'The Love Space Demands', *Independent*, 7 October.

Gardner, Lyn (1986), 'City Limits Interview: Yvonne Brewster', *City Limits*, 21–27 February.

Gilroy, Paul (1987), *There Ain't No Black in the Union Jack: The Cultural Politics of Race and Nation* (London: Hutchinson).

Godiwala, Dimple (2006), 'Alternatives Within the Mainstream: British Black and Asian Theatres – An Introduction', in Dimple Godiwala (ed.), *Alternatives Within the Mainstream: British Black and Asian Theatres* (Newcastle: Cambridge Scholars Press), pp. 3–18.

Goodman, Lizbeth (1993), *Contemporary Feminist Theatres: To Each Her Own* (London: Routledge).

Igweonu, Kene (2011), 'Interculturalism Revisited: Identity Construction in African and African-Caribbean Performance', in Kene Igweonu (ed.), *Trends in Twenty-First Century African Theatre and Performance* (Amsterdam and New York: Rodopi), pp. 61–84.

—(2013), 'Keeping it Together: Talawa Theatre Company, Britishness, Aesthetics of Scale and Mainstreaming the Black-British Experience', in Patrick Duggan and Victor Ukaegbu (eds), *Reverberations Across Small-Scale British Theatre: Politics, Aesthetics and Forms* (Bristol: Intellect), pp. 81–98.

Ince, Laurel B. (1986), '*An Echo in the Bone* by Dennis Scott', *Caribbean Times*, 14 July.

Iqbal, Nosheen (2011), 'Talawa Theatre Company: The Fights of our Lives', *Guardian* [online], 29 May, available at www.guardian.co.uk/stage/2011/may/29/talawa-theatre-company-25th-anniversary [accessed 27 October 2011].

Johnson, David (2001), 'The History, Theatrical Performance Work and Achievements of Talawa Theatre Company 1986–2001', PhD Thesis, University of Warwick. Available at <http://wrap.warwick.ac.uk/3070/> [accessed 15 January 2014].

McLauchlan, Deborah (1993), 'From Mississippi Delta', *City Life Manchester*, 12 May.

McMillan, Michael (2006), 'Rebaptizing the World in Our Own Terms: Black Theatre and Live Arts in Britain', in Geoffrey V. Davis and Anne Fuchs (eds), *Staging New Britain: Aspects of Black and South Asian British Theatre Practice* (Brussels: Peter Lang), pp. 47–63.

Morgan, Joy (1993), 'From Mississippi Delta', *Weekly Journal*, 15 April.

Osborne, Deidre (2006), 'Writing Black Back: An Overview of Black Theatre and Performance in Britain', *Studies in Theatre and Performance* 26:1, pp. 13–31.

Phillips, Caryl (1986), 'Historical Reverberations', *Race Today* 17:3, p. 26.

Solanke, Adeola (1989), 'The Head Without a Cap', *New Statesman & Society*, 10 November, pp. 41–2.

Talawa (c.2013), About Talawa [online], available at www.talawa.com/about_talawa.php [accessed 12 October 2013].

Talawa Theatre Company Archive (c.1986), 'Final Costs – The Black Jacobins' Production Accounts for *The Black Jacobins* [Production and Project Accounts, 1986–2005], TTC, 2/2/1.

—(1989a), letter from Ian Brown to Mary Lauder, 31 March 1989, TTC, 9/1/1.

—(1989b), 'Why *The Importance of Being Earnest*? Because it is a Brilliant Play', programme for *The Importance of Being Earnest*, 15–27 May, TTC, 8/3/3/4.

—(1989c), 'This Unusual Earnest', press release, 19 June, TTC, 8/2/3.

—(1989d), programme for *The Gods Are Not to Blame*, 31 October–25 November, TTC/8/3/3/6.

—(1991), programme for *Antony and Cleopatra*, 16 May–15 June, TTC, 8/3/3/9.

—(1993a), letter from Lyn Gathercole to Angela McSherry, 21 October, TTC, 9/1/2.

—(1993b), press releases for *The Lion* by Michael Abbensetts at the Ward Theatre Foundation, Kingston, Jamaica, 3–13 November, TTC, 8/2/12.

—(1994), Yvonne Brewster, 'Projections and Options: January 1995 – December 1997', 18 June, TTC, 1/2/1.

—(c. 1996a), Talawa, 'History of Talawa', various histories and profiles of the company (Company Histories, 1996–2004), TTC, 1/8/1.

—(c. 1996b), Talawa, 'Policy of Talawa Theatre Company', various histories and profiles of the company (Company Histories, 1996–2004), TTC, 1/8/1.

Ukaegbu, Victor (2006), 'Talawa Theatre Company: The "Likkle" Matter of Black British Creativity and Representation on the British Stage', in Dimple Godiwala (ed.), *Alternatives Within the Mainstream British Black and Asian Theatres* (Newcastle: Cambridge Scholars Press), pp. 123–52.

NOTES ON CONTRIBUTORS

Jacqueline Bolton is Lecturer in Drama and Theatre at the University of Lincoln, UK. She has written for the journal *Studies in Theatre and Performance*, is the editor of the Methuen Drama Student Edition of *Pornography* by Simon Stephens, and has contributed a chapter on his work in the Methuen series *Modern British Playwriting: 2000–2009*, (London: Methuen Drama, 2014).

Kate Dorney is Senior Curator of Modern and Contemporary Performance at the Victoria & Albert Museum, UK. She is the author of *The Changing Language of Modern English Drama 1945–2005* (2009), co-author (with Frances Gray) of *Played in Britain: Modern British Theatre in 100 Plays* and co-editor with Ros Merkin) of *The Glory of the Garden: Regional Theatre and the Arts Council 1984–2009* (2010) and the peer-reviewed journals *Studies in Theatre and Performance* and *Studies in Costume and Performance*. She researches and publishes widely in the field of modern and contemporary theatre practice in Britain.

Sara Freeman is Assistant Professor of Theatre at the University of Puget Sound, USA. Previously she taught at the University of Oregon, Illinois Wesleyan University, and Columbia College in Chicago. She holds a PhD in Theatre from the University of Wisconsin-Madison. Her historical scholarship concerns alternative British theatre and contemporary playwrights, and she maintains an active creative practice as a director and dramaturg. She co-edited *International Dramaturgy: Translation and Transformations in the Theatre of Timberlake Wertenbaker* (2008) and *Public Theatres and Theatre Publics* (2012) and has published chapters in *Decades of Modern British Playwriting: The 1980s* (London: Methuen Drama, 2012), *Readings in Performance and Ecology*, and *Querying Difference in Theatre History* (2012). She is contributing chapters to the forthcoming collections *Conspicuous Work: Theatre, Performance, and History in Process* and *Staging the Maternal*. She won the Gerald Kahan Award from the American Society for Theatre Research in 2007 for an article on Joint Stock Theatre Company published in the journal *Theatre Survey*.

Michael Fry is Deputy Director of East 15 Acting School, University of Essex, UK. He was previously Senior Lecturer in Theatre at Coventry University, Artistic Director of Floorboards Theatre Productions, Great Eastern Stage and Not the National Theatre and Visiting Professor at Washington and Webster Universities. He has directed over 150 productions at regional theatres and opera companies, and in London at the Young Vic, Lyric Hammersmith, the Gate, the King's Head and Soho Theatre. International projects have toured to Ireland, Italy, France, Romania, Estonia, South Africa and China. His plays and adaptations have been performed in theatres throughout England, America and Australia and are published by Methuen Drama, Samuel French and Oberon. His study of adaptation, *Proliferation and Prejudice,* is due to be published in 2016.

Sarah Gorman holds the post of Reader in the Department of Drama, Theatre & Performance at Roehampton University, London UK. Her research focuses on contemporary feminist performance and European/North American experimental theatre and Live Art. Her book *The End of Reality: The Theatre of Richard Maxwell and the New York City Players* was published in 2011. She is the author of numerous reviews, articles and chapters having had work published in: *Feminist Review, Performance Research, Contemporary Theatre Review, New Theatre Quarterly, AngloFiles, Western European Stages* and *Studies in Theatre and Performance.* Her Reading as a Woman blog can be found at http://readingasawoman.wordpress.com.

Kene Igweonu is Senior Lecturer in Performing Arts at Canterbury Christ Church University, UK. His interests cover African and African-diaspora theatre and performance, as well as cultural and performance theory. His current research and practice focus particularly on somatic practices in performance training, issues of identity in performance and cross-art practices. He is a member of the editorial boards of *African Performance Review (APR), South African Theatre Journal (SATJ)* and *Jibilika: Journal of Performing and Creative Arts.* He is the founding convener, and currently co-convener of the African and Caribbean Theatre and Performance Working Group of the International Federation for Theatre Research (IFTR) and an elected member of the IFTR Executive Committee. Dr Igweonu has published extensively on African theatre and performance. He has written several entries on Nigerian theatre for the forthcoming *Cambridge Encyclopaedia of Stage Actors and Acting.* Earlier works includes *Trends in Twenty-First*

Century African Theatre and Performance (2011). His latest work is a three volume co-edited book-set published under the general title *Performative Inter-Actions in African Theatre* (2013).

Graham Saunders is Reader in Theatre Studies at the University of Reading, UK. He is author of *Love me or Kill me: Sarah Kane and the Theatre of Extremes* (2002), *About Kane: the Playwright and the Work* (2009), *Patrick Marber's Closer* (Continuum, 2008) and co-editor of *Cool Britannia: Political Theatre in the 1990s* (2008) and *Sarah Kane in Context* (2010). He is Principal Investigator for the five year AHRC funded '*Giving a Voice to the Nation': the Arts Council of Great Britain and the Development of Theatre & Performance in Britain 1945–1994* and co-investigator on the three year AHRC funded project *Staging Beckett: The Impact of Productions of Samuel Beckett's Drama on Theatre Practice and Cultures in the United Kingdom and Ireland.*

He is the author of numerous articles and chapters having had work published in *Contemporary Theatre Review, Modern Drama, New Theatre Quarterly, Studies in Theatre and Performance* and *Theatre Research International.*

INDEX

This index covers theatre companies in all chapters. Terms are indexed by commonly known abbreviation or in full.